Praise for *Global HR Competencies*

From Africa

"I live by a simple leadership philosophy: the business is ours to manage... the future is ours to create. The most important aspect of our business is not grades, processing plants and headgears. It is people: People are the Business... Our Business is People. Dave Ulrich and his co-authors understand this key concept in the most profound sense. They bring this perspective to bear in this important book about HR practices from around the world."

—Mark Cutifani, CEO: AngloGold-Ashanti

"With the world of business going through rapid change on a global scale, technical know-how has emerged as the key driver behind competitive advantage. However, in order to ensure that company cultures are tailored for sustainable success, HR professionals must be best positioned to build organization cultures for competitive advantage and people centricity. Africa, in particular as the world's second-largest continent and home to over a billion people, needs to use technological solutions to improve the quality of life in the communities in which organizations operate. It is my firm belief that the global HR competencies and best practices identified throughout *Global HR Competencies: Mastering Competitive Value from the Outside In* will provide an invaluable resource to HR leaders in crafting sustainable organizations in a world of fast moving technological change and innovation."

—Paul Norman, Chief Human Resources & Corporate Affairs, MTN Group

"At last . . . an articulate and well-defined global standard for what makes an effective HR professional. This is a seminal, groundbreaking publication, thoroughly researched and based on the live realities facing organisations around the world. Dave Ulrich is the most respected expert on the HR profession. He and his global colleagues have produced a compelling publication that will challenge HR professionals to once again raise their games. Our rapidly evolving world demands excellence and enhanced performance. In a world of increasing economic, social and political volatility, this book defines the HR competencies that drive sustainable business success across the world. The insights from *Global HR Competencies* are invaluable and challenge us from the 'outside-in'. Essential reading for all HR professionals."

—Shirley Zinn, Deputy Global Head, Human Resources
Standard Bank Group and HR Director of Standard Bank SA

From Australia

"The book brings important research to life with the injection of regional context and local knowledge, turning the findings into lessons for the profession globally."

—Peter Wilson, National President, Australian Human Resources Institute

"The HR mantra for leaders is to pursue life-long learning. This book is a must read as it describes the evolving role of HR. It surprisingly identifies the Technology Proponent as a critical area in which HR professionals may add substantial value. This is clearly one area for future learning and growth."

—Ian Hedges, General Manager, People Hanson

"HR practice in a global context is a topic that all HR practitioners must master given the world is now at every organization's doorstep. This book helps HR practitioners to not only understand global HR competencies and best practices but to appreciate the similarities and differences in these competencies and practices across global regions."

—Mike Dawson-Smith, Manager Human Resources, City of Melbourne

From China

"Tencent has grown tremendously in recent years in both size and complexity. As the leader of Human Resource function, one of my key challenges is to make sure my Human Resource team is well equipped to cope with these growth and transformation challenges. This book provides a pragmatic guide regarding the competencies that HR professionals must master to excel in today's business world."

—Xidan, SVP HR, Tencent Holdings Limited

"Developing high value-adding HR strategies is a hot topic among HR and business executives. This book illustrates the strategic capabilities and professional competencies that HR professionals should have. This is an invaluable resource, especially for HR management and companies involved in business transformation."

—Jerry Li, Asiainfo Linkage VP, BMS&HR

"As TCL strives to become a global firm, we face tremendous challenges in developing our leaders and enhancing organization capabilities to execute new strategic initiatives. *Global HR Competencies* provides a definite roadmap to upgrade the competencies of our HR professionals who play vital roles in the transformation of TCL. My greatest appreciation to the authors for providing both the gold standard in global HR competencies as well as a compelling overview of how these competencies apply to China. Outstanding!"

—Bo Lianming, President, TCL Corporation

"*Global HR Competencies* reveals how Human Resource functions in successful organizations can play a highly strategic role. This important book inspires HR professionals to understand what competitive values they should pour their hearts into. By embracing these six competencies, HR professionals will move their careers and their companies forward to high levels of performance."

—Angel Yu, Vice president, Partner Resources, China,
Starbucks Coffee Company

From Europe

"Human centered leadership—creating the conditions for people and organisations to be effective and grow—will be the key to sustainable competitive advantage in the global economy. Business and HR leaders need to raise their game in this respect. This book will help them do this and transform their people from being their most unpredictable business assets to their most valuable ones!"

—Stefan Jacoby, President & CEO of Volvo Car Corporation

"It was once said that where you stand on an issue depends on where you sit. But no matter where you sit either in growth markets or developed markets *Global HR Competencies: Mastering Competitive Value from the Outside In* is an invaluable guide to boosting the understanding of the nuanced role the HR function plays in different markets. Another highly informative book by Ulrich, Brockbank, Younger, and company!"

—William S. Allen, Group Senior Vice President, Group HR A.P. Møller-Mærsk

"This book builds on the strong body of research undertaken over many years by the University of Michigan Business School and The RBL Group to examine the linkage between HR competencies and their impact on business performance within the broader global societal trends. Moving the short-term tactical contribution of HR to operational enterprise performance is a welcomed focus. The opportunity to position HR as the interpreter of global external societal dynamics as it relates to shaping human relationships at work is an exciting and important direction for the HR field."

—Hugh S. Mitchell, Chief Human Resources & Corporate Officer,
Royal Dutch Shell plc

"This is a rallying cry to business and HR leaders to live the 'outside in'. It is also a series of smart lessons on how to do it. It is rooted in what is happening in our ever faster changing world. Through extensive global research and many insightful examples, it shows where HR can play and must play to contribute real value to the enterprise. Consistently provocative, the updated competencies are excellently crafted to challenge HR on where it spends its time and what capabilities it develops."

—Andrew Gibson, Senior Vice President, Human Resources,
Kraft Foods Europe GmbH

From India

"*Global HR Competencies: Mastering Competitive Value from the Outside In* is an excellent research-based account of how contemporary HR practices are helping corporations across the world excel and globalize. Wayne Brockbank and Dave Ulrich's book is a must read for CEOs and HR professionals alike."

—Adi Godrej, Chairman, Godrej Group
President, Confederation of Indian Industry

"Wayne, Dave, and their global colleagues have the abilities to hold you spellbound and make sure you learn. Putting the current business challenges into context, this book explores the increasingly complex global interplay of technology, environment, and the accelerating change in business paradigms, giving us an 'outside-in' view. Enormously educative and indeed spellbinding!"

—KV Kamath, Chairman of the Board, Infosys

"This book scientifically and systematically highlights the HR competencies needed in the future to create sustainable organizations of excellence. It provides a new and critical 'Outside In' perspective, so relevant in today's context. The blend of research and case studies coupled with thought leadership of Dave, Wayne, and their global colleagues provides invaluable universal and regional insights for management practitioners. I am also delighted to see the role played by National HRD Network, India in getting the Indian perspective and, indeed as a matter of pride, that the book gets released when NHRD is celebrating its twenty-fifth year."

—TV Rao, Chairman, TVRLS; Professor, IIMA;
Founder, President, National HRD Network

From Latin America

"This book results from the largest global effort to identify the competencies that currently allow HR professionals to create value for their organizations, considering the specific characteristics of the regions in which they operate. Given the importance of such understanding in today's business context, this book should be read by any HR professional who has a true interest in the standards of excellence of the HR function in each region, and by senior line managers who aim to collaborate with their HR departments to develop a people-based competitive advantage."

—Eduardo Villar, HR VP, Hochschild Mining

"*Global HR Competencies* will become one of those books that is a defining point of a discipline. It opens the door to a new world for all HR professionals, making it the best road map ever written to help identify and implement HR practices and professional skills that have high impact on business. This book will help HR professionals to contribute to an area of business where great help is needed."

—Carolina Florez Stutz HR Vice President, Oracle, Latin America Division

"This research fundamentally challenges the traditional internal focus of HR. In an environment where continuous and unpredictable change has become the norm, the internal line-of-sight becomes problematic. Only those HR leaders who are able to incorporate a robust external market perspective into their HR programs will ensure fundamental competitive advantage to their organizations and greater business success for their customers and shareholders."

—Miguel Li Puma, Americas Talent Management VP, Boehringer Ingelheim

From the Middle East

"The domain of Human Resources is continuously evolving as a competent advantage in the global arena. This book sets the scene for perfect alignment that will help HR management in articulating company growth strategy with the needed organization capabilities. The beauty of the research given in this book is that global competencies that it defines provide HR professionals with the futuristic mindset so that they compete globally despite the local sociographic changes in today's volatile business environment."

—Abeer Al-Omar, Senior Executive Administration & Corporate Services, EQUATE Petrochemical Company

"*Global HR Competencies* book defines the HR competencies that will greatly assist any Saudi company achieve its strategic goals and objectives through full utilization of its human resources."

—Khalid S. Al-Mudaifer, President & CEO, Ma'aden Saudi Arabian Mining Co.

"This book by Wayne, Dave and their global colleagues is a great step forward in transforming HR into the strategic business partner it needs to be. It provides clear guidance to HR professionals on what competencies—as individuals and as a function—they need to cultivate in order to meet and exceed the rising expectations that business has of HR. Their work is a terrific asset to the HR professional."

—Mohammed Mubarak Al Hajeri, Executive Director, Human Resources, Abu Dhabi Investment Authority

From North America

"Dave Ulrich and his colleagues at RBL and at the University of Michigan have captured, in their usual prescient manner, the HR challenges and opportunities companies face as they seek to expand their businesses across the developed, developing, and emerging marketplace spectrum. This is a 'must read' for any leader who is responsible for managing global businesses. The financial crisis of 2008 underscored the fact that the world is now, for better or worse, tightly connected and interrelated. *Global HR Competencies* sheds light on the importance of HR practices that are adaptable and designed to create value based on keen insights at the local level. For the HR practitioner, this book will illuminate and expand the notion of geographic diversity and the essentials of getting and staying in touch with local norms and trends."

—Dennis W. Shuler, Chief HR Officer and Senior Vice President, The Kellogg Company

"The insights and ideas of Dave Ulrich and his colleagues continue to challenge HR leaders to build competencies and drive HR practices that maximize business impact in a fast-paced, global marketplace. This latest study is a 'must read' for any HR professional working to build an organization capable of achieving sustainable business success in today's dynamic environment."

—*Lynanne Kunkel, Vice President of Human Resources, North America,*
Whirlpool Corporation

"In this book you will find several examples of what we did to grow an organization that started with $1.5 billion in unsecured debt and grew it to a recent sale value of more than $8.9 billion. My only regret is that this book gives away some of our closest held secrets of competitive advantage. Since the beginning of my first day as CEO, it has been my privilege to have a trusted advisor in Human Resources. Dale Lake stood by my side guiding me through the complexities of human behavior and the complex human emotions resident in the workplace at the employee level and the Board table. Through my HR advisor I was able to use a performance priority system taught by him to decipher a code of complex abilities that define who we are as individuals. As a CEO I learned how to maximize the performance of my teams. My HR advisor taught us to be visionary and to actualize an organization 'built to change.' This book captures those insights."

—*Mayo Schmidt, President & CEO, Viterra*

From Turkey

"We are highly aware of the importance of having highly competent HR professionals and a high performing HR department in creating value for our business. We have always been good at managing our finances, but we are now equally good at managing our human resources. How do we know? Because our people are really executing the strategy and we are enjoying unprecedented growth. How did we do that? By making sure our HR team walks in the direction set in this book by the indisputable thought leaders in the field. Thank you for the comprehensive research and this invaluable book."

—*Burak Basarir, President, Coca-Cola Bottlers, Turkey*

"I recommend this book to all leaders who desire to understand what they should expect from their HR function to create intangible value. No need to say it is a must read for HR professionals who want to learn what they need to know, be, and do to meet the rising expectations from HR. The competencies here are universal. We will make sure our HR people in Turkey and in all our businesses abroad have them, thus creating competitive advantage for us wherever we are."

—*Murat Ulker, Chairman of the Board of Directors, Yildiz Holding*

"It is a privilege to do HR in an organization where the CEO sees the HR as his copilot. Our CEO knows that if he manages the people side of the equation as well as the finance side, we will be invincible. We are making sure that we arm our HR people with the latest knowledge and practices in the field, so we are the winners at all times. This book you are holding is an important part of our ammunition."

—*Basak Karlidag, Vice President, Human Resources, TeliaSonera, Eurasia*

Global HR Competencies

Mastering Competitive Value from the Outside In

Dave Ulrich
Wayne Brockbank
Jon Younger
Mike Ulrich

New York   Chicago   San Francisco   Lisbon   London
Madrid   Mexico City   Milan   New Delhi   San Juan
Seoul   Singapore   Sydney   Toronto

The **McGraw·Hill** Companies

1 2 3 4 5 6 7 8 9 0   DOC/DOC   1 8 7 6 5 4 3 2

ISBN: 978-0-07-180268-0
MHID: 0-07-180268-1

e-ISBN: 978-0-07-180269-7
e-MHID: 0-07-180269-X

McGraw-Hill books are available at special quantity discounts to use as premiums and sales promotions, or for use in corporate training programs. To contact a representative, please e-mail us at bulksales@mcgraw-hill.com.

This book is printed on acid-free paper.

CONTENTS

PREFACE
DAVE ULRICH

We were asked recently if we liked the human resources (HR) field, which we do. But we also like to observe, think about, monitor, and improve organizations. We believe that organizations sustain what they do because of their internal HR processes. Organizations have the capacity to turn individual skills into collective successes. It is through organizations that political, business, religious, education, and health agendas are accomplished. HR offers us a lens through which we understand and upgrade both individual abilities and organization capabilities.

To master HR in today's technologically connected and rapidly changing environment requires insights into global communities. A credit crisis in Greece affects not only the European political coalition but also stock prices in Asia and America. The Arab Spring electrifies social movements worldwide. Brazil's election of a new president signals to companies around the world that they can enter the Latin American market, and Argentina's decision to nationalize an oil company signals the danger of socializing private enterprise. China's need for energy affects oil prices worldwide. And the list goes on.

HR practices have adapted to this ever-increasing global market. The selection of schools from which to hire must include both local and global universities. Managing diversity refers as much to global perspectives as to race and gender. Talent development often includes placing people on global assignments either as expats or on temporary teams. Compensation systems must adapt to local conditions yet maintain global principles. Communication includes sensitivity to time zones, language, and local cultures. Organization structures attempt to focus on local requirements but have global scale.

HR professionals need to recognize and master changing global expectations and create HR practices that help individual and organizational behavior adapt accordingly. Recent insights into HR suggest that HR should be outside in, meaning that HR professionals need to understand global, social, technological, economic, political, environmental, and demographic trends; to align their HR work with external customers, investors, regulators, and communities; to help shape and drive business strategies; and to create individual abilities, organization capabilities, and sustainable leaderships. These increased HR expectations require new HR competencies.

Why We Wrote *Global HR Competencies*

Drawing on a truly global data set, this unique book examines how HR professionals integrate across external, stakeholder, strategic, and organization levels in each major region of the world. It complements *HR from the Outside In,* which reports the overall findings of our research and their implications for the HR profession.

Never before has the field of HR been able to examine both global expectations and local requirements for HR with data from both HR professionals and their associates. This book reflects standards of excellence from each global region, defining excellence not just in terms of HR impact on short-term individual and business performance but also in terms of sustainable impact on customers and society as a whole.

To provide a regional perspective on global HR expectations requires collaboration across global boundaries. We are privileged in this book to have the partnerships necessary for such a perspective. This book is based on the sixth round of the Human Resource Competency Study (HRCS). This research collects data on 140 HR competencies from HR professionals and their HR and non-HR associates. In the current round of the study, we have data from more than 20,000 individuals around the world. The sponsors of the 25-year research agenda have been the University of Michigan and the RBL Group, but the research is carried out through regional partners. Each of these partners helped collect data and coauthored chapters in this book about the HR requirements in their regions.

We asked the regional partners why they chose to participate in this research. Their answers below confirm a commitment not only to improving global HR competencies but also to creating regional excellence.

- *Africa.* "We were excited to participate in this study for a variety of reasons, but mainly because the study recognizes Africa as an equal member of the global business community. It also focuses on the contribution of HR to business sustainability and growth, based on innovation and an embedded culture of excellence." —Elijah Litheko, chief executive officer, Institute of People Management (the first and largest such organization in Africa)
- *Australia and New Zealand.* "This project plays a major part in the identification and articulation of competencies for the HR profession in Australia as benchmarked against the profession globally. The competencies are then aligned across all activities conducted by the Australian HR Institute, including course development and accreditation and professional membership." — Anne-Marie Dolan, manager, Development & Research, Australian Human Resources Institute (the only national association representing HR and people management professionals, with more than 19,000 members)
- *China.* "Although tremendous economic uncertainty exists in today's world, CEOs in China must move forward regardless of these conditions to position their enterprises for future growth and manage business risks. We were glad to participate in this study as we believe that HR management will play a critical role in helping corporate leaders to achieve these goals." —Rick Yan, president and CEO, 51job, Inc. (a recruiting company that reaches out to millions of people in China each week)
- *Europe.* "As a national HR organization, our aim is to support our member companies in their pursuit for success. We do that by helping them in developing their HR practices and competencies. The HRCS has for many years been regarded as the state of the art when it comes to HR competencies' driving practices and performance. The possibility of delivering value to our members in Norway—and to the HR community in Europe—in such a way made us excited to participate in this study." —Håvard Berntzen, senior

advisor HR, HR Norge (Norway's largest HR and management professional network, with 2,800 members from both the private and public sector)

- *India.* "With India emerging as a key global player, the HR profession in India is continuously benchmarking with the best in the world, and it is here that the HRCS survey fits in. Having collaborated with the University of Michigan in earlier surveys, NHRDN was keen on this partnership to benefit from the richness, scope, and diversity of the survey, and thus value-add to its members and the larger HR fraternity." —Dhananjay Singh, executive director, National HRD Network (India's leading community for HR professionals, with more than 12,500 members)

- *Latin America.* "We have been a partner for Latin America since 1997 and are delighted to have participated in the most global of all editions of the HRCS. Economic growth and social changes in our region present important challenges related to HR management, which will need to be addressed by competent and informed HR professionals. The data collected allow for connecting the Latin American HR profession to global standards, while acknowledging our region's unique characteristics." —Alejandro Sioli, professor of Organizational Behavior and Human Resource Management; and Michel Hermans, assistant professor of Organization Behavior and Human Resource Management, IAE business school of Austral University (one of the leading business schools in Latin America, with accreditation of multiple agencies and a strong executive education program)

- *The Middle East.* "Prior to HRCS Round 6, there was a scarcity of data from the Middle East on the big-picture aspects of the HR profession and its contribution to organizational success, economic growth, and social change. With the region experiencing a period of rapid changes—politically, socially, and economically—and with associated major issues relating to the utilization of human capital, the Arab HR Professional Association Group was excited with the prospect that the HRCS would provide a credible tool that would help define the roles of HR practitioners and provide some form of measure that could be used for monitoring HR trends and correlations with economic and social change." —Fouzi Abdulrahman Bubshait, a Saudi national with extensive experience as a leader and HR manager with leading Saudi organizations; and Andrew Lindsay Cox, an Australian with a background in project and quality management, and several years' experience in the region

- *North America.* "Our program is known not just for research and masterful teaching but also for action that makes a difference in the real-world workplaces of the leaders who come to us. The HRCS engages in all three of these important components of our work. It is a meaningful research project for the HR and academic communities; it is readily incorporated into our HR executive programs through the teachings of Dave and Wayne and their colleagues; and HR practitioners around the world incorporate these new ideas into their organizations to positive results." —Melanie Weaver Barnett, chief executive education officer, Ross School of Business, the University of Michigan (which has been rated as the number one program for HR executive education in various publications over the past 20 years)

- Turkey. "Even though more Turkish universities have started offering HR programs, their output is still too limited to guide the HR practice in Turkey. Thus organizations and HR people in need of research-based knowledge turn mostly to North American sources. However, in that case successful implementation requires serious adaptation to fit the distinct characteristics of Turkish business context and culture. We were excited to participate in this study because it gave us an opportunity to guide the HR practice." —Pelin Urgancilar, principal at the RBL Group (which has been a sponsor of the HRCS for the past quarter century)

Who This Book Is For

This book addresses HR professionals and leaders on every continent. We appeal to those who are interested in knowing how to add value through HR in their own regions as they understand and apply HR best practices from around the world.

HR professionals from all multinational corporations will find this book valuable in understanding how their field adds value in different regions. It will also help headquarters HR professionals know how to best develop and employ their HR professionals from every continent.

Line managers in multinational organizations will find value in understanding what to look for in competent HR professionals, what HR agendas add most value, and which key issues to address in adapting headquarters' HR agendas in local business settings.

Undergraduate and graduate students and academic researchers in HR, organizational behavior, organization design, international business, and business strategy will find this book useful as they seek to understand the commonalities and differences in how human and organizational issues are addressed around the world. Students from emerging economies might find this book especially important in expanding their perspectives on personal development and on HR's value in their respective settings. Given that many emerging economies are growing faster than developed economies, students from developed countries will find this book valuable in expanding their global understanding and their career options.

Business executives and HR professionals considering expanding operations into new regions and markets will find this book to be a useful template for designing and implementing high-impact HR functions to facilitate the firms' growth.

How the Book Is Organized

Part One of the book discusses the changing global business landscape and the way HR requirements have responded. Chapter 1 reviews how HR professionals deliver value. It describes the 25-year history of the HRCS and shows how these competencies shape both the personal effectiveness of HR professionals and the business performance of their employers. Chapter 2 presents a global perspective on HR competencies. It reports the overall findings of the sixth round of the HRCS.

Part Two (Chapters 3 through 11) covers nine major regions of the world: Africa, Australia and New Zealand, China, Europe, India, Latin America, the Middle East, North America, and Turkey. Each of these chapters describes the business challenges and HR expectations in its region, with the following outline:

- Regional social, economic, political, environmental, technological, and demographic trends
- Regional business trends
- Regional organization trends
- Regional HR trends
- Regional competencies of HR professionals based on the sixth round of the HRCS

Each regional chapter is written by HR experts with extensive experience in that region, and it includes specific examples of how HR delivers value within that region. At the same time, it offers a shared global perspective using a common framework for HR competencies based on the global HR competency research.

Part Three of the book summarizes and integrates these regional differences and looks to the future. Chapter 12 compares and contrasts HR practices within each region and identifies local differences and global commonalities. Chapter 13 offers a perspective on what is next in HR.

This book offers a living example of the inevitable global–local paradox. We offer a global standard for what makes an effective HR professional. This global standard was derived from research across local regions, but the basic principles and expectations for HR professionals occur in a global setting and have global commonality. At the same time, we are keenly aware that doing HR requires local adaptation. HR work in the Middle East is different from that in Latin America or Europe. Because we have local insights on a global standard, we can begin to accurately portray what it takes to be an effective HR professional working in a region but playing a global game.

Who Has Helped with This Book

We are grateful to many people for their work on this book. We appreciate the authors of each chapter. We are thankful for their working on a very tight time schedule to discern their regional business challenges, to examine their unique data, and to draft their chapters. This book was done in record time. We appreciate the support from RBL staff who helped coordinate this work, particularly Kaylene Allsop, Elisa Visick, Sally Jensen, and Justin Britton. We are most appreciative of the 20,000-plus respondents to the 45-minute survey. Their willingness to complete the survey enabled this book. We are very grateful to Melanie Barnett, Kim Cameron, and Allison Davis-Blake at the Ross School of Business at the University of Michigan, which has sponsored this study for 25 years. We realize that our insights on HR have been developed from thought leaders who shaped our ideas and from hundreds of clients and participants in executive programs who have taught us how to turn ideas into actions.

As always, we are grateful to Hilary Powers, our "write knight," who has the talent of translating rambling ideas into coherent statements. She has worked particularly hard on this manuscript with authors from many backgrounds and native languages.

Mostly, we are grateful to our families who have been more than patient with our passions for this field and this book. Wendy, Nancy, Carolyn, and Melanie have been remarkably supportive partners in all that we do.

PART ONE

THE CHANGING GLOBAL BUSINESS LANDSCAPE AND HOW HR REQUIREMENTS HAVE RESPONDED

CHAPTER 1

OVERVIEW AND LOGIC

1

Wayne Brockbank

This book focuses on the competencies and practices that characterize high-performing HR professionals and businesses. We address this issue on both a global and a multiregional scale. That is, several chapters focus on the HR world as a whole. Others focus on specific parts of the world: Africa, Australia and New Zealand, China, Europe, India, Latin America, the Middle East, North America, and Turkey. These chapters examine conditions in each region or country, discussing their implications for business in general and for HR practices in particular. The common point of reference for each chapter is the Human Resource Competency Study (HRCS), which is the world's longest ongoing research on HR competencies and practices. It has generated the largest data set on these issues, considered both globally and on a regional basis.

Tata Group: HR Competencies in Action

The Tata Group, headquartered in Mumbai, India, is the wealthiest conglomerate in India, with 424,365 employees and annual revenues of US$83.3 billion.[1] In 2009, the Reputation Institute ranked it as the eleventh most reputable company in the world.[2] It is an ideal experience to open this book because it has been remarkably effective at balancing complex paradoxes: diversification versus integration, global versus local, economic performance versus social contributions, family legacy versus professional management, and competing through scale versus innovation. It is a role model for any company coping with the contradictions of the twenty-first century. It is also an example of how HR helps confront the organizational challenges inherent in modern life.

The Tata Group consists of 95 companies in seven business sectors: information technology and communications, engineering projects and services, steel and other materials, services (including five-star hotels and life insurance), energy, consumer products, and chemicals.[3] Thus, it is one of the world's most diversified conglomerates. Despite this diversification, it also works to find ways to use commonalities to enhance efficiencies, distribute best practices, provide more unified customer-facing experiences, and sustain the powerful Tata brand.

In 1991, Rajan Tata became chairman of Tata. At that time about 5 percent of Tata's revenue came from outside India. Today about 66 percent of its revenue is from outside the country. This remarkable expansion has come about through a combination of organic growth (as with Tata Consulting Services) and acquisitions (as with Tata Automotive). From 2004 to 2011, Tata acquired almost seven companies per year on average.[4] The most visible of these was Jaguar-Land Rover, acquired in 2008 for US$2.3 billion. In the midst of such growth, Tata works diligently to retain local leadership and line talent. It has gained a reputation for working closely with local government, union, and community leaders to ensure that its acquisitions result in a win-win situation for all stakeholders. Tata managers seek to connect to the society and environment in which they operate.

A noteworthy aspect of Tata is the manner in which it balances its economic and social performance. Its vigorous and sustained financial performance and work ethos are well known. Tata is also strongly committed to improving the quality of life in the communities it serves, building community schools and clinics, founding and supporting universities and institutes, providing scholarships to underprivileged but high-potential students, and helping fund dozens of nongovernmental organizations (NGOs). This philanthropic orientation is not just embedded in its collective psyche, it is also embedded in the ownership structure that was established by the founding father of Tata.

In emerging economies, privately held firms tend to be dominated by individual families.[5] For many years Tata's senior management came from the Tata family, but the Tata board has recently appointed someone from outside the family, Cyrus P. Mistry, as deputy chairman and heir apparent to the position of chairman. He was thoroughly vetted by the board as someone who has an outstanding academic background, has participated effectively on the boards of several other companies, is insightful about the future of business in India, has a vision of the global economy, is humble, and has the values necessary to run the Tata group.

Economy and Innovation in Tata

Tata does a remarkable job at competing on the bases of both scale and of innovation. Given India's large population and high rate of poverty, it is not surprising that the "wealth at the bottom of the pyramid" concept would originate there.[6] Within this environment, Tata has mastered scale and disciplined cost control as exemplified by the US$2,500 car, the Nano. At the same time, the company's history reveals a hotbed of innovation.[7]

- 1893: The invention of ring spindles for textile manufacturing
- 1902: India's first luxury hotel (the Taj Mahal)
- 1932: India's first airline

    And Tata's legacy of innovation continues today.

- 1995: India's first branded jewelry
- 2002: The world's slimmest designer watch
- 2007: India's first teraflop supercomputer
- 2008: India's first full-length 3-D animated film

    Because of Tata's ability to maneuver through such paradoxes, Bloomberg *Businessweek* has rated it sixth among the world's most innovative companies, right behind Apple, Google, Toyota, GE, and Microsoft.[8]

HR in Tata

Tata's HR practices play important roles in its success. Some of the impact of HR has been directly through HR professionals and departments; some has been through the partnership of HR with senior executives who help set the tone and direction of the companies' HR policies.

From the beginning, Tata's founders, Jameset Tata and his son Dorab, recognized that the company's ability to achieve its potential depended heavily on its ability to recruit the best talent. In the company's early years, they established the India Institute of Science. This early investment in human capability has been followed by the Tata Institute of Fundamental Research, the Tata Institute of Social Sciences, the JRD Tata Ecotechnology Centre, the Energy and Resources Institute, and many others.

From Tata's inception, balancing economic success with a nascent expression of corporate social responsibility became the company's norm. For example, in 1932 Dorab placed nearly all of his personal wealth in a trust that now accounts for 66 percent of the Tata Group's ownership. The Tata Trust was created to give back to the community with a mandate to be used "without any distinction of place, nationality or creed."[9] As stated by Satish Pradhan, executive vice president of HR, "We have to be profitable but we go beyond. The purpose of our business is to give back to the community. This is a basic value."[10]

This quality is reinforced by HR practices, including the recruitment of people who embrace this legacy and by implicitly evaluating people on both "talking the talk and walking the talk." In addition, Tata conducts Tata Administrative Service (TAS), a comprehensive developmental program for 25 to 30 of Tata's high-potential employees. Offered annually, it includes a three-month stint in rural areas where participants undertake community-improvement initiatives. They return with a greater appreciation of Tata's social values and the social relevance of economic success.

The various Tata companies share a dominant HR logic. Line managers and HR executives jointly identify key industry trends and the sources of competitive advantage that are required in their respective companies. They then translate these sources of competitive advantage into specific cultural attributes and accompanying behaviors that are required in the business. The generic process is adapted to local conditions so as to avoid a one-size-fits-all mentality, but the intent is the same: to enable HR to add substantive support to the company's sources of superiority over its rivals in the context of market realities.

Tata's headquarters HR plays several roles in contributing to the performance of individual companies and to the group as a whole. It is the custodian of the group values: integrity, understanding, excellence, unity, and responsibility. Headquarters HR executives work with HR leaders across the group to set and ensure standards of excellence within the company's HR community. They sponsor regular meetings of the company HR heads to facilitate internal benchmarking and sharing of best practices. The headquarters HR unit also sponsors the group HR Internet portal.

A number of other HR practices enables Tata to balance its paradoxes as a group and as individual companies:

- People with specific technical skills are transferred from one group company to another. This seeds best practices and provides opportunities for professional growth.
- Tata has developed a business- and values-centered leadership framework that is applied to the recruitment, development, evaluation, and compensation of each professional, as well as to succession planning. This framework is shared across group companies and contributes to building the Tata leadership brand.
- For many years, the Tata Management Training Centre has likewise contributed to the development of TMTC key leaders throughout the group companies. Its renowned general management program, the Tata Group Executive Leadership Seminar, is designed and delivered by faculty from the Ross School of Business, at the University of Michigan. Participants come from companies across the group and are taught the best concepts and practices in specific areas that are integrated into a general manager's agenda.
- Tata has developed two major initiatives that also cut across business lines: Tata Quality Management (TMTC) and Tata Business Excellence. These programs are likewise taught and reinforced at TMTC.
- Tata prides itself on finding and hiring the finest minds in India, regardless of caste, nationality, or religion. The internal job-posting program is designed to minimize the nepotism and under-the-table payments that are prevalent in some parts of India.

The Tata experience exemplifies the emerging challenges that face HR professionals and the opportunities that, along with agendas and competence, will allow HR leaders to respond. Thus, the company provides the context within which we write this volume.

The World of HR Today

We share a deep commitment to the potential of HR to add substantial value as a source of competitive advantage. When HR focuses on creating human talent and organizational capability that connect to customers and lead the competition, it has the ability to be fundamental to major business outcomes: market share, revenue growth, profitability, and sustainability. This is not hyperbole or a statement of faith; it is an observation based on our 25 years of empirical research.

In addition, the world of business is going through dramatic transformations on a global scale.[11] The good news for HR is that we know its work matters most under conditions of change.[12] The bad news is that HR professionals do not have to look for change; it is looking for them across a wide variety of fronts:[13]

- Interconnected and interdependent globalization
- Growth of emerging markets and the subsequent shift from low-cost labor as the primary differentiator to high-quality products and innovation
- Growth of economic wealth in developing economies
- Growth of international investments
- Mandates for global sustainability
- Growth in the global population, primarily in developing countries
- Increase of middle-class purchasing power, 80 percent of which will come from emerging markets in Asia
- Continuation of the information revolution
- Radical obsolescence of technological know-how
- Internet-based networking—more than 30 percent of the world's population has Internet access in early 2012, and the proportion is only likely to rise

- Greater regulation with concurrent growth in market-based competition
- Customization of technological platforms
- Reduced cost and enhanced speed of global communication

The Purposes of HR

In this context, we have developed a distinct point of view concerning the purposes of HR. We see six high-level purposes through which HR adds value to the business:

- *HR professionals should be the best thinkers in their companies about human and organization issues.* HR professionals usually agree with this position; however, line executives frequently tell us that it is not actually true in their organization. They sometimes suggest that HR is more of an internal police function, that HR professionals serve as process facilitators or transactional administrators and focus more on internal HR issues rather than critical business problems. Nevertheless, we strongly contend that HR professionals *should* be the intellectual architects designing talent and organization agendas for their organizations.
- *HR professionals must be equal partners with line executives to accomplish the organization's purposes.* Suppose that the CEO indicates that the firm should go in one direction, while the compensation system rewards people for going in a different direction. Which direction will people choose?[14] If such a disconnect occurs, the influence of leaders and the influence of the collective HR practices will cancel each other out and the competition wins. Thus, it is imperative that HR and line leaders be yoked together and headed in the same direction as partners.
- *HR needs to be responsible for both the talent agenda and the organization agenda.* The talent agenda calls for having the best individuals in the industry as defined by customer and competitive requirements; the organization agenda defines how people work together, how they think, and how they behave together to create the competitive capabilities. It is not sufficient to have talented individuals. Talented individuals must function in a cultural

environment in which they can make optimal use of their knowledge, skills, and abilities.

- *HR can and should contribute substantially to revenue growth.* A basic principle of economics is that nothing you do inside a firm means much unless it helps bring in cash from the outside. If there is no demand for a product, its economic value is zero, no matter how much of it you make. Therefore, HR professionals must have a line of sight to the outside customer. This argument is the basic premise of this book's companion volume, *HR from the Outside In.* If HR is to be a partner to the business and if the customer of the business is the outside customer, HR's line of sight must also run outside to that customer.

- *HR needs to create and sustain economic intangibles that are valued and rewarded by capital markets.*[15] Such intangibles include:
  - Keeping promises by delivering consistent and predictable results
  - Articulating a compelling strategy for the future of the business that encourages and supports customer intimacy, product innovation, and geographic expansion
  - Investing in core competencies by identifying and providing concrete investments in people and money
  - Building organization capabilities such as collaboration, speed, accountability, learning, leadership, or shared mindset.

- *HR should see itself as a fundamental source of competitive advantage—and create practices that support that view.* Since the beginning of the industrial revolution, core technical knowledge has been the fundamental source of competitive advantage in almost every industry. For example, if you're in the automotive industry, does your firm have the technical knowledge to design and build a car? In the pharmaceutical industry, does your firm have the technical knowledge of molecular structures of medicines that can treat diabetes? The problem is, of course, that the shelf life of technical knowledge has drastically shortened in the past couple of decades. If your firm knows something, your competitors probably know it as well. If technical know-how is no longer a source of competitive advantage, then what is?

The final frontier of competitive advantage is no longer what your firm knows but what your firm is able to create. So you need to address some new questions: Does your firm have a culture that fosters creativity, innovation, and learning? Does it have the requisite cultural capabilities of flexibility, adaptability, and agility? Does it have a culture that is nimble, fast, and proactive? When technical know-how was the source of competitive advantage, engineering was the way you built that competitive advantage. But in an age of technological turbulence, when company cultures must be tailored for sustainable success, you need to look beyond engineering and ask, "Which department should have the best thinkers and creators of the cultural agenda?"

Years of research strongly indicate that HR is the answer.[16] In this age of technological churn, HR becomes an ultimate locus for building competitive advantage.

Purposes and Vision of the Human Resource Competency Study

Over the 25 years of this study, we have sought to contribute to the progress of the HR profession by pursuing five purposes:

- We want to understand, at a basic level, the competencies that exist within the HR profession. What are they? How are they bundled into useful categories for development and application?
- Which of these competencies have the greatest impact on personal effectiveness as seen by those who are most familiar with an individual's functioning as an HR professional?
- Which of these competencies have the greatest influence on business results? In selecting this focus, we differentiate between the competencies that are basic entrance requirements into the field and those that make successful HR professionals.
- How is the HR field as a whole evolving? Over the years of the study, we have gathered enough data about HR professionals to identify the

trends that have a reasonable probability of taking HR into the future. For example, we have found that a small but important number of HR activities are rarely done very well, but when they are done properly, their impact on business success is substantial—making them potential sources of competitive advantage. This is what we have sought, and this is what we have found.

- How can competencies be defined and standards raised on a global scale? As business has become more global, so has the HR function. In nearly all companies, HR departments have responded to the mandate to expand their global perspectives and capabilities. In some companies, HR has even led the globalization charge.

Not too many years ago, most HR best practices and publications originated in North America. It is now becoming clear that many best HR practices are being developed and implemented throughout the world by thoughtful, business-focused HR professionals. With this volume, we hope to help facilitate a greater understanding of the HR field on a global scale by tapping into the world's largest database on the competencies and practices that add the greatest value.

HRCS Research Methods

From its inception, the HRCS was designed in close cooperation with leading practitioners, line managers, HR associations, and academicians. HR and line managers have knowledge, skills, abilities, and experience that make their involvement in these processes important. Prominent academicians are up to date on the emerging research, theories, and concepts of organization and HR.

Before the first round of the survey in 1987 and each subsequent one (in 1992, 1997, 2002, 2007, and 2012), the research team went through a three-step process. First, we examined the relevant literature on business trends, HR practices, and competencies. Second, we interviewed hundreds of HR professionals, line executives, and academicians and consultants in individual interviews or in semistructured focus groups. Third, in the rounds following 1987, we focused on those items that were most important from the preceding years.

After these preparatory activities, we constructed the survey for each of the six rounds. Since we want to examine which competencies are related to both individual effectiveness and business success, we developed measures for two outcome variables. We measured individual performance, or personal effectiveness, by asking both HR and non-HR associates of the HR participant, "Compared to other HR professionals you have known, how does this participant compare?" Business success was measured using an aggregate index of seven dimensions: profitability, labor productivity, new product development, customer satisfaction, attraction of required employees, regulatory compliance, and answers to the question, "Compared to the major competitor in your industry, how has your business performed financially for the last three years?"

We also asked questions concerning HR department issues: Which stakeholders receive the greatest focus from the HR department? What are the focal activities of the HR department? How effective is the HR department overall? What is the influence of the HR department relative to other functions?

In every round of the study, we have applied a 360-degree methodology. HR participants completed a survey on themselves. They also selected a set of associates who were familiar with their functioning in the field and did the rating. Some of them were HR professionals, and many were non-HR clients, including line executives. Thus, we ended up with three categories of respondents: the HR participants themselves, their HR associates, and their non-HR associates. This is a much richer approach than relying on any one category of respondents.

Over the years of the research, the survey has become increasingly global. We have been honored by the involvement of outstanding colleagues from around the world. Our 2012 research advances the global range of the study by including the leading HR professional organizations in Australia (AHRI),

Table 1.1   HRCS Respondents by Research Round

	1987	1992	1997	2002	2007	2012
Business Units	1,200	441	678	692	413	635
HR Participants	1,407	751	664	1,192	1,671	2,628
HR and Non-HR Associates	8,884	3,805	2,565	5,890	8,414	17,385
Total Respondents	1,200	4,556	3,229	7,082	10,063	20,013

China (51job), India (NHRD), Latin America (IAE), the Middle East (ASHRM), Northern Europe (HR Norge), South Africa (IPM), and Turkey (SCP), and through our own extensive networks in North America, including the Ross School of Business at the University of Michigan.

Overall, we have collected information from more than 55,000 respondents in more than 3,000 businesses, including more than 20,000 individual respondents in 2012. (See Table 1.1.)

This table vividly illustrates the point that the results don't just represent HR people talking about what they think matters; they also include insights from those outside HR.

Over the years we have seen distinct and useful trends in respondent characteristics, as detailed in Table 1.2. In our sample there are an increasing number of women, more educated but with less work experience, who work as individual contributors. There has also been an increase in the proportion of functional HR specialists and a decrease among the HR generalists in the sample. The proportion of individuals from smaller and medium-size companies has grown. This gives a better mix of participants from companies of different sizes so that we are able to generalize the implications of the findings for HR professionals in all businesses.

Table 1.3 gives the response rate by geographical regions, showing that the data set is representative of every major part of the globe. While the data set is tilted disproportionately toward North America, it nonetheless constitutes the largest database of its kind in every geographical region—even those with only relatively modest response rates. As far as we know, this data set is the largest of its kind in the world.

Table 1.2   Characteristics of the Human Resource Competency Data Set, Rounds 1 to 6

HR Participant Characteristics	Round 1 1987	Round 2 1992	Round 3 1997	Round 4 2002	Round 5 2007	Round 6 2012
Gender:						
• Male	77%	78%	70%	57%	46%	38%
• Female	23	22	30	43	54	62
Education:						
• High school degree	3%	7%	4%	4%	9%	3%
• Associate college degree	5	7	6	9	12	7
• Bachelor degree	48	43	42	42	37	39
• Graduate degree	44	43	48	45	41	51
Level in HR Department						
• Individual contributor	20%	24%	29%	24%	28%	34%
• Manager of individual contributors	36	41	34	34	30	39
• Director of managers	36	29	30	31	20	19
• Top manager	8	6	7	11	21	7
Company Size:						
• 1–499	15%	17%	22%	25%	31%	19%
• 500–999	10	9	13	15	14	33
• 1,000–4,999	25	22	34	33	28	10
• 5,000–9,999	11	12	11	9	6	10
• Over 10,000	39	40	20	18	20	28

(continued on next page)

Table 1.2   Characteristics of the Human Resource Competency Data Set, Rounds 1 to 6 (continued)

HR Participant Characteristics	Round 1 1987	Round 2 1992	Round 3 1997	Round 4 2002	Round 5 2007	Round 6 2012
Years in HR:						
• 5 years or fewer	10%	14%	13%	25%	24%	25%
• 6–9 years	14	19	15	18	20	18
• 10–14 years	26	24	21	22	23	25
• 15 or more years	50	43	51	35	32	32
Primary Role:						
• Benefits, medical, and safety	6%	5%	5%	4%	3%	3%
• Compensation	5	4	4	6	6	7
• HR planning, strategy, and affirmative action	6	8	5	8	14	14
• Labor relations	6	8	5	6	5	4
• Organizational development, research, and effectiveness	2	5	3	13	7	9
• Recruiting	3	6	4	4	6	11
• Training and communication	7	14	6	12	9	11
• Generalist	61	45	60	48	49	40

Table 1.3   Respondents by Geographical Region

	% of Respondents
United States and Canada	35
Latin America	16
Europe	12
India	8
Asia—China	7
Asia—Other	7
Australia and New Zealand	6
Turkey	3
Middle East	2
Africa	1

In Table 1.4, we break down the response rate by industry in each region. The data set has strong representation from service, manufacturing, and banking, but the regional differences are interesting. The Middle East sample is strongest in the chemical industry (including petrochemical). Australia is strongest in public administration. Europe and Asia are strongest in the banking sector. Africa is strongest in services. Finally, Turkey is strongest by far in the wholesale and retail sectors.

With this data set in hand, we then set to work on the analytical processes. To achieve the objectives of the study, we applied several statistical tools: central tendency analysis, factor analysis, and regression analysis.[17] To more easily interpret the relative impact of competency domains and factors on individual effectiveness and business success, we then scaled the regression beta weights to 100 points.

Evolution of the Human Resource Competency Model

Over time, our findings have evolved as business dynamics and HR have changed. As a result, our basic competency model has changed with each round of research.

Table 1.4 Response by Industry and by Region (Percent)

Industry	Total	U.S. and Canada	Latin America	Europe	China	Australia and New Zealand	India	Turkey	Africa	Asia	Middle East
Agriculture	1	1	1	1	0	2	1	0	1	0	1
Banking	15	6	14	28	10	14	2	11	16	26	12
Chemicals	3	3	2	5	5	1	2	1	1	1	20
Construction	3	1	6	6	3	2	3	1	0	1	1
Food	4	6	7	4	1	4	2	6	4	0	2
Manufacturing	20	22	14	14	29	5	31	26	12	13	17
Mining	3	2	9	1	0	1	0	0	4	0	8
Pharmaceuticals	5	9	8	2	3	1	3	24	37	2	0
Public Administration	4	3	0	6	1	28	0	0	7	2	1
Services	31	37	29	19	36	31	43	3	51	45	32
Utilities	5	4	5	3	2	6	10	1	3	1	3
Wholesale/Retail	7	7	5	9	11	6	1	25	1	7	1

Figure 1.1   *1987 HR Competency Model*

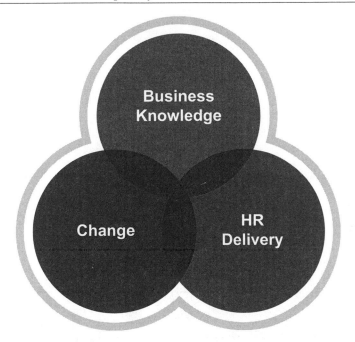

In the 1987 model, three main categories of HR competencies emerged from the data: knowledge of the business, delivery of HR practices, and management of change. At that time, HR was stepping out of its traditional roles of driving transactional processes and pursuing functional practices and was beginning to engage in the business and in helping it manage the turbulence that was just beginning. (See Figure 1.1.)

In 1992, personal credibility emerged as an important domain for HR professionals, a requirement for being allowed onto the business playing field. Credibility was a function of working well with senior leaders, communicating with excellence, and delivering results with integrity. As the world passed through the fall of centralized economic models in India, China, and Russia, change management became more heavily weighted. In the midst of a more globally competitive business environment, HR professionals in high-performing firms were spending more time and effort on strategic issues, whereas those in low-performing firms continued to focus heavily on operational-level issues (see Figure 1.2).

Figure 1.2   1992 HR Competency Model

In 1997, cultural management made its debut in the Human Resource Competency Model. As a critical capability, cultural management addressed the organization's collective knowledge, thought patterns, and integrated actions. In high-performing firms, HR professionals played a central role in identifying and implementing organizational cultures that helped the firm win in the marketplace and successfully implement its business strategy.

As culture emerged, so did another important empirical trend that gave substance and direction to culture and became a harbinger of the future direction of the HR field. We were able to verify that HR professionals in general had relatively low knowledge of external market dynamics. However, HR professionals in high-performing firms knew significantly more about external business realities (that is, customers, competitors, industry trends, and globalization) than did their counterparts in low-performing firms. We were able to verify the importance of HR having an external line of sight and not merely an internal one (see Figure 1.3).

Figure 1.3   *1997 HR Competency Model*

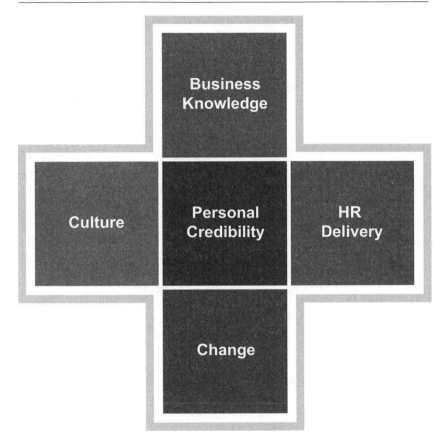

In 2002, HR's role as a strategic contributor asserted itself (see Figure 1.4). The strategic contributor competency domain consisted of an integration of fast change, strategic decision making, and market-driven connectivity. Market-driven connectivity was a concept new to the HR field. As far as we know, this category had not been identified by any previous competency work. This factor consisted of HR professionals identifying important information from the business environment, amplifying that information across the organization, providing the tools that unify the organization around key market information, and reducing the presence of the types of less important information that frequently block attention to more critical market information. By so doing, HR professionals helped their organizations successfully navigate changing customer, competitive, and shareholder requirements.

Figure 1.4   *2002 HR Competency Model*

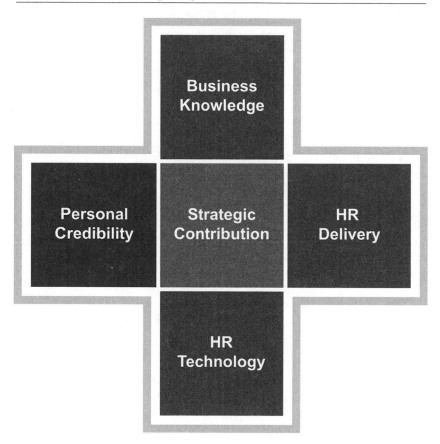

In 2007 we found that building organization capabilities had become a defining feature. This was an integration of three domains. First, as strategic architects, HR professionals helped formulate and implement the customer-centric business strategy. Second, they built organization capabilities as empirically represented by culture and change management. Third, they aligned talent and organization design activities with the organization capabilities that were, in turn, required by the customer-centric business strategy. We found that to optimize this integration, HR professionals had to excel more than ever before as credible activists in driving business results. Interestingly, non-HR associates had greater expectations for HR professionals to be focused on the external customer than HR professionals did of

Figure 1.5   *2007 HR Competency Model*

themselves. We also found an important integration between talent management and organization design—which indicates that the current trend toward framing the HR agenda entirely in terms of talent management to the exclusion of organization design will probably result in a suboptimal contribution to the business. (See Figure 1.5.)

Overview of the 2012 findings

In 2012, we have identified six domains of HR competency. These are represented in Figure 1.6.

- *Credible activist.* HR professionals in high-performing firms function as credible activists. They do what they say they will do. Such results-based integrity

Figure 1.6   *2012 HR Competency Model*

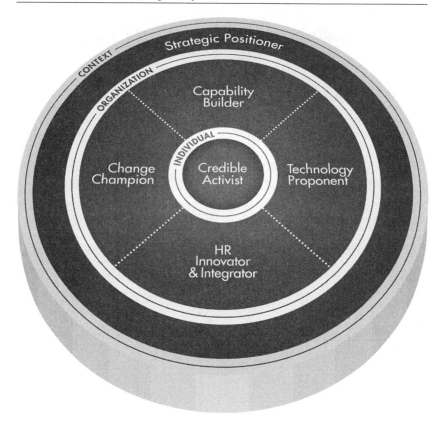

serves as the foundation of personal trust that, in turn, translates into professional credibility. They have effective interpersonal skills. They are flexible in developing positive chemistry with key stakeholders. They translate this positive chemistry into influence that contributes to business results. They take strong positions about business issues that are grounded in sound data and thoughtful opinions.

- *Strategic positioner.* High-performing HR professionals understand the global business context—the social, political, economic, environmental, technological, and demographic trends that bear on their business—and translate these trends into business implications. They understand the structure and logic of their own industries and the underlying competitive dynamics of the markets they serve, including customer, competitor, and supplier trends. They then apply this knowledge in developing a personal vision for the future of their own company. They participate in developing customer-focused business strategies and in translating the business strategy into annual business plans and goals.

- *Capability builder.* At the organization level, an effective HR professional creates, audits, and orchestrates an effective and strong organization by helping define and build its capabilities. Capability represents what the organization is good at and known for. These capabilities outlast the behavior or performance of any individual manager or system, and might include innovation, speed, customer focus, efficiency, and the creation of meaning and purpose at work. HR professionals can help line managers create meaning so that the capability of the organization reflects the deeper values of the employees.

- *Change champion.* Effective HR professionals develop their organizations' capacities for change and then translate that into effective change processes and structures. They ensure a seamless integration of change processes that builds sustainable competitive advantage. They build the case for change based on market and business reality, and they overcome resistance to change by engaging key stakeholders in key decisions and building their commitment to full implementation. They sustain change by ensuring the availability of necessary resources—time, people, capital, and information—and by capturing the lessons of both success and failure.

- *HR innovator and integrator.* At the organization level, the major competencies of effective HR professionals are their abilities to integrate HR practices around a few critical business issues. The challenge is to make the HR whole more effective than the sum of its parts. High-performing HR professionals ensure that desired business results are clearly and precisely prioritized, that the necessary organization capabilities are powerfully conceptualized and put into operation, and that the appropriate HR practices, processes, structures, and procedures are aligned to create and sustain those capabilities. As they do so with discipline and consistency, they help collective HR practices reach the tipping point of impact on business results. They also innovate new HR practices, processes, and structures that continually direct HR more fully toward business results.

- *Technology proponent.* For many years, HR professionals have applied technology to their basic work. HR information systems have been applied to enhance the efficiency of processes including benefits, payroll processing, healthcare funding, record keeping, and other administrative services. In this HRCS round, we see a dramatic change in the implications of technology for HR professionals. At the organization level, high-performing HR professionals are now involved in two additional categories of technological application. First, HR professionals are applying social networking technology to help people stay connected with one another. They help guide the connectedness of people within the firm and the connectedness between people outside firms (especially customers) with employees inside the firm. Second, in the high-performing firms, HR professionals are increasing their roles in the management of information. This includes identifying the information that should receive focus, bundling that information into usable knowledge, applying that knowledge to key decisions, and then ensuring that these decisions are clearly communicated and acted upon. This is a newly emergent competency through which HR professionals will add substantive value to their organizations.

These HR competency domains and their implications for personal and business performance are examined in greater detail in Chapter 2.

CHAPTER 2

THE GLOBAL PERSPECTIVE

2

Jade White and Jon Younger

To properly ground the global findings of the 2012 Human Resource Competency Study (HRCS) data and the implications for HR professionals, it is useful to start with what organizations must do if they wish to perform well in a dynamic and fast-changing global economic, social, and political landscape.

The concept of globally connected economies became real and concrete when the Great Recession began in 2008 in the United States and quickly spread around the world, drawing economies across Europe and Asia down with it. It showed its teeth when a hedge fund manager in London cornered the market for cocoa beans, driving up the cost of hot chocolate in Australia.[1] The nascent power of social media was tested and confirmed when Facebook and smart phones provided the technology to connect students and dissidents, encouraging the Arab Spring and the downfall of autocracies in Egypt, Tunisia, and Yemen. The 30 million people online at Skype at any given moment, the 900 million monthly users of Facebook, or the 3 billion searches a day on Google show that technology now enables ubiquitous information and global relationships and makes each person a citizen journalist.

In general, it is helpful to group the contextual factors facing modern organizations into six categories, forming the acronym STEPED:

- *Social.* Personal lifestyles are changing in regard to families, urbanization, ethics, religion, and expectations of well-being.
- *Technological.* New devices and concepts enable new products, services, communication patterns, and relationships; they create, destroy, and reinvent whole industries.

- *Economic.* Cycles of the economy shape consumer and government confidence. For example, the Great Recession of 2008 has had a profound impact on corporate and personal risk tolerance.
- *Political.* Regulatory and political shifts change the roles and expectations of government; for example, we have seen profound tectonic changes in the politics of Europe, the Middle East, and Africa in the past few years.
- *Environmental.* The green movement is reshaping the roles and responsibilities of companies and countries.
- *Demographic.* The *New York Times* reported recently that the percentage of white births has fallen below 50 percent in the United States; the global Muslim population is growing at 2 percent per year, significantly faster than other religious groups overall.[2]

Table 2.1 shows a subset of trends within the STEPED factors, along with the organizations that took advantage of those trends as well as those that missed them.

In times past, HR was not seen as responsible for helping the organization monitor, understand, and respond to external factors and trends except as they pertained directly to HR services such as recruiting, training, pay, and retention. Other functions would have been held responsible. Much has changed.

As we pointed out in Chapter 1, the fundamental role of HR is to create value. We see HR as a business within the business that is focused on converting strategy and goals into culture, talent, and leadership. In doing so, HR must be conscious of a set of paradoxical requirements. The first of these is the need to take an outside-in mindset. This means applying the discipline to monitor and identify key external trends and emerging stakeholder expectations, and to convert these into organizational requirements, priorities, and internal actions. The broader set of paradoxes is described in Table 2.2.

Dealing with these paradoxes has generated exciting changes for the HR profession. Innovative HR practices are emerging in the BRIC and N11 countries, across Asia, Africa, and Latin America and driving new developments in traditional HR practice strongholds in the United States and Western Europe. Some years ago, top companies would focus on a few well-regarded

Table 2.1   *Impact of External Trends*

Trend	Opportunities in the Periphery	Who Took Advantage	Who Missed It
Social	Sports and new age drinks	Snapple, Gatorade	Coke, Pepsi (initially)
	Popularity of reality shows	Cable	TV networks
	Upscale online purchasing	Gilt Groupe, Net-a-Porter	Traditional department stores
Technological	Digital revolution	Apple and iPad	Music industry
	White LED lighting	LED companies	Lightbulb manufacturers
	Open-source software	Linux, IBM	Microsoft and Sun Microsystems
	CD-ROM encyclopedias	Microsoft	Encyclopedia Britannica
	Rapid spread of GSM	Nokia	Iridium
Economic	Overnight package delivery	FedEx, UPS	USPS, United Airlines
	Search engine potential	Google	Microsoft
	Discount point-to-point airlines	Southwest, Ryanair, and EasyJet	United, Delta, Lufthansa
Political	Generic AIDS drugs in Africa	Pharmaceutical companies in India	Major global pharmaceutical companies
	Social discontent in Venezuela	Hugo Chavez	Establishment (PDVSA)
Environmental	Hybrid cars	Toyota, Honda	General Motors
Demographic	Return to family time (through gaming for all ages)	Nintendo (Wii)	Sony (Playstation), Microsoft (Xbox); (both adapted systems later)

Table 2.2   *Paradoxes of Organizational Life*

Paradox	Requirement
Outside and in	HR must turn outside business trends and stakeholder expectations into internal actions.
Global and local	HR must have both a global perspective and local insight.
Business and people	HR should focus on both business results and human capital improvement.
Organization and individual	HR should target both organization capabilities and individual ability.
Process and event	HR is about sustainable and integrated solutions, and each activity (for example, a training, communication, staffing, or compensation program) needs to reflect that.
Future and past	HR should shape the future of the organization while respecting its heritage.
Strategic and administrative	HR must attend to long-term strategic practices as well as day-to-day administrative processes.

places to find great HR talent, such as PepsiCo, Exxon Mobil, IBM, General Electric, and Procter and Gamble (P&G). Now recruiters are as likely to go to companies like Lenovo in China, ICICI in India, Atlantica Hotels in Brazil, and Alexander Forbes in Africa. CHRO (chief human resource officer) roles are being sought after and regularly filled by business leaders from other functional domains—not to meet a rotational quota but because these leaders see the strategic contribution of a high-performing HR function. Graduates of top business schools are actively choosing a career in HR. Graduate programs in HR management are being created in leading universities.

Competency Domains

As promised in Chapter 1, this chapter explores the six competency domains identified in the 2012 round of the HRCS: credible activist, strategic positioner, capability builder, change champion, HR innovator and integrator, and technology proponent. Each offers insight into the skills and activities that offer most promise for HR professionals and departments.

Credible Activist

In the 2007 round of the HRCS, the credible activist domain was central to developing a reputation as a high performer in HR. In that research, four factors contributed to the category:

- *Delivering results with integrity.* The judgment required to define the right priorities along with the skill to address priorities in the right way.
- *Sharing information.* The ability to communicate effectively in person and in writing, coupled with the knowledge of which colleagues to communicate with.
- *Building trust.* The development of a broad and deep network of strong relationships across the organization and certainly beyond HR.
- *HR with attitude.* The sense of when to take the initiative or even challenge the status quo to increase strategic contribution to the organization.

In the 2012 round, credible activism again emerged as a crucial global competency for high performance in HR. However, we observed some meaningful shifts in what credible activism means and requires (see Table 2.3).

The most important element of building a reputation for credible activism is *earning trust through results*, followed closely by *influencing and relating to others effectively*. Not far behind is the perception of continuous personal and professional improvement—through self-awareness and taking action to continue to grow and develop functional and interpersonal skills. Finally, high-performing

Table 2.3   Credible Activist: Factor, Mean Score, and Impact on Individual Effectiveness and Business Success

Factor	Mean Score (out of 5.0)	Individual Effectiveness	Business Impact
Earning trust through results	4.36	28%	25%
Influencing and relating to others	4.24	28%	26%
Improving through self-awareness	4.08	26%	30%
Shaping the HR profession	4.13	18%	19%
Overall R^2		.405	.056

HR professionals are seen not only to do effective HR but also to move their own effectiveness forward in their teams, their organizations, and in the broader professional communities.

Credible activism is the domain in which HR professionals in our population score highest. It has the highest mean among the six competencies. We know that the high scores for credible activism are consistent for both HR and non-HR (line) respondents; both HR and line participants recognize its importance. It is also the highest-rated HR professional competency in every region. However, it is not the principal correlation with business success; for that, we must look to other competency domains. Thus credible activism is the doorway to competence—necessary but not sufficient, the foundation but not the home.

Strategic Positioner

High-performing HR professionals think and act from the outside in. In the past 25 years, the outside-in concept has evolved from knowing the company financials to adapting strategies to serving stakeholders to responding to business conditions.

From 1987 through 2007, our research found (as others have advocated) that HR needs to know the business to be effective. We have proposed a business literacy test for HR professionals that would confirm they had the basis for informed dialogues with their colleagues:

- What is our largest competitor and why do people buy from it?
- How did our organization perform last year? What is forecast for this year?
- Who sits on our board of directors?
- What is our market share? Is our market segment growing or shrinking?
- What are the emerging technology trends facing our industry?
- Who are our largest customers and why do they buy from us? How many customers did we gain last year? Lose?
- Who are our primary competitors? What do they do better than we do? Why do customers buy from them? What do we do better than they do? What do customers value most?
- What social and political trends might be disruptive to our industry?

In the 2012 HRCS round, "knowing the business" evolved into the strategic positioner domain. We chose the word *positioner* intentionally. Most of us have used some type of global positioning system to find out where we are on the face of the earth. Likewise, as strategic positioners, HR professionals help their organizations know where they fit in the context of business trends and stakeholders.

When HR professionals know and translate external business trends into internal decisions and actions, they create value. Strategic positioning significantly raises the bar for HR professionals. For example, Halliburton's CHRO Mahesh Puducheri moved himself and key members of his team from Houston to Dubai to improve their focus on Halliburton's emerging market needs.

At this point, an HR professional who cannot read and interpret financial statements, contribute to strategy, recognize and serve external stakeholders, and anticipate and react to business trends simply will not fully contribute to business discussions. It is not enough to just learn finance or strategy. The strategic positioner competency domain includes three factors:

- *Interpreting the global context.* Attending to and understanding the key environmental factors (the STEPED factors) that influence the performance, opportunities, and challenges facing the organization now and in the future.
- *Decoding customer expectations.* Applying context assessment to interpret what the global context means for the target customers of the organization. What do customers expect from the organization with respect to products and services, cost, responsiveness, problem solving and physical access, and ongoing support?
- *Cocrafting a strategic agenda.* Working with both line managers and functional colleagues to convert the Outside In to a comprehensive strategic response that fully addresses key people requirements.

Table 2.4 provides the global findings for these factors.

HR professionals are generally better at cocrafting a strategic agenda (3.96) than interpreting the global context or decoding customer expectations

Table 2.4   *Strategic Positioner: Factor, Mean Score, and Impact on Individual Effectiveness and Business Success*

Factor	Mean Score (out of 5.0)	Individual Effectiveness	Business Impact
Interpreting global context	3.83	29%	30%
Decoding customer expectations	3.83	29%	37%
Cocrafting a strategic agenda	3.96	42%	33%
R^2		.332	.062

(3.83). The table also shows that cocrafting a strategic agenda is more important to professional effectiveness ratings than to business success (42 percent to 33 percent). Business success comes more from the ability to decode customer expectations (37 percent) and convert these expectations into aligned and integrated HR systems and practices. The data suggest that HR professionals may come across as more professionally effective by displaying knowledge of finance and strategy, but they do more to drive business results when they work with stakeholders (particularly customers) and business context.

Capability Builder

In the 2007 round, the competency domain of culture and change steward encompassed both capability building (culture) and change leadership. In the 2012 round these two domains revealed enough individual importance to divide. For capability builder we found 18 competencies clustered into three factors, as outlined in Table 2.5.

The global findings show that capability building is made up of three interrelated and important factors:

- *Capitalizing on organization capability.* The first step for HR contribution in capability building is to identify what the organization is good at and known for now, and what organization capabilities are key to future organizational success. This is the factor on which HR professionals are rated most positively (4.03).

Table 2.5   Capability Builder: Factor, Mean Score, and Impact on Individual Effectiveness and Business Success

Factor	Mean score (out of 5.0)	Individual Effectiveness	Business Impact
Capitalizing on organization capability	4.03	36%	32%
Aligning strategy, culture, practices, and behavior	3.94	36%	37%
Creating a meaningful work environment	3.94	28%	31%
R^2		.31	.074

- *Aligning strategy, culture, practices, and behavior.* This factor covers the process of converting the abstract into the real. Articulating current and future capabilities is an essential first step. But, unless converted into practice—into what is real—it does no good. HR professionals convert potential capability into reality by aligning HR systems and practices in ways that build awareness, create experiences that reinforce capability, and reward individuals who best exemplify the capabilities in how they work and interact with internal employees and with target customers and other external stakeholders. For example, the French energy company Total S.A. depends for growth on its ability to build strong collaboration with governments in the countries in which it operates.

- *Creating meaningful work environments.* HR professionals can help create meaningful work environments that reinforce requisite capabilities. At present, HR professionals are somewhat better at diagnosing required capabilities (4.03) than establishing them or creating meaningful work settings (3.94).

Change Champion

We label this domain "change champion" and not "change agent" for two important reasons. First, the agent of change often initiates but does not necessarily follow through. Second, an agent acts on behalf of someone else

Table 2.6   *Change Champion: Factor, Mean Score, and Impact on Individual Effectiveness and Business Success*

Factor	Mean score (out of 5.0)	Individual Effectiveness	Business Impact
Initiating change	3.94	53%	46%
Sustaining change	3.91	47%	54%
R^2		.296	.066

but does not take personal ownership for change. The chosen term proposes that we envision change champions as people who both start and follow through with change.

We have identified 11 specific knowledge and behavior items that characterize the change champion domain. These items statistically cluster into two factors, *initiating change* and *sustaining change*, as shown in Table 2.6.

These data offer additional insights on the process of change. By separating initiating from sustaining change, the data suggest that HR professionals have two challenges. The first is to get change started effectively.

- *Initiating change.* Initiating change means getting started, turning pressures for change into change initiatives, and taking first steps to move change forward. Our research showed that seven competencies define the extent to which HR professionals initiate change:
  - Ensure that key leaders are aligned around major change initiatives.
  - Help employees at all levels understand why to change—and why now.
  - Create a sense of urgency.
  - Identify and overcome sources of resistance to change.
  - Help set the direction of change with clear outcomes.
  - Build commitment of key people to support change efforts.
  - Articulate the key decisions and actions required for success.
- *Sustaining change.* The second factor is creating the conditions, and demonstrating the persistence, to ensure that change is sustained over time. Sustaining change means sticking with initiatives, making sure that desired changes happen, and delivering outcomes from the change. Our research

identified three specific behaviors that HR professionals can demonstrate to help sustain change:

- o Ensure the availability of resources to stick with the change (money, information, technology, and people).
- o Monitor and communicate progress of change processes.
- o Adapt learning about change to new settings.

As change champions who sustain change, HR professionals have to make sure that changes last by implementing sustainable disciplines into their organizations.

The point that jumps out from the data in Table 2.6 is that HR professionals need to initiate change if they wish to be seen as personally effective. To drive business success, however, they need to ensure that change is sustained. At present, most HR professionals are better at initiating or starting change than at making sure the desired changes survive, continue to develop, and have impact over time. Until this balance changes, HR is apt to be perceived as overly influenced by management fads and fashions.

HR Innovator and Integrator

The HR innovator and integrator domain is closely associated with that of talent manager and organization designer, which was identified in the 2007 round of the HRCS. In that round, five factors contributed to the talent and organization domain:

- Ensuring today's and tomorrow's talent
- Developing talent
- Shaping organization
- Fostering communication
- Designing reward systems

In the 2012 HRCS research, the emphasis on talent and leadership continues unabated, but with an interesting shift. It is not sufficient to create good

Table 2.7   *HR Innovator and Integrator: Factor, Mean Score, and Impact on Individual Effectiveness and Business Success*

Factor	Mean	Individual Effectiveness	Business Impact
Optimizing human capital through workforce planning and analytics	3.95	22%	21%
Developing talent	3.83	16%	19%
Shaping organization and communication practices	3.94	23%	21%
Driving performance	3.87	19%	19%
Building leadership brand	3.87	20%	20%
R^2		.331	.078

systems of workforce planning, talent development, leadership, and organization design. The stakes have been raised in 2012. Innovation becomes a more critical factor, driving a focus on more efficacious ways to deliver talent, leadership, and organization. And integration—the best system—is reinforced.

The factors of HR innovator and integrator are outlined in Table 2.7.

HR innovators and integrators define workforce requirements, develop employees, and shape organization and communication practices. In several areas, however, we see a fairly significant and certainly interesting evolution of expectations. Workforce planning and analytics are a far more intense focus in the current formulation. Driving performance is a more significant factor in 2012. A strong element of the competency domain is building leadership brand: an organization's reputation for systematically developing strong leaders and leadership. This is new to the research. Although talent management has always included leader selection and succession as a key factor and leadership development as an essential aspect, the focus on leadership as a distinctive organization capability (and the role of HR professionals in building this capability) is powerful and clear.

The impact of HR innovator and integrator on ratings of HR professional performance is significant. As with credible activism, high performers tend to be seen in positive terms when they score well as HR innovators and integrators.

However, the business impact of HR innovator and integrator is more significant; this domain has the largest impact on business performance, explaining 19 percent of the variance.

The factors of this domain are complex enough to warrant discussion in considerable detail.

Optimizing Human Capital

Optimizing human capital through workforce planning and analytics is the first factor. Effective HR professionals perform four key tasks:

- *Define critical strategic roles.* Workforce planning defines the key roles and resources that disproportionately drive organizational performance. HR professionals support strategic contribution when they help leaders understand the roles that drive the greatest value, the opportunities to think differently and innovatively about resourcing, and the ways to convert these insights into an organization plan.
- *Conduct the SWOT.* Defining resource needs must be informed by assessment of current strengths, weaknesses, opportunities, and threats. HR contributes most by auditing the state of the workforce, clarifying needs for change, and building the plan.
- *Buy, build, or do both.* Some organizations such as P&G and Exxon Mobil are committed employee developers and resist hiring senior staff from outside.[3] Other organizations such as Siemens tend to buy experienced talent (that is, bring it in from outside). Still others, such as Goldman Sachs, combine these strategies, supplementing campus hiring with selective experienced hires. HR plays an important role in exploring what the organization does today, how successfully it performs, and which changes are needed to ensure that it has the people it needs for the future.
- *Manage the change process.* This means initiating the process in a way that facilitates success. It also requires involving the right individuals, providing effective information and homework, and considering contingencies—and then monitoring and sustaining performance by reviewing the effectiveness of decisions made and anticipating potential problems.

Developing Talent

When it comes to developing employees, the focus is on both how and how well the organization is growing the technical, organizational, and interpersonal skills needed for people to have productive and satisfying work lives. The actions that make up this factor are standard-setting, assessment, investing in talent, and follow-up.

- *Setting a standard.* Competence begins by identifying the required competencies to deliver future work. Rather than focus on what has worked in the past by comparing low- and high-performing employees, more recent competence standards come from turning future customer expectations into present employee requirements. HR professionals help general managers create a theory or point of view on competencies that leads to a set of employee standards. The simplest test of the competence standard is to ask target or key customers, "If our employees live up to these standards, would they inspire confidence from you in our firm?"
- *Assessing individuals and organizations.* With standards in place, competent employees deliver results in the right way—and the right way is defined by the competence standards. Forward-thinking organizations are increasingly seeking outside perspectives on performance, as well as internal collegial views. This helps individuals know what to do to improve and provides valuable input to the organization about how to design and deliver HR practices to upgrade talent.
- *Investing in talent improvement.* Individual and organization gaps may be filled by investing in talent. In our work we have found the following six investments can help upgrade talent.
  - Buy: recruiting, sourcing, and securing new talent into the organization
  - Build: helping people grow through training, on the job, or in life experiences
  - Borrow: bringing knowledge into the organization through advisors or partners
  - Boost: promoting the right people into key jobs
  - Bounce: removing low performers
  - Bind: retaining top talent through opportunity, reward, and nonfinancial recognition

When HR professionals create choices in these six areas, they help individuals and organizations invest in future talent.

Shaping Organization and Communication Practices

Organization is not the boxes on a chart but a set of operating protocols reinforced through relationships that combined into what we call capabilities. Our colleague Dave Hanna has leveraged an approach we find particularly helpful:

- What is the business result we are trying to achieve?
- What capabilities must be in place for the business result to be achieved and sustained over time?
- How do we activate these capabilities through HR systems and practices?
- How do we implement change in a way that reinforces this virtuous cycle?
- How do we measure and monitor effectiveness and efficiency?
- How do we ensure alignment over time?

Shaping organization and communication practices has the highest rating for professional effectiveness in this domain (23 percent) and is tied with other factors for greatest impact on business success.

Driving Performance

The 2007 global findings did not explicitly address performance management; however, in this round the importance of performance management in innovative and integrated HR contribution is strongly reinforced. Effective HR professionals play a number of critical roles in driving performance:

- *Establishing clear performance standards.* Effective HR professionals ensure that employees understand what performance is expected and why. Communication creates a line of sight between the individual employee and external stakeholders. Stories that describe the real impact of performance on customers are particularly powerful. For example, British Petroleum (BP) did an excellent job of making the impact of the U.S. Gulf cleanup meaningful to its employees by engaging them in relief efforts and drenching the organization with information about the effect of the spill on residents' lives. GE Medical Systems makes the impact of work on customers real by introducing its employees to cancer survivors.

- *Establishing a clear process of performance assessment, with well-defined performance metrics.* It is essential that the performance management process be effective, efficient, and transparent: who does what, when, how, and with what information or metrics in place.

- *Providing rich feedback on strengths and needs for improvement and development.* Relevant and meaningful feedback is the foundation for development. We see a shift from 360-degree feedback to what has been called 720-degree feedback, coupling the internal information with approaches that directly involve customers, suppliers, and other external stakeholders.

- *Rewarding and recognizing good performance.* Driving performance depends on the combination of financial rewards and nonfinancial acknowledgment or recognition of achievement. We recommend the following principles in developing effective reward and recognition schemes:
  - *Equity.* Employees who contribute more value to the organization should receive more rewards.
  - *Transparency.* How rewards are determined should be clear. The perceived fairness of the system is undercut when the measures and decisions are opaque.
  - *Meaningfulness.* Rewards should be meaningful to the individual. For example, some employees may be more interested in time off, others in financial reward, and others in new opportunity or challenge.

- *Teaching employees and line managers skills in providing and receiving feedback.* Effective performance management is based on skills in giving and receiving feedback. Top organizations don't take feedback skills for granted; rather, they reinforce these skills through regular education.

- *Adapting performance standards to changing strategic demands.* HR plays a critical role in keeping performance standards accurate and relevant. Standards should flow from strategic goals. As goals change, standards must follow, or the organization will find itself rewarding people for the wrong behaviors.

- *Dealing with nonperformance in a fair and timely way.* How the organization deals with nonperformance is important. Nonperformance must be dealt with respectfully and fairly—and above all promptly. The organization's response to high and low performance sends a message to all employees about the value of performance, the fairness and transparency of the system, and the importance that the company places on meeting its goals and serving customers.

Building Leadership Brand

The last factor for HR innovator and integrator is leadership brand.[4] Over the past several years, The RBL Group research on leadership effectiveness has identified a seminal shift in thinking about leadership and talent. A more strategic focus for leadership development should focus less on the skills of individual managers and more on leadership as an organization capability: the ability of an organization to develop leaders at all levels who reinforce confidence in the future and are branded by the distinctiveness of their competence.

A leadership brand has two key elements. The first of these is leadership competence in the fundamentals of being in charge, what we call the "leadership code."[5] The second consists of the differentiators—the things that make a leader reflect and exemplify the character of a specific firm.

We view the development of a powerful leadership brand as a six-step process, sketched in Figure 2.1.

Table 2.8 outlines actions HR professionals and their leaders can take to help their organization develop a working leadership brand.

Technology Proponent

Technology proponent is an interesting and important addition to the competency domains identified in earlier rounds. In 2007, operational execution was a critical factor in HR performance and contribution: effective delivery of both administrative and strategic services. As technology has enabled and transformed HR performance, it has become increasingly important for HR to be tech-savvy, recognize the important contribution that technology can make, and propose and promote technology solutions appropriately.

Figure 2.1   *Developing a Leadership Brand*

Table 2.8   *Promoting Leadership Brand*

Top Priority for Improvement	Potential Actions for HR Professionals	Potential Actions for HR Leaders
Create a business case that leadership matters.	Identify the need for stronger leaders and leadership and their value for growth, customer satisfaction, and risk management.	Make leadership an explicit aspect of strategic discussions: do we have the leadership to implement the strategy?
Articulate the definition of an effective leader.	Identify areas of agreement and disagreement regarding leadership differentiators.	Align leadership standards with strategic requirements.
Assess leaders against a set of criteria.	Assess leaders and audit the assessment process.	Ensure a consistently demanding and rigorous process.

Table 2.8   *Promoting Leadership Brand (continued)*

Top Priority for Improvement	Potential Actions for HR Professionals	Potential Actions for HR Leaders
Invest in future leaders.	Use databases such as the RBL and Hewitt's Top Companies for Leaders to define how the best companies develop leaders.	Make global benchmarking a regular part of reviewing effectiveness .
Measure or track leadership effectiveness.	Identify areas of integration and where better integration is needed.	Audit the leadership development process: how can we improve?
Integrate leadership development efforts.	Assess opportunities to improve innovation and integration of HR practices.	Involve customers and investors in assessing leaders.

Technology proponent is rated lowest among competency domains in professional effectiveness (3.72), but it has a significant impact on business success (18 percent of HR's total impact). Thus, this domain represents a major opportunity for improvement and increased value added. Table 2.9 provides the statistical breakdown of the factors of the technology proponent domain.

Improving Utility

Improving utility of HR operations though technology covers a wide range of activities. The automation of HR functions such as payroll, performance appraisal, and employee benefits can deliver efficiency; introducing employee self-service can increase it further. But this is only the starting point. The capacity for digitization of employee information, organizational roles, and workflow across functions opens up enormous opportunities for HR to improve its management of employee information and experience. For example, American Express has empowered its customer care professionals by providing a flexible technology platform that enables these employees to trade work shifts with one another on their own, without reference to supervisors, allowing people to improve their work–life balance.

Table 2.9   *Technology Proponent: Factors, Mean, and Impact on Individual Effectiveness and Business Success*

Factor	Mean (1–5)	Individual Effectiveness 100%	Business Impact 100%
Improving utility of HR operations	3.72	2.9	5.0
Leveraging social media tools	3.68	2.7	4.7
Connecting people through technology	3.77	4.6	6.3
R^2	3.72	12%	18%

Using Social Media

Social media tools offer a lot of advantages. In recent years social media and supporting technologies have emerged as a platform for companies to engage with employees, customers, and partners. Many companies have a page in Facebook to connect with customers, and they use videos and blogs on social media platforms to communicate about their work cultures and present new opportunities to the external world. For example, Intel has a video on YouTube, and Deutsche Bank has developed a report called "Unofficial Guide to Banking" that both demystifies banking for customers and attracts new recruits.[6]

Social media are also emerging as a way to connect employees with customers. Beyond simply addressing customer problems, these platforms are becoming a knowledge hub for collaboration among employees and customer staff to solve problems and generate new ideas to improve products and services. In essence, the traditional customer word-of-mouth is now spoken on social media platforms. And businesses cannot afford to ignore this new reality. A few years back, for example, some Dell laptops caught fire unexpectedly. The phenomenon was more intensely tracked on the social media sites than anywhere else, and Dell was able to use the same platform to grasp the source of these problems and address them rapidly.

Nonetheless, few organizations use social media well. According to Gartner Research, only 5 percent of organizations take advantage of social media to collaborate with customers to improve their processes.[7] It is clear that this is still an evolving technology. Hence, it should not be a surprise that this factor rates low in business impact in our results.

Connecting People Through Technology

Of all the findings in the 2012 round of the HRCS, none is perhaps more dramatic—or more counterintuitive—than the "connecting people through technology" factor of the technology proponent domain. The reasoning for this conclusion is reasonably straightforward. All technology proponent factors have the lowest personal effectiveness scores of any of the domains by noticeable margins. While connecting people through technology scores highest of the three domain factors, the differences among the three are small. The high drama occurs in impact on business success. Connecting people through technology has the greatest effect on business success of any factor of any domain. It is simultaneously where HR professionals have the worst scores and where they can have the greatest impact. This is essentially the definition of potential competitive advantage.

The survey items that comprise this factor indicate a comprehensive communications strategy that can be expressed in the framework set out in Figure 2.2.

HR professionals who can use social tools and other technology to translate and filter market information (from the outside) into efficient and effective internal decision making and actions will offer their organizations a decided competitive edge.

Figure 2.2   Communications Strategy

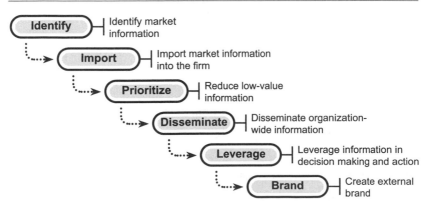

Overall Findings

Despite the regional variations discussed later in this book, we are struck by the consistency of findings across geography and industry. Although there are certainly differences on the margin, these data speak eloquently to the increasingly global nature of HR competency expectations, professional effectiveness, and the business impact of HR contribution. Table 2.10 makes this point clearly.

These are the key points from the data:

- Credible activist is the highest rated competency domain in every region.
- Technology proponent is the lowest rated competency domain in every region.
- The degree of variation across regions is important and material, but generally smaller than might be expected.

Globalization Trends

The continuing globalization of HR and the growing impact of globalization on HR competency expectations and competency assessment can be attributed in part to the increasing professionalization of HR. No longer is HR seen as the backwater of organizations, nor is it generally regarded as merely an administrative, transactional function. In addition, both information and employment cross national boundaries more and more easily.

Professional Effectiveness and Business Impact

A particularly powerful finding of the 2012 HRCS round is the asymmetry of ratings of HR professional effectiveness and business impact. As Figure 2.3 points out, there are interesting differences between the factors that drive the perception of professional effectiveness and the factors that contribute directly to business impact.

This matrix provides a vivid representation of the relationship between current HR effectiveness and business success. Note that credible activist factors are in the upper left-hand corner, indicating that they are performed at

Table 2.10   Mean Competency Domain Ratings by Region

	Overall Total	Africa	Australia and New Zealand	China	Europe	India	Latin America	Middle East	U.S. and Canada	Turkey
Strategic Positioner	3.89	4.09	3.95	3.78	3.82	3.83	3.85	3.84	3.99	3.73
Credible Activist	4.23	4.46	4.31	4.18	4.14	4.19	4.18	4.19	4.35	4.04
Capability Builder	3.97	4.18	4.05	3.87	3.90	3.96	3.94	3.92	4.08	3.82
Change Champion	3.93	4.14	3.96	3.84	3.85	3.92	3.91	3.87	4.03	3.76
HR Innovator & Integrator	3.90	4.09	3.96	3.82	3.81	3.89	3.84	3.82	4.02	3.76
Technology Proponent	3.74	3.84	3.70	3.74	3.61	3.82	3.70	3.72	3.82	3.64
Overall Mean	3.96	4.16	4.01	3.88	3.87	3.94	3.91	3.90	4.07	3.81

Figure 2.3   *Prioritizing HR Competence Actions Based on Current Effectiveness and Business Impact*

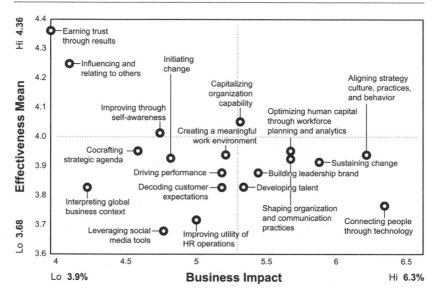

a high level of effectiveness but have less influence on business success. By contrast, the factors that have the greatest impact on business success are, in order of importance:

- Connecting people though technology (domain: technology proponent)
- Aligning strategy, culture, practices, and behavior (domain: capability builder)
- Sustaining change (domain: change champion)

Sum Greater than the Parts

These data are consistent with another, equally interesting finding from the global sample. Overall, individual HR professional effectiveness explained approximately 8 percent of the HR impact on business performance. However, the effect of the HR department was considerably greater, explaining over 30 percent of HR contribution. In short, attention to HR professional skills and knowledge is an important factor in HR achievement, but only where HR professional skills are joined with HR department effectiveness and efficiency does the HR function truly contribute.

Table 2.11 reports the focus on and relative impact of these actions on business performance, with some fascinating results.

Table 2.11   Focus of HR Department

Question: To what extent are the following true of your HR department?

	Mean	Relative Weighting
Interacts effectively with the board of directors	3.67	7.7%
Has clear roles and responsibilities for each of the groups within HR (service centers, centers of expertise, embedded HR)	3.65	7.6%
Matches the structure of the HR department with how the business is organized	3.64	7.8%
Ensures that HR initiatives enable the business to achieve strategic priorities	3.62	9.7%
Develops an HR strategy that clearly links HR practices to business strategy	3.61	9.2%
Ensures that the different groups within HR work effectively with each other to provide integrated HR solutions	3.50	8.2%
Effectively manages external vendors of outsourced HR activities	3.49	8.3%
Invests in training and development of HR professionals	3.46	7.3%
Ensures that HR is a cultural role model for the rest of the organization	3.42	8.4%
Holds line managers accountable for HR	3.38	8.2%
Connects HR activities to external stakeholder expectations (customers, investors, and so on)	3.25	8.9%
Tracks and measures the impact of HR	3.22	8.8%
Multiple Regression R^2		

Conclusion

The global findings of the 2012 round of the HRCS point out that HR is a global village, increasingly connected by shared perspectives on HR performance requirements and current skills, knowledge, and contribution. HR professionals must focus from the outside in, build strong relationships with internal and external stakeholders, lead and manage change, build capability within their organizations through innovative and integrated HR practices, and use technology strategically and creatively for both efficiency and organizational connectivity.

PART TWO

THE WORLD'S NINE MAJOR REGIONS: THEIR BUSINESS CHALLENGES, HR COMPETENCIES, AND COMPETITIVE PRACTICES

AFRICA

3

Justin Allen and Elijah Litheko

June 16, 1976, was a cold day in Soweto township. Fifteen-year-old Refentse marched with her fellow students to protest the oppression of the apartheid regime, chanting and yelling at the police as they glared back at the youths. Suddenly, the police opened fire. "They didn't give any warning. They simply opened fire. . . . And small children, small defenseless children, dropped down like swatted flies. . . . "[1] The world seemed to explode around her, and when the dust settled, several of her friends lay bleeding in the dirt. Refentse has never forgotten the horror. That day she promised herself that she would some how and in some way change the world. She would find a way to create opportunity for everyone.

Thirty-five years later, Refentse sat at her desk in the Sandton area of Johannesburg and thought back on the dark days of apartheid, and the many hard years that followed. But the world had changed, at least in part, and now she was the new head of HR in a large manufacturing and distribution company with offices throughout Africa—and she had an entirely new dilemma in front of her. Refentse was tired. The CEO had just returned from a conference and told her that it was HR's job to build both talent and organization capability. He said he expected her to prepare a comprehensive HR strategy and to present her initial approach to him within one week. What could she do?

Reaching into the past, she knew what to do . . . she would take to the streets! "Moipone," she called out to her assistant, "please make appointments for me to visit every office to meet with our leaders in Nairobi, Accra, Gaborone, Lagos, and here in Sandton. I need to talk to our people. I need to understand the situation on the ground. It's time to change the world again."

Introduction to HR in Africa

This chapter is a window into the field of HR in Africa. The saga of the confluence between people and work in the continent is made up of millions of stories like Refentse's, where individuals seek to find meaning and create value at the abrupt intersection between the history of nations and their individual lives. We hope this work will increase understanding and shed light on the context in which African HR professionals work each day.

Before we attempt to either extrapolate on individual experiences such as Refentse's or hypothesize about regional phenomena, we must first take a moment to recognize the vast and complex diversity of the 54 African nations. We know that any attempt to bundle all of Africa into one homogenous homily is inherently suspect. However, trusting that the views we offer in the following pages will be taken in context, we hope that our rendering of the HR scene in Africa is a helpful starting point.

Socioeconomic Conditions in Africa

As the world's second-largest continent and home to more than a billion people, Africa has a long, proud history of innovation, hard work, collaboration, and—more than anything else—the capacity to survive and thrive despite difficult circumstances. The landmass alone is impressive: the continent of Africa is large enough to fit all of China, the United States, Mexico, India, Peru, France, Spain, Sweden, Japan, Germany, Norway, Italy, New Zealand, the United Kingdom, Nepal, Bangladesh, and Greece within its borders.[2] Despite the continent's size and diversity, a broad-brush sketch of its social, political, market, organizational, and talent trends will provide a useful backdrop for the HRCS data.

Overview

While most nations look back to the Industrial Revolution as the foundation of their modern-day work and management practices, Africans most often recollect the oppression of European invasion, occupation, and colonization that raged about the same time, during the final quarter of the nineteenth century. In a desperate grab for natural resources and an effort to offset burgeoning trade deficits, the colonizers partitioned Africa according to their whims and greed, regardless of the conflict their arbitrary boundaries created within existing local tradition. Consequently, while the Western world was tinkering with free enterprise and capitalism, colonizers in Africa relied heavily on the military and police to increase productivity, and a dictatorial style reminiscent of those colonizers often pervades modern business management in Africa to this day. Meanwhile, local leaders who are successful in getting the best from their people tend to be strong relationship-builders and influencers, a skill-set honed over generations of finding opportunity among captors.

When colonial territories finally gained independence after World War II, the sudden departure of colonists from Africa left a significant infrastructural, educational, and economic void for incoming African governments and local business leaders to fill. For example, the World Bank reports that when DR Congo gained independence in 1960, it had just 16 post-secondary-school graduates among a population of 13 million.[3] Meanwhile, when constitutional measures to promote long-repressed local traditions and values were introduced at independence, these practices were unavoidably jumbled with the cultures created in European colonialism. The most frequent results have been the volatility, corruption, and violence that still hobble African enterprise.

Notwithstanding the difficult hand it has been dealt, Africa is rising. Economic investment, especially recent infusions of capital from Asia, has increased during the post–cold war era, and 30 African countries are now measured in the Global Competitiveness report. Rwanda, for example, has improved 40 places in the past five years (from a ranking of 110 to 70) and has 13 measures in the top 10 countries globally.[4] Additionally, Africa has many excellent universities—including 50 in the top 15 percent of the 20,000 registered universities globally.[5] And perhaps most significantly, the International Monetary Fund has suggested that Africa will host as many as 7 of the 10 fastest-growing economies in the world by 2020.[6] More and more Africans are returning home to take advantage of the increasingly recognized realization that Africa is the new global investment frontier.

Talent and Organization Trends

While Africa is rising from a macroeconomic perspective, the struggle to build personal economic freedom continues to be an individual battle as well. Over the years, limited economic and education opportunities coupled with tumultuous economic conditions have caused unemployment rates in many African countries to become excessively high. This lack of employment opportunities, particularly among youth (ages 18 to 35) and women, has been widely regarded as the force behind the recent uprisings in North Africa. Despite the difficulty, growing numbers of Africans are obtaining a solid education from universities both outside and inside Africa. Meanwhile, the majority who are unable to obtain secondary or tertiary levels of education are increasingly looking for opportunities to build competence while on the job.

Increasing individuals' competence at work appears to be the key to building a sustainable labor pool in Africa, and organization structures are beginning to transform across the continent in ways that make on-the-job learning feasible. Although the colonial command-and-control, top-down organizational design tends to be the norm, some of the best African companies are seizing the unique opportunity to draw upon past traditions of clan-based societies to build organization cultures that promote learning and growth.

Case Studies as Context

The following case studies ground the picture of Africa in reality. Our samples include MTN, a large multinational with headquarters in South Africa; TechnoServe, a high-impact enterprise that provides business support services for local small and medium-size enterprises throughout Africa; and the Ouelessebougou Alliance, a local government partnership that uses human and physical resources interventions to increase livelihood measures in villages in Mali. These organizations also provide examples related to the research-based recommendations presented later in this chapter.

MTN: Telecommunication Services in Africa

With more than 164 million subscribers in communities across Africa and into the Middle East, MTN is emerging as the leading provider of telecommunications in emerging markets. It was founded in South Africa in 1994—a time when many international organizations failed to see sustainable opportunity in Africa—and it has grown exponentially since, with 2011 revenues totaling more than US$15 billion. MTN leaders agree that the company's unique combined expertise in human resources and technology has enabled its current success and will empower future opportunity.

After 15 years of growth and facing depressed financial markets, MTN's 2009 leadership team knew they needed to be clear about the group's strategy and align all systems to ensure future success and expansion. In a seminal series of meetings, they reiterated that their strategic driver in Africa was their position as the lowest-cost operator, and they decided to invest in HR systems and technology to remain profitable while operating in price-sensitive emerging markets. With this mandate during the past three years, MTN has invested in performance and recognition systems, leadership development systems, and communication systems. In terms of the HRCS work, MTN shows particular strength in the HR innovator and integrator domain and in the technology proponent domain.

HR Innovator and Integrator

With a clear strategy in mind, MTN leaders identified a number of innovative initiatives to pull their people together and integrate their systems with their strategy. For example, the MTN Y'elloStars program allows employees to nominate individuals and teams who have displayed exceptional behaviors across four MTN recognition categories. Submissions in each category are rated by a panel-evaluation process, and the winners proceed through quarterly, annual, and then regional and overall winners in each of the recognition categories. Although relatively simple, the YelloStars program has been highly successful. The program gives staff various means of recognizing one another as individuals or as teams and has been instrumental in helping MTN drive its values and performance-based culture.

Technology Proponent

To address the difficulty of maintaining consistency and employee engagement across long distances and multiple technology platforms, MTN launched a group-wide intranet it calls MTN Connect. The solution involved the integration of off-the-shelf digital software and formed a new communication and technology platform to build a digitally-connected employee base across 21 countries. MTN Connect became the access point to host and share relevant group information and up-to-date internal news, and the place to collaborate and share insights with colleagues throughout MTN. MTN Connect offers several benefits:

- A single platform accessible to all 35,000 colleagues
- An easy-to-access spot for company policies, frameworks, and documentation
- An increase in the quality and speed of organizational learning and collaboration through an integration of social media tools and the formation of online communities relating to specific topics
- External talent attraction and recruitment tools such as web-enabled career sites, CV hosting capabilities, and young-talent-attraction multimedia communication and marketing campaigns

MTN has led the way for mobile technology to leapfrog landline infrastructure in Africa, enabling thousands of people to gain access to the Internet and global markets. Building on this tradition, HR at MTN has bypassed old legacy HR systems and delivered a solution that further narrows the digital divide between employer, employees, and customers. Although not without its own challenges, MTN is a strong example for international companies seeking to penetrate African markets, and also for African companies looking to grow throughout Africa.

TechnoServe: Building Capability and Championing Change

While MTN is an archetype for large companies in Africa, TechnoServe (www.technoserve.org) offers a model for small- and medium-size enterprises (SMEs). TechnoServe is an international nonprofit with operations throughout Africa, as well as in Latin America and Asia, TechnoServe's mission is to improve economic viability for SMEs while enabling self-reliance and increased capacity among their suppliers and employees.

TechnoServe identifies entrepreneurs and SMEs with growth potential that warrants human capital investment and then offers business development support, including financial literacy, governance guidance, market strategy, and people strategy. The TechnoServe model is based on the premise that building organization capability is the ticket to long-term growth and business survival in Africa. In other words, if an enterprise has the systems, processes, and people necessary to become very good at one or two key strategic focus areas and align these systems to meaningful work, it will be much more likely to see long-term financial success and its employees and suppliers will be much more likely to see long-term improvements in their lives. TechnoServe shows particular strength in the capability builder and change champion competency domains.

Capability Builder

The TechnoServe team first works with SME owners to clarify their strategic direction and ascertain the capabilities the SMEs will need if they are to deliver on their strategies over time. TechnoServe then looks to identify improvement areas with the entrepreneurs and employees to meet both the business goals and goals aimed at improving the employees' lives. Solutions can range from introducing quality-assurance practices to upgrading financial management systems, but regardless of what the solutions are, employees must be able to articulate how their newfound initiatives help them build organization capability. In this manner, SMEs are able to enhance their long-term sustainability.

Change Champion

Making change happen in any culture can be difficult, but such efforts tend to be especially challenging among SME employees in Africa. Perhaps this is due to multiple initiatives these employees have seen come and go over the years, or perhaps it is because change efforts are based on Western incentive systems rather than incentives more likely to be meaningful to Africans. To break the change barrier, TechnoServe works with leaders in SMEs to identify external mentors, who act as change champions. Rather than offering a theory or academic model for change, these mentors guide leaders on a journey and demonstrate resilience in the face of ambiguity and change. These individuals are most often local professionals who have been successful and who understand the challenges SME leaders face in their local context. To supplement the mentoring relationship, TechnoServe provides training, coaching, and individual experiential learning to help lead change.

Given that SMEs provide the large majority of formal employment opportunities in Africa, understanding how to improve their business results by building human capital is critical. While most SMEs are too small to have large formal HR departments, the general principles still apply, and organizations like TechnoServe are showing the impact people solutions can have on sustainable economic development for businesses and individuals.

The Ouelessebougou Alliance: Public-Private Sector Partnerships

The implementation of "human resources work" in Africa doesn't always fit the mold common among large corporations based in Europe, Asia, or North America. Broad-based HR information systems (HRIS) implementations and large-scale corporate initiatives are rare. Rather, implementation of the HR model is often modified in Africa to fit the informal economy and family or tribal businesses.

With that in mind, much employment in Africa occurs on the street or village level, and the Ouelessebougou Alliance, named for the town in Mali where it is based, offers a model of best practice in this important category. The alliance is a small partnership between local government, local enterprise, and a nonprofit that employs human and physical resources interventions to increase livelihood measures among villagers, supporting the local informal economy.

Mariama "Tenengnini" Diakite, a human services field worker with the Ouelessebougou Alliance, exemplifies the HR competencies outlined in our research. She is not called an "HR business partner," but that is what she is. During more than 10 years as an employee with the alliance, Tenengnini has demonstrated excellence in building trust as a credible activist while helping decode the context around her to cocraft a strategic agenda for change.

Strategic Positioner

Shea nuts grow in abundance in Mali, and with the right training and tools, workers can transform the oil from these nuts into profitable shea butter, a commodity sold on the international market to be used in cosmetics and lotions. One of Tenengnini's roles as part of the alliance was to work with local village leaders to increase training and help people find access to tools that will help them produce the quality needed on the international market. However, Tenengnini faced two major roadblocks. First, she lacked the credibility and clout she needed to get the attention of the village leaders. She quickly found that regardless of how important her solutions were to the livelihood of the villagers, she got very little traction because she was a woman without the right family history. Second, once trained, many villagers fell ill or had family members who became sick, so they were no longer able to use their newfound skills to provide for their families.

Assessing the situation, Tenengnini intelligently identified the needs of her stakeholders and worked with her colleagues at the alliance to develop a plan for success. In short, her plan was to find a way to reduce illness so as to gain the trust and respect of the village elders and their people. This allowed her to work with them more closely to help them find sustainable economic solutions in the shea butter industry for the villagers. Although it appears simple on the surface, the process she followed to develop her plan is the same one we see outlined in the strategic positioner domain of our competency study: clarify the context you work in, outline stakeholder needs, and develop an agenda for action. For HR professionals worldwide the process is called "best practice"; for Tenengnini, it was just instinctively the right thing to do.

Credible Activist

With a strategic plan in hand, Tenengnini was prepared to work. She knew that if she could prove success in just one village, she would gain credibility to work in all the surrounding villages. In the rural areas of Mali, one in five children dies before reaching age five, killed by a preventable disease such as dysentery, measles, or malaria. Tenengnini and her colleagues decided to tackle malaria with mosquito nets as their solution. Selling nets is one matter. Convincing people to sleep under the uncomfortable nets in 40 to 50 degrees Celsius temperatures (104 to 122 degrees Fahrenheit) is a completely different matter. So, just as an HR leader might do in a large manufacturing facility during a major change effort, Tenengnini addressed them all one by one, working closely with the people to present the virtues of mosquito nets in terms they understood. Finally, after a year of building relationships in one village, she was able to decrease its rate of malaria by 87 percent. Now much healthier, the villagers were able to dedicate time to their livelihoods, and Tenengnini gained credibility to work with village elders in other villages, promoting both the importance of mosquito nets *and* the production of exportable shea butter.

Review and Discussion of the 2012 HRCS Africa Findings

Prior to this round of the HRCS, very little research on the continent's HR practices had been conducted, and the reports that exist often focus on a specific company or region. Our data add to the growing body of research on African HR, and we are excited to provide a clearer topographical survey of the HR landscape in Africa.

While we consider this to be the most significant study on HR competencies in Africa to date, we also acknowledge the limitations in the data, given our sample size, especially when considering the immense size of the continent and its vast diversity of culture and people. We cannot claim that our sample represents every HR professional in every country across Africa. However, we are confident that the data provides an excellent baseline from which to begin exploring the strengths and improvement opportunities among African HR professionals. Consider the HRCS results in light of your own experiences with African HR professionals, and draw your own conclusions as you analyze the information.

Profile of an Effective HR Leader in Africa

Given the turbulent sociopolitical environment many Africans were raised in, the typical HR leader in Africa often combines a cacophony of life experience with a deep understanding of humans' need for tolerance, acceptance, and purpose. A key finding is that the best HR leaders in Africa are brilliant at initiating change and relating to others.

Gender and Experience

Africa—like India, the Middle East, and Latin America—is a region where men still dominate the HR profession. As noted earlier, the large majority of HR professionals in the world are women. However, in developing economies, including Africa, men are still the dominant force. This trend has been shifting to a more balanced mix over the past several years, and Africa leads developing economies in its ratio of females to males, but the gender demographic in Africa still lags the global norms with 54 percent male and 46 percent female.

Meanwhile, when overlaying gender distribution with tenure in HR, increasing numbers of African women are in the "0–5 years of experience" and "6–10 years of experience" category. Currently, a plurality of African HR professionals has more than 15 years' experience (32 percent), with men making up the majority of these professionals. Given gender trends in the workforce and the eventual retirement of the more experienced workers, we anticipate females will dominate the profession in Africa within 5 to 10 years.

Size of Business

As noted earlier, many now see Africa as the world's most attractive region for investment.[7] Nonetheless, relatively few large businesses have taken root, discouraged by lack of infrastructure and by uncertain political stability. Consequently, the majority of HR professionals in Africa are working in SMEs, with roughly 50 percent of all HR professionals working in companies with fewer than 1,000 employees. This is significantly different from most other regions of the world and requires a specialized skill set for HR professionals in Africa.

Competency Domains

Comparing global averages with Africa-specific data offers interesting insights. Table 3.1 shows that across the board African mean scores in each of the HR competency domains are higher than global mean scores. In fact, African mean scores are not only higher than average global scores, they are higher than mean scores in any other region in every single domain. This may be surprising to some. However, the underlying values and beliefs of culture play a significant role in the approach participants take when answering questions in a 360-degree assessment. Based on qualitative data, including personal interviews and experience working with HR professionals from around the world, we conjecture that the significantly high African scores may be reflective of a cultural bias for saving face and putting your best foot forward. With this in mind, it is helpful to control for regional ratings bias by evaluating comparisons within Africa itself to identify areas of perceived strengths or weaknesses.

Table 3.1 Domain Mean Scores Comparison: Africa

	Strategic Positioner	Credible Activist	Capability Builder	Change Champion	HR Innovator & Integrator	Technology Proponent
Africa domain mean score	4.09	**4.46**	4.18	4.14	4.09	**3.84**
% of African mean total	16.49	**17.98**	16.85	16.69	16.49	**15.48**

Two intriguing trends emerge when examining the difference between African and the global percentage-of-mean figures:

- *Pillar in credible activist.* It is clear that raters view African HR professionals as significantly more proficient in the credible activist domain than in other domains. From movements like the Arab Spring in Northern Africa to individual stories like Tenengnini and the Ouelessebougou Alliance, Africans seem to know instinctively what to do to build trust and move things forward.
- *Notable concern in technology proponent.* The opposite is true for technology proponent, where African HR professionals are seen as significantly weak compared with those in other domains. As shown in the MTN example, strength in technology is an anomaly in Africa that offers opportunity for competitive advantage to those who build strength there.

Key Strengths and Opportunities

Refentse's story at the beginning of the chapter highlights the childhood conditions in which many African HR professionals developed their stamina and strength. Although we use the Soweto riots of 1976 as a specific example in our illustration, African HR professionals across the continent have faced similar crucibles in their lives where they honed fundamental skills and developed critical competencies during long years struggling for survival and fighting for opportunity. In this segment we explore the strengths African HR professionals can leverage, as well as opportunities where they can improve for continued growth.

Strength 1: Credible Activist (Influencing and Relating to Others)

African HR professionals received their second-highest relative scores in the factor "influencing and relating to others," which is found in the credible activist domain. (See Table 3.2. Note that although "earning trust through results" is the highest overall score in Africa's credible activist domain, when compared with the global dataset, 5.46 percent is a relatively low score. In other words, respondents in other regions of the world generally give much higher scores in "earning trust through results" than African respondents give. We address these results in more detail later in the chapter.) As noted in all three case studies, African HR professionals seem to have an innate ability to influence and relate to others. They are very good at building relationships, understanding the intricacies of human relations, reading nonverbal and underlying messages, and demonstrating empathy.

The best HR professionals in Africa are those who understand how to relate to people from a variety of backgrounds and know how to influence them to get results. In fact, it is important to note that *all* of the factor scores in this domain are relatively high. This skill-set is complementary to African scores on the factor "initiating change," as discussed below.

Table 3.2   Credible Activist Factor Comparison

	Earning Trust Through Results	Influencing and Relating to Others	Improving Through Self-Awareness	Shaping the HR Profession
Average response for Africa	4.52	4.48	4.33	4.44
Relative response compared with all factors for Africa	5.46%	5.42%	5.23%	5.37%

Strength 2: Change Champion (Initiating Change)

In the area of initiating change (a factor of the change champion domain), Africa ranks among the top. Table 3.3 outlines the supporting data. This is the trait TechnoServe applies to push for change in the SME markets. In most developing economies, HR leaders are seen as individuals who need to be told what to do and who are averse to risk, but our data combined with our experience working in Africa show that African HR professionals thrive on initiating change and looking for new approaches and new solutions.

The combined data in Tables 3.2 and 3.3 suggests that African HR professionals are adept at dealing with ambiguity and are more likely than others in the field to initiate change and challenge the status quo.

Strength 3: Strategic Positioner

African HR leaders receive relatively high marks in two of the three factors of the strategic positioner domain (see Table 3.4). We highlight this domain as an area to build upon because of its impact on driving business results. The best HR professionals in Africa use their abilities to relate to others to reach out to customers and employ their influencing abilities both inside and outside the business.

Table 3.3   Change Champion Factor Comparison

	Initiating Change	Sustaining Change
Average response for Africa	4.16	4.09
Relative response compared with all factors for Africa	5.03%	4.94%

Table 3.4   Strategic Positioner Factor Comparison

	Interpreting Global Business Context	Decoding Customer Expectations	Cocrafting a Strategic Agenda
Average response for Africa	4.01	4.05	4.18
Relative response compared with all factors for Africa	4.85%	4.90%	5.05%

Influencing and relating to others, initiating change, and decoding customer expectations are three areas in which African HR professionals are seen as highly proficient. Knowledge of these strengths is critical, and individual HR professionals in Africa should regard them as strengths to build upon. International recruiters and business leaders should also capitalize on these strengths when searching for HR professionals who can manage well across boundaries and influence coworkers, drive change, and make clear connections with customers.

Improvement Opportunity 1: Technology Proponent

Africa has quite low scores in the technology proponent domain (see Table 3.5). This is an interesting trend given that other developing economies (such as in India, China, and Turkey) have high scores in both improving HR operations through technology and connecting people via technology. Awareness of this weakness is important, and African HR leaders would do well to increase their technological prowess and thereby propel their regions into accelerated economic opportunities.

If Africa is truly the next big investment opportunity in the world, African HR leaders must learn to leverage any and all technological solutions available to them. Certainly, while many small African companies cannot afford to implement large ERP systems, as demonstrated in the MTN example, the proliferation of cloud computing and social networking enables lone HR professionals to identify applications that can change the way work is done and the way people interact with one another. Most of these applications require relatively little setup time and can be purchased for fees that fit the budgets of small African businesses. If HR professionals can learn to take advantage of technology, they will play a significant role in the transformation of the region.

Table 3.5   Technology Proponent Factor Comparison

	Improving HR Operations	Connecting People via Technology	Leveraging Social Media
Average response for Africa	3.86	3.92	3.73
Relative response compared with all factors for Africa	4.67%	4.74%	4.51%

Improvement Opportunity 2: Change Champion (Sustaining Change)

While initiating change is a strength for African HR professionals, the companion factor (sustaining change) can be a relative weakness (see Table 3.3). As seen in the TechnoServe example, unless champions are identified to carry changes through time, many African leaders will simply spend time starting new initiatives and pushing to change the system, while failing to focus on ensuring the changes actually take place. Consequently, they will probably lose credibility and their strength in initiating change will be undermined.

As demonstrated by Tenengnini, sustaining change requires discipline and an ability to execute well and provide focus over time. This discipline can come in the form of a tool as simple as a checklist that is reviewed regularly. Whatever the mechanism, African HR professionals must improve their abilities to sustain change over time and therefore make sure they provide the results they have committed to deliver to their stakeholders.

Improvement Opportunity 3: A Cautionary Note on Trust

Although African HR professionals receive high overall scores in the credible activist domain, when compared with other regions of the world, they have a low score in one of the domain's factors: ensuring trust through results.

Clearly, Africa's lower trust score is an average of many scores, and we have worked with many HR professionals who maintain extremely high levels of trust and have solid integrity. However, the trust trend is real and must not be taken lightly by African HR professionals. We offer this cautionary note based on the data and suggest that all HR professionals, regardless of their geography, examine their own behavior to ensure that they maintain high levels of trust by fulfilling all the obligations they commit to and by delivering results.

Conclusion: Driving Business Results in Africa

It is always helpful to be aware of our strengths and opportunities for improvement, and it is even more helpful to know which competencies will have the greatest impact on our ability to deliver results. Therefore, one of the most important questions in our study was, "Does effective HR work have a positive impact on business performance?" The resounding answer is, "yes". Our data shows that the combined influence of the six HR competency domains has a 14 percent impact on business results in Africa (0.144 R^2). This is significant, given the many other variables that affect business performance. Meanwhile, regardless of the data, the case studies in this chapter demonstrate that whether in a large company like MTN with thousands of employees or in a small organization like the Ouelessebougou Alliance, when all is said and done, the fundamental take-away is that HR excellence in Africa drives business results.

Throughout this chapter we have evaluated the context in which HR work is done today, shared best practice case studies, and outlined our data which points to strengths, weaknesses and opportunities for HR professionals in Africa. We close where we began: just as Refentse was able to build upon a difficult past to create future growth, we are convinced that HR professionals and HR organizations in Africa can stand upon the foundation of their past to build a brighter future. We have great hope for the future of Africa. We have great confidence in the HR professionals who will continue to help Africa rise up.

CHAPTER 4

AUSTRALIA AND
NEW ZEALAND

4

Anne-Marie Dolan and Alan Nankervis

The ongoing discourse concerning the global convergence or divergence of human resource management (HRM) strategies, systems, and practices suggests that elements of both persist in all national contexts, including those of Australia and New Zealand.[1] However, their influence varies, depending on economic, political, and social factors, the dynamism of local industry sectors, and the nature of industrial-relations systems. The stage of evolution of the HRM profession and the associated competencies of HR professionals are also crucial characteristics everywhere.

Australia's Business Environment

Australia is simultaneously the largest island and the smallest continent in the world, with just under 22.5 million people, or 0.3 percent of the world's population, and 1.8 percent annual growth.[2] Its gross domestic product (GDP) in 2010 amounted to nearly US$916 billion.[3] This represents approximately 1.3 percent of global GDP, and its economic growth rate was a modest 2.6 percent.[4] The economy was formerly based on agriculture and manufacturing, but since the 1970s it has shifted toward resources and services, with reduced focus on manufacturing due to more competitive labor costs in regional countries. In the resources sector, minerals are the most important contributor—especially in Western Australia and Queensland, with burgeoning markets in China and India. The demand from these markets has led to scarcity of both skilled and semiskilled labor, which has attracted workers from other Australian states and sectors, thus creating important workforce imbalances. Meanwhile, the significance of agriculture has declined as acquisitions and mergers have replaced small farms with large conglomerates, many of which are foreign-owned. Overall, Australia's financial, economic, and labor markets are now substantially influenced by and responsive to outside forces.[5]

Australia's workforce is culturally diverse as the result of ongoing immigration, most recently from Asia, and its current unemployment level hovers around 5 percent.[6] Employment rates vary by age; with almost 61 percent of those between 15 and 24, 79.5 percent between 25 and 54, and 61 percent between 55 and 64 in full-time jobs.[7] In the 15- to 24-year-old age group, many potential workers have chosen to pursue further education to enhance their career opportunities, and the majority of these undertake part-time or casual work to finance their studies. Many of these workers are employed in the services sector, notably in retail and hospitality. Approximately 25 percent of Australians are employed on a part-time basis; many of these are women. There is also a growing proportion of casual employees in the retail, tourism, and hospitality sectors, together with many contract positions in the resources sector.

Australia has a strong adversarial industrial-relations system with complex conflict–resolution procedures inherited from its British origins. Until the 1980s, frequent industrial actions including strikes and go-slows constrained productivity and competitiveness. However, this system has been transformed in recent decades because of industry restructuring, government and union imperatives of cooperation rather than confrontation, and declining union membership (currently 15 to 20 percent of the workforce, depending on the industry sector). Union membership has been consistently higher in the public than the private sector in Australia.

All these factors provide Australian HR professionals with both pressures and opportunities—and consequently with challenges to their present and future roles and competencies. Australia's HRM model has been categorized as "transnational-hybrid," encompassing both the more formal and standardized HRM systems employed in large foreign and domestic corporations and public sector agencies, and the more informal functions used by small and medium-size organizations.[8]

HRM at Luxottica

Luxottica's HR function has received accolades within Australia and has delivered the strongest retail results in its global business (fashion eyewear) in the past.[9] Winning countless individual and team-based HR, people management, and business leadership awards (including the 2009 Australian Human Resources Institute Award for HR Impact), the team delivers impressive results in a tough retail environment with a typically part-time workforce.

One key to Luxottica's HR strategy, and HR's recognition within the organization as a true business partner, is the use of success metrics in performance management, talent acquisition, and leadership development profiles.[10] It tailors global initiatives to the region, as with OneSight, a program that provides free vision care for people who cannot afford it and helps fund research into the prevention of optical diseases.[11] Locally, Luxottica has rolled out the program widely, including to remote indigenous communities in Australia through partnership with the National Rugby League. Overall it has assisted more than 185,000 individuals. Utilizing changing industrial and employment legislation to address local skill shortages in optometry, Luxottica Retail Australia has worked with the 457 visa program (an Australian government visa waiver initiative) to recruit optometry staffs from overseas, building the legislation's requirements into employment contracts and policies so as to ensure that the demand for optometry staffs can be met. The success of Luxottica's HR function locally is demonstrated in the application of its practices in the global business, including the performance-management and talent-management processes.

Characteristics and Implications for HRM in Australia

HR professionals in Australia are generally well educated, with either undergraduate or postgraduate qualifications in relevant fields, and women are in a majority in the profession.[12] An integrated system of vocational and tertiary education provides a comprehensive range of trade and professional courses, which are accredited by the Australian Human Resources Institute (AHRI). The HR function in most Australian organizations has been described as "bureaucratic-service," whereby professionals act as service providers to line management as "business partners" and coordinate the outsourced services of external providers.[13]

Ongoing industry restructuring has demanded dynamic HR responses to issues such as talent attraction and retention, multiskilling and redeployment, the amendment of employment conditions, and union negotiations. The diversity of the workforce, reflected primarily in its multicultural and inter-generational characteristics, requires creative and constant management, while providing significant opportunities for nurturing innovation and adaptation. An interesting example of this approach in Australia is provided by SA Water, a privatized corporation that supplies water-related services to South Australia. Faced with an aging workforce (average age: 48), it instituted a formal demographic review to address potential skills shortages. The outcomes of the review included a four-year apprenticeship program, a two-year graduate program, and a series of traineeships and cadetships. It has resulted in a drop in the company's median workforce age to 42 and a significant reduction in employee turnover rates. This program does a great deal to maintain the talent pipeline and transfer knowledge from older staff to younger trainees; it has reduced SA Water's exposure to skill shortages and other problems in the workplace.[14]

New Zealand's Business Environment for HRM

While considerably smaller in size than Australia's and less diverse in its range and breadth of industry sectors, New Zealand's economy has grown consistently over the past decade. The country's less complicated political structure (a unicameral rather than bicameral legislature and two rather than three layers of government: national and local, with no state level intervening) has helped successive New Zealand governments adapt to changing global and regional economic demands more easily than their Australian counterparts. In particular, they have significantly modernized their former adversarial industrial-relations system, resulting in more equitable and transparent processes for both employers and employees, even though (as in Australia) unions are still an important factor and dangerous to challenge.[15] However, union densities in New Zealand have also declined considerably over the past few decades to around one-fifth of the workforce. These reductions in union membership have been attributed to increases in the middle class and to the more individualistic perspectives of Gen X and Gen Y employees.

As in Australia, the New Zealand workforce is heterogeneous, with 33 percent born overseas, and it has an increasingly large service sector (71 percent in 2006). Unemployment levels in New Zealand hover around 3 to 4 percent, with identified skills shortages in fields such as accounting, finance and management, hospitality and tourism, and some skilled vocations (such as doctors, engineers, and architects). There is also a noticeable brain drain from New Zealand to Australia resulting from perceptions of greater career opportunities in the latter, not unlike the situation between Canada and the United States.

New Zealand's IIRM model has been described as "emergent-development," with its higher proportion of SMEs practicing less formal HRM processes and a greater use of external recruitment agencies for attracting and selecting talent. Nevertheless, researchers have noted that many New Zealand organizations encourage employee participation and are concerned about job satisfaction, often giving individuals substantial leeway to control their day-to-day work.[16]

Contemporary Global, Regional, and Local HRM Challenges

Australia and New Zealand share many of the HR challenges discussed in other chapters of this book, including the demands presented by the globalization and regionalization of business. Accordingly, there are associated demands on HR professionals to demonstrate their contributions to these developments, including aspirations toward the application of global best practices in their own context.

As early as 2003, AHRI research defined the seven major issues confronting businesses in Australia (and by inference New Zealand as well): persistent skills shortages in specialist areas and a concomitant difficulty with labor supply, short- rather than longer-term planning, difficulty with harnessing technology, pressure for legislative compliance, budget constraints, and low productivity.[17] The report concluded, "Challenges presently confronting business in Australia require HR to become a proactive strategic contributor."[18] Despite numerous challenges in the global and regional business environments since then, including global economic crises, rising unemployment rates, and the aging of the workforce in many regions, this imperative remains high on the Australian and New Zealand HRM agenda. A recent white paper, for example, summarized the key challenges faced by local HR professionals in the foreseeable future.[19] New Zealand HR professionals also face similar challenges, largely parallel to those confronting HR professionals in other developed countries:

- Global competition
- Technological and communication breakthroughs
- Employee personal flexibility
- Skills convergence in multidisciplinary environments
- Macroeconomic and demographic changes
- Global best practice in HRM
- Changing business standards
- Government imposition of regulations "to quell public fears"

While Australia and New Zealand face competition from U.S., U.K., and European Union companies (and also from the growing Southeast and East Asian economies), they also have interesting opportunities. For Australia at least, the current boom in China and India has provided a seemingly insatiable demand for its mining resources. This has led to what some have described as a "two-speed economy;" however, with a booming mining sector balanced by significant downturns in retail and manufacturing. Skilled workers in the latter sectors have often left their employers to seek lucrative contract jobs in mining, thus further increasing the skills gaps in the manufacturing and retail sectors.

The white paper referred to earlier also presents the Top 10 HRM challenges: managing talent, improving leadership development, managing work-life balance, managing demographics, becoming a learning organization, managing globalization, improving employee engagement, increasing the alignment between employee performance and rewards, managing change and cultural transformation, and finally, managing corporate social responsibility (CSR).[20] These challenges, it maintains, require the following HR roles, which are associated closely with the competencies discussed later in this chapter:[21]

- Workplace transformers
- Work–life integrators
- Next-generation talent managers
- Performance rewarders
- Learning architects and builders
- CSR stakeholder marshals
- Engaging communicators
- Diversity champions
- Regulatory wizards

Each of these roles requires an underlying set of competencies that are the basis for any Australian HR generalist. These competencies are detailed in the AHRI Model of Excellence developed in 2007 and based on the 2007 round of the HRCS, along with other research on HR in Australia that included interviews with senior HR practitioners and CEOs.

AHRI Model of Excellence

These are the competencies of the current AHRI Model of Excellence:

- *Business Driven.* The need for the HR practitioner, regardless of level or specialization, to understand the nature of the business as well as the political, legislative, and economic environment within which it operates and the economic drivers that lead to its success.
- *Strategic Architect.* The need for the HR practitioner to take knowledge about the organization and its drivers and develop a people strategy that complements the organization's strategy and contributes to its business outcomes.
- *Stakeholder Manager.* The need for the HR practitioner to have an understanding of the needs of all stakeholders to the business (including employees,

customers, shareholders, unions, funding bodies, and government) and to ensure that HR strategy and practice helps the organization meet those needs.

- *Workforce Designer.* The need for the HR practitioner to plan, attract, develop, retain, and manage a workforce that supports current and future organizational objectives.
- *Expert Practitioner.* The need for the HR practitioner to maintain and develop personal knowledge, skills, and experience; to apply that expertise to executing the people strategy; and to develop or acquire additional expertise for the HR function as required.
- *Credible Activist.* The need for the HR practitioner to develop networks and circles of influence within the organization and to deliver the HR message with credibility and conviction.
- *Culture and Change Agent.* The need for the HR practitioner to understand the culture the organization requires to achieve desired business outcomes, to identify where change is required to achieve those outcomes, and to drive that change appropriately.

This version of the model has been applied to the HR profession in Australia through AHRI's accreditation of higher education HR curricula and AHRI professional membership levels. The model continues to evolve. A new version of the model, scheduled for release in 2012 to 2013, will be based on the 2012 HRCS round, along with further Australian research to be conducted by AHRI. It is anticipated that this version will continue to align with the HRCS model and reflect the new emphasis on the technology proponent domain that is identified in the global survey.

Review and Discussion of the 2012 HRCS Australia–New Zealand Findings

The sample of HR professionals from Australia and New Zealand did not clearly differentiate between the two countries. This was unfortunate because the countries differ in the types of organizations that employ HR professionals, the roles that they assume, their diverse HRM models, and their industrial relations contexts. However, the impressive size of the global sample did not permit microanalysis between countries in the same region. Therefore, the following discussion reports on the Australia–New Zealand region overall, with some accompanying comments on potential differences between the two countries. The sample size was 6 percent of total global participants, in contrast to 13 percent from Europe, 16 percent from Latin America, and 36 percent from the United States and Canada. Comparisons based on such disparate samples will inevitably attract critiques, although general observations provide a useful snapshot of HRM professionals' roles and competencies within diverse regional or national environments.

The study shows that Australian and New Zealand HR professionals include a proportion of women (59 percent) similar to that of their U.S. and Canadian, European, and Turkish counterparts, but a considerably larger proportion than in India, Latin America, Africa, and the Middle East. In contrast, women dominate the Chinese HR profession. While not a surprising outcome, this observation reflects the development of the profession in Australia and New Zealand from its primarily female-dominated roots in personnel management to its current more gender-balanced strategic role. Earlier studies had similar findings but cautioned that the developing gender balance during that period might have led to career divisions between male and female HR professionals, with the former assuming more of the strategic and managerial roles.[22] To date, there is no clear evidence either way on this issue in either country, but it might be expected that the application of Equal Employment Opportunity legislation would mitigate such developments. An earlier AHRI study found that Australia had a relatively equal age distribution of HR professionals, with 29 percent between ages 26 and 35, 28 percent between 36 and 45, 28 percent between 46 and 55, and fewer than 10 percent over 56 years of age—representing a healthy balance between early, mid-, and later-stage careerists.[23]

HR Participant Characteristics

Perhaps of more relevance to the roles and competencies of HR professionals in Australia and New Zealand is the finding on their qualifications and professional experience. More than 70 percent have either a four-year degree in

HRM or a postgraduate qualification, while18 percent have an associate's degree from a vocational or technical training institution, and 12 percent have only completed secondary school. An earlier Australian study was less impressive, reporting only 61 percent of participants with either undergraduate (32 percent) or postgraduate (29 percent) degrees, and the rest with only high school or vocational qualifications.[24] It was also able to probe a little deeper, finding that of those with university qualifications more than two-thirds had HRM-specific degrees, and that the HR professionals surveyed considered the most relevant subjects in their degrees to be those focusing on HRM, strategic HRM, and industrial relations.[25]

Given the relatively rapid development of the HRM profession in Australia and New Zealand over the past two decades, accompanied by a significant growth in vocational and higher education qualifications and associated AHRI/NZHRI accreditation, these findings are impressive. In particular, the fact that a large majority of participants have undergraduate or postgraduate qualifications is a tribute both to the educational institutions and to the HR professional bodies in both countries. However, in comparison with other regions in the study, the HRCS study shows that HR professionals in this region include the highest proportion of high school and associate's degree holders, and among the lowest proportions of graduates.

The Australian and New Zealand HRCS sample was disproportionately represented by large organizations; an AHRI study indicated a more even balance between large and smaller organizations.[26] This may be important since competencies such as strategic positioner, change champion, capability builder, and HR innovator and integrator are more evident in larger organizations than might be expected in SMEs.

With these qualifications several additional generalizations can be made about HR professionals in Australia and New Zealand. There is a reasonable gender balance, although women still predominate among HR professionals, and the majority of them work for larger-size organizations rather than smaller ones. Most are qualified at least to the undergraduate (and sometimes postgraduate) degree level, but a smaller proportion are only high school graduates, most likely those who entered the profession at a time when more advanced qualifications were not required. There is also a broad spread of work experience, from fewer than 5 to more than 15 years.

HR Professional Competencies

With a mean of 4.01 across the six HR competency domains, it can be concluded that Australian and New Zealand HR professionals in this study are performing a combination of high-level functions consistent with the expectations of strategic HRM theory. However, given the respondents' concentration in larger-sized organizations, this was not especially surprising. Of these competencies, the highest ratings were given to credible activist (4.31) and capability builder (4.05). In both these cases, the proportions were above the global mean overall but marginally lower than those for the African and the U.S.-Canadian samples.

Comparable value was given to the competencies of change champion (3.96), HR innovator and integrator (3.96), and strategic positioner (3.95). The lowest rating was allocated to the technology proponent competency (3.70), a surprising finding, as it was lower than the overall mean.

While the competency domain of capability builder may have strategic implications, in general, this competency might be expected to reflect more operational purposes including workforce planning through such techniques as talent attraction and retention, job redesign, human resource development, and employee consultation. Many Australian and New Zealand organizations have sought to build workforce capabilities through a combination of voluntary redundancies, more sharply focused recruitment and selection processes, flexible rewards and remuneration programs, and (where permissible under the relevant legislation) the replacement of permanent by contract or casual employment conditions.

The National Australia Bank (NAB) provides an excellent example of the employee consultation aspect of the capability builder competency. In the face of severe national and regional competition, NAB decided that it needed to break down its former hierarchical decision-making style and move toward a more collaborative approach. Thus, it designed a program called World Café, which encompassed proficiency pathways, development pathways mapping, new induction courses, a capability toolkit, and a "thoughts in action" online forum. The outcome was a reduction in employee-initiated turnover from 46.5 percent to 34.5 percent over 12 months, along with significantly improved employee engagement. NAB also provided generous employment packages to help retain people with the scarce and high-demand talent to fill specialist and managerial positions.

The 2012 HRCS findings also provide relatively strong support for the competencies of strategic positioner and HR innovator and integrator, which are arguably most reflective of the vertical alignment of business and HR strategies, with the representation of HR professionals at senior management and board levels. Although earlier AHRI and NZHRI studies have indicated that only a relatively small proportion of HR professionals in Australian and New Zealand organizations have a seat at the board table, the 2012 HRCS study is more positive, suggesting at the least that HR professionals themselves feel that they have the trust of senior management and the confidence and competence to perform more strategically (credible activist). Given the rapid changes occurring in both countries—including mergers and acquisitions, increasing regional and global competition, significant sector shifts, and the demand for new employee skills—these HR competencies have become crucial for organizational renewal and even survival.

As noted earlier, a particular challenge faced by Australian and New Zealand organizations and their HR professionals is the so-called two-speed economy in Australia. The increased demand for mining resources accompanied by decreased demand in other sectors will require sophisticated business acumen and comprehensive yet flexible HR plans. Such HR plans will need to be based on aggregated data from HR information systems, accompanied by pertinent program evaluation systems to justify their contributions to organizational performance. A prime example here is in the Australian and New Zealand retail industries, where not only have many jobs been lost to regional competitors with lower labor costs, but new technologies, such as customer self-scanning, have also significantly reduced the demand for semiskilled labor while increasing the demand for more sophisticated employee skills.

Transfield Services is one company whose use of HR metrics has allowed it to successfully address its challenges. Applying HRIS data aligned to the bottom line, it has demonstrated the returns for the company from the people employed.[27] In integrating 27 businesses acquired over eight years of operation, Transfield uses best-practice human capital metrics to identify better scale effectiveness and thus achieve success in the organization. A dashboard, developed in-house, has allowed the company to save tens of millions, providing more value for shareholders.

Technology Proponent Competency Domain

The relatively low rating with respect to the technology proponent domain reported in this region is perhaps the most surprising finding because both countries have generally been perceived as among the earliest adopters of new technology. Thus, it might have been expected that younger HR professionals with tertiary qualifications would be eager to embrace the benefits of new technology as a vehicle for their strategic, operational, and administrative functions. Certainly there is evidence that new technology is employed in such techniques as employee kiosks, information systems, online training and development, and innovative recruitment processes, including access to Facebook and Twitter.[28] However, the finding might be a reflection of the inability of HR professionals to evaluate the potential or to communicate their understanding of the value of such technologies to their managerial counterparts. While HR may not be able to clearly demonstrate the business case for using different technologies in the workplace and integrating them into work processes, the case is being driven by individual employees whose personal usage of new technology and social media platforms carries over into their professional lives.

In a recent survey by telecommunications company Optus, IT and HR decision makers from more than 320 medium-size to large Australian organizations noted that more and more workers, especially younger ones, are demanding authorization to use their own devices at work.[29] So while this data showed a relatively low rating for HR generally as technology proponents, it appears that the demand from employees who have already incorporated new technologies into their personal lives is driving the adoption of social media, tablets, and mobile technologies by their organizations.[30] One company that has used new technologies successfully is Deloitte, whose Bamboo smartphone application provides employee information to HR practitioners for use during disasters so they can contact employees, check on their safety, and call for help if needed. This application was used to great effect during the recent Queensland floods, where Deloitte HR practitioners were able to communicate constantly with their employees.[31]

HR Competencies and Effect of HRM on Business Performance

Drilling deeper into the six HR competency domains, both strengths and some future challenges are revealed in the 2012 HRCS study. Thus, with respect to the strategic positioner competency, the primary strengths include the ability to interpret the global business context and to devise appropriate HRM strategies in association with senior managers. These are important skills within a dynamic regional business environment, which is becoming increasingly competitive for resources and labor, and which has undergone significant transformation with respect to industry shifts, employee skills requirements, and cross-regional business operations. Susan Ferrier, HR director of the legal firm Allens Arthur Robinson and winner of the AHRI Dave Ulrich HR Leader of the Year Award, is a good example of a strategic positioner who has driven a people strategy contributing to the success of the law firm. Ferrier designed and delivered a strategy, planned for three years at a cost of AU$60 million, that was designed to transform the firm's culture and business results. It included a performance and award strategy and a capability framework to build engagement within a high-performance culture.[32]

Similarly, demonstrating the HR integrator and innovator competency, the Australian and New Zealand participants considered that they possessed the ability to ensure trust through demonstrated business outcomes based on HR functions, and to design HR programs that were appropriate to business requirements. Again, the linkages between such various HR activities as talent attraction, HR development, employee retention, and career development are crucial components of a comprehensive HRM plan that meets the present and future needs of their organizations.

Bupa, a healthcare services provider, illustrates these competencies. It has linked employee performance with clients' outcomes through a program it calls Personal Best. The program set out to transform internal performance benchmarks into client-based criteria. Employees were encouraged to identify three client-based commitments each quarter as their personal best achievements, using either individual client or community-based goals. These were recognized each quarter as Legends and attracted appropriate rewards. The program has resulted in greater client satisfaction, higher staff engagement scores, and discernible improvements in profitability levels, with the program contributing to a 27 percent improvement in 2009 and a 20 percent improvement in 2010. The program has also resulted in a drop in the manager attrition rate from 30 percent to 10 percent. It thus represents both a multiple-stakeholder HRM approach and a successful attempt to seamlessly link performance with rewards and recognition systems.

In the 2012 HRCS round, Australian and New Zealand HR professionals exhibited strengths as capability builders. This competency domain focused primarily on the abilities to capitalize on organization capabilities and to align strategy, culture, and practices in creating a meaningful work environment. These are key features of strategic HRM theory, and they reflect participants' abilities to design programs that benefit both their employers and employees. Such programs in Australia and New Zealand often include competitive rewards and compensation schemes, career enhancement techniques, leadership development projects, innovative job design, and work–life balance activities. These are often complemented by extensive human-capital planning and the development of comprehensive HR metrics systems (technology proponent and HR integrator and innovator domains) that are employed to demonstrate the effectiveness of single or multiple HRM activities.

Mercy Health, a private health-services provider, has employed such programs effectively. In response to employee attraction and retention issues within a female-dominated workforce (90 percent), the company devised a comprehensive HR strategy for enhanced flexibility in employee working conditions. The strategy included a supportive parents' network for employees on maternity or paternity leave, a database of such employees who might be interested in part-time work prior to return to full-time employment, school-holiday activities, and a childcare referral program. Employees responded with reduced turnover, and almost 100 percent have returned from parental leave instead of staying out of the workforce to care for their new children. Close to 80 percent of employees have taken up a flexible work arrangement.

Challenges and Opportunities Raised by the HRCS Study

Challenges raised by HRCS 2012 for HR professionals in the Australia–New Zealand region are associated with specific competencies, such as the abilities to decode customer expectations, to improve through self-awareness, and to influence stakeholders other than customers and employees—that is, investors, the community, and line managers. In the past, some HR professionals have focused on proving the value of their activities to senior managers at the expense of connecting more closely with the operational needs of line managers or the community within which their organizations do business. Several research studies in Australia have suggested the former, but there is also some evidence that many large organizations in Australia and New Zealand are attempting to reach out to their communities through focused local recruitment and corporate social responsibility initiatives, and that HR professionals are jointly involved with other senior managers in these endeavors.

The Resilience@Law program provides a great example of HR professionals working with multiple stakeholders within a community to benefit not just individual organizations but an industry sector as a whole. Through this initiative, five top-tier Australian law firms (Allens, Blake Dawson Waldron, Clayton Utz, Freehills, and King & Wood Mallesons) collaborated on an initiative designed to improve psychological well-being in the profession. Responding to some significant statistics on depression and suicide in the sector, the five firms worked with the University of New South Wales and the Council of Australian Law Deans to develop the program, which helps working lawyers, graduates, and students handle the pressures they face and the associated mental health issues. Although it is in its early stages, the program has attracted attention in the sector and is helping to raise awareness of the issues and the potential for further collaboration to reduce the incidence of mental illness in the profession.

Apart from the competencies of individual HR professionals, the 2012 HRCS study reveals some interesting information about the effectiveness of HR departments as a whole on business performance in the Australia–New Zealand region. HR departments had high scores on such components as effective interaction with boards of directors, clear roles and responsibilities, external vendor management, and the horizontal alignment of all HRM programs. PepsiCo ANZ demonstrates how the Australian HR function of a global business can deliver integrated HR practices with a measurable impact on the company's performance in the region. With high turnover and lower-than-optimal levels of engagement, driven by an "unrelenting focus on productivity and results" that led to unsustainable costs to the business, the Lead the Way cultural change program was implemented in 2009.[33] It identified key areas of leadership, employee recognition, and communication to be addressed. Designed around a cultural change road map aligned to John Kotter's change model, the initiative strongly relied on communication and recognition of employee contribution to organizational outcome, creating greater levels of engagement, empowerment, and excitement.

In the 2012 HRCS round, HR departments scored lower on items such as the implementation of HR initiatives that enable the business to achieve strategic priorities, acting as a cultural role model, and closely matching the structure of the HR department to the structure of the organization. While some of these findings diverge from those for individual HR professionals discussed earlier in this chapter, they nevertheless present challenges that need to be addressed as a component of comprehensive HRM strategies and processes. Perhaps part of the explanation for these perceived limitations lies in the focus of some HR departments in Australia and New Zealand on designing strategies and programs to address business priorities and collecting and disseminating data that demonstrate their financial value at the expense of managing other important internal linkages. In Australia, Telstra was for several years overly focused on the reduction of overall staffing costs through voluntary (and sometimes forced) redundancies at the expense of employee morale, until it realized that more balanced approaches were required to retain talented performers. Some airlines and banks in both Australia and New Zealand have experienced similar problems.

Conclusion

Australia and New Zealand have similarities and differences in their business contexts, but they generally face the same overall global and regional challenges. However, Australia's business environment is characterized by larger organizations than those in New Zealand.

Their industrial relations systems have undergone significant transformation in the past few decades, leading to more cooperative approaches and declining union densities. At the same time, industry in both countries has seen shifts away from manufacturing and agriculture and toward services, and—particularly in Australia—toward the resources sector. These industry developments, combined with new employee attitudes and aspirations, have led to workforce challenges including specialist skills shortages and increased employee demands.

Australian and New Zealand HR professionals are gender-balanced and generally well qualified although there are some concerns about the aging of the professionals. HR professionals rated highly in the credible activist and capability builder competencies. They had above-average ratings in the change champion, HR integrator and innovator, and strategic positioner competencies, but they were below the already low global average in technology proponent competence.

Specific challenges for HR professionals include their abilities to manage multiple stakeholders and their capacities for self-awareness. HR departments also face some issues with respect to their abilities to implement strategies that match organizational priorities and to act as cultural role models.

CHAPTER 5

CHINA

ARTHUR YEUNG AND WANG TAO

5

Haidilao Hotpot Restaurant (HDL) has recently captured a lot of media attention and generated heated discussion on social media—especially Weibo (a Chinese version of Twitter). Exaggerated comments like "HDL is unstoppable" and "No one can beat HDL" circulate widely. Many prominent Chinese business leaders also speak highly of HDL's personalized and excellent service.

HDL started in 1994 as a hot pot chain restaurant and grew rapidly over the years, with revenue reaching RMB1.5 billion (about US$240 million) in 2010, a net profit rate of 16 percent and more than 10,000 employees. HDL's success is not attributed to secret recipes or unique cuisine but to differentiated services. Many first-time customers are amazed by the large crowd of people willing to wait in the restaurant lounge. While waiting, these people have fun and enjoy free Internet, snacks, drinks, and even complimentary nail service or shoe polishing. The waiters are extremely friendly and detail-oriented; they provide hot towels every 15 minutes, refill customers' drinks, and in addition to those basic services, they send faxes, help take care of babies, buy ice cream from nearby supermarkets, and waive the bill if the service is unsatisfactory. Many of these services go far beyond the standard operating procedures prescribed by HDL, but the company does not object. HDL employees are empowered and encouraged to meet and exceed customer needs in whichever ways possible.

If you look at the profiles of typical HDL employees, their backgrounds are remarkably humble. They receive relatively little education, come from poor and remote provinces, and are referred by friends or family members to work at HDL. Yet they are motivated to serve because at HDL they are able to "change their fates by their hands," as succinctly described by HDL founder Zhang Yong, who insists on offering a fair and transparent work environment for each employee regardless of his or her background.[1] All HDL employees clearly understand that their well-being as individuals and as teams is closely tied to their extraordinary service to customers. Rapid promotions, salary increases, and bonuses are distinctly linked to customer satisfaction. In addition to the emphasis on customers, HDL also goes the extra mile to take good care of its employees, as Zhang Yong deeply believes in the relationship between employee satisfaction and customer satisfaction. HDL offers employee benefits far beyond the industry standard, including air-conditioned apartments within a 20-minute walking distance, an educational allowance for children, and living stipends for employees' parents. When we interviewed an employee as to why she is so motivated to serve, her answer was straightforward: "Because Big Brother Zhang [the nickname for Zhang Yong within the company] treats me very well."[2]

While HDL is innovative in many of its management and HR practices in China, it also represents a broader trend in how Chinese firms are transforming in the changing business environment. With the new banner of "sustainable growth" as the development strategy for China, many companies are starting to consider how to treat employees, customers, shareholders, the environment, and the community in ways that promote long-term success; how to run businesses to create more value; and how to make better use of both manual and knowledge workers to gain a competitive advantage. This chapter outlines the latest developments in HR practices and competencies in China in the context of changing environmental trends and corporate transformation.

Key Environmental Trends in China

The rapid expansion of the Chinese economy (with a compound annual growth rate of 10.8 percent in the past three decades) has seemed miraculous to people in other parts of the world. However, this fast growth—characterized by export-driven and investment-led policies—has serious costs in terms of environmental pollution and high consumption of energy and raw materials, as well as low wages and minimal benefits for workers, tension with trading partners, and other difficulties. In recent years, as articulated in the Twelfth Five-Year Plan, the Chinese government has clearly signaled the following changes:[3]

- A gradual shift from an export-driven to a consumption-driven economy, with the minimum wage increasing 13 percent per year to both ensure the well-being of workers and increase their purchasing power and ability to consume.
- An increase in the service sector by 4 percent (to account for 47 percent of GDP within the next five years) to reduce the heavy reliance on manufacturing.
- An increase in R&D expenditures (to 2.2 percent of GDP) to encourage the shift from being the world's factory to being a hub for R&D, high-end manufacturing, and the service sector in the coastal regions.
- A reduction in the GDP growth target (to 7.5 percent in 2012, which is far below the growth trajectory based on recent years' output) to provide adequate time and resources for the planned transformation.

The message is clear. The Chinese economy will not be sustainable based on its historical growth model of leveraging low-cost labor, polluting heavily, and creating friction with its trading partners. The government is committed to changing the course of China's development. As government at both the national and regional levels take a visible hand in guiding the direction of the Chinese economy and business environment through a combination of tax benefits, grants and incentives, and legal and policy requirements, corporations will probably align their business strategies with the new opportunities and challenges these government actions create.

Weakening demand in U.S. and European markets has forced many export-oriented Chinese firms to rethink how to compete and grow their businesses in ways beyond the mass production of low-cost products. At the same time, the Chinese domestic market has become crowded and competitive. The rapid market expansion in recent decades has also attracted a lot of multinational firms that not only manufacture but also sell and design products and services locally. Adding to the pressure, instead of being satisfied with serving high-end affluent customers and well-developed tier-one cities, many multinational firms are starting to penetrate middle- and even low-end market segments in tier-two or tier-three cities. This creates direct competition between global and local firms in many industries.

Another important factor is the change in companies' costs. Not only are labor costs rising fast (with an annual increase of 13 percent in the minimum wage), but so are raw material and energy costs. While the number of workers entering the market every year is huge, the demand for high-caliber, experienced professionals and management talent still far exceeds supply, leading to high talent turnover and escalating salaries.

Strategic Transformation of Chinese Firms

All these environmental trends are accelerating the transformation of many Chinese firms in two ways: Firms are moving from low-cost manufacturing to higher value-added technology and service, and from operating inside China to growing globally.

Many Chinese firms have no choice but to transform themselves. As labor costs rise and the export market weakens, using the old "big scale, low cost" model to grow a business is increasingly difficult. Midea, one of the leading air-conditioning manufacturers in China, with approximately RMB100 billion (about US$15.87 billion) in revenue in 2010, exemplifies such a transformation. When China can no longer offer low cost and when Midea can no longer leverage large economic scale due to shrinking overseas demand, the company's new strategic priorities are to enhance product innovation, using Apple as a role model; to improve efficiency through automation and lean manufacturing rather than massive amounts of low-cost labor; and to expand globally under its own brand name rather than through OEM (original equipment manufacturer) manufacturing. The goal is to both improve profit margins and create sustainable growth. Similar stories can be heard at many manufacturing firms located in the Pearl Delta and Yangtze Delta regions, where labor costs are escalating, the RMB is appreciating, and export demand is weakening.

Meanwhile, after establishing a strong foothold in the Chinese market, many firms in China also aspire to be global players for both defensive and offensive reasons. China is already an important part of the global business world. To operate in markets with global competitors, Chinese firms need to build up their capabilities and grow in scale to compete with global giants both inside and outside China. Through mergers and acquisitions, direct investment, and strategic alliances, Chinese firms are learning to better leverage resources like technology and talent, and capture new market opportunities beyond China. Companies such as Huawei, ZTE, Lenovo, Wanxiang, Midea, TCL, China Mobile, Haier, and ICBC are pursuing this path with different degrees of success.

In short, many Chinese firms are growing up. They started in low value-added activities such as manufacturing and final assembly, but now they are moving toward higher value-added activities like innovation, services, and branding. They have also moved from operating primarily inside China (doing OEM business for multinational firms or selling products locally) to establishing business operations like R&D centers and sales and marketing offices outside China. The ultimate objective is to shift from success in the sheer scale of production to being a strong global competitor. Such a transformation, however, imposes exacting demands on leaders, as these are new territories that many Chinese firms haven't yet explored.

Knowledge Workers as a New Source of Competitiveness

The implication of these transformations for HR is clear: Chinese firms need not only more talent but also better talent. To switch from low-cost manufacturing to higher value-added technology and to develop a distinct brand, Chinese firms need to make good use of the country's knowledge workers, who are still relatively inexpensive in global terms, even though they cost more than manufacturing workers. Firms need to use these knowledge workers to engage in R&D, product development, marketing, and technical support. To compete with global giants inside and outside China, Chinese firms also need to design and manufacture products on par with those of the global giants in terms of both technological capabilities and product quality, but with a significant price advantage to compensate for weaker branding. All these demands require Chinese firms to use HR differently to create new competitive advantages. Two pioneering examples insert are as follow:

- Sany Heavy Industries is currently the largest construction equipment manufacturer in China, competing directly with global giants like Caterpillar, Komatsu, Volvo, and Hitachi. Founded in the early 1990s, Sany now outperforms all global competitors in China based on its differentiated service, product quality, and technological capability. What enabled Sany, a latecomer to the market, to close the technological gap between it and the global giants? As Xiang Wenbo, president of Sany Heavy Industries, explains: "Sany can leverage the abundant supply of hardworking, smart, and relatively cheap engineers in China. In the United States or Western Europe, most top-notch talent nowadays goes to investment banking, internet, or consulting firms. Equipment manufacturing is not an attractive industry for the best talent. However, in China, the best high school graduates always go on to study engineering in Chinese universities. We are still able to get the best talent in our field in China. Also, compared with our competitors in the developed economy, our engineers only cost about one-fifth as much in total compensation. With the availability of the best talent that is hardworking and relatively low-cost, we can design products that are technologically sophisticated."[4] As a result, Sany's equipment has been used in demanding circumstances such as the rescue of Chilean mine workers in 2010, the response to the recent Japanese earthquake and tsunami disasters, and the construction of the world's tallest building, the Burj Khalifa, in Dubai.
- Mindray, the leading medical diagnostic device company in China, designs and manufactures four lines of diagnostic products including patient monitors and ultrasound scanners. Started in 1991, the company now outperforms all global giants (such as GE, Philips, and Siemens) in its product

lines in China. What enables Mindray to succeed in China? The key is its ability to create more value for its customers than its competitors can by designing products that are highly customized to the Chinese market and different customer segments (15 or 16 models in each product line versus 7 or 8 models in its competitors' lines). Mindray also offers affordable and prompt maintenance services (on-site service within 24 hours, free replacement of equipment if it cannot be fixed after two or three attempts), and sells its products for 20 to 30 percent less than its competitors. The combination of differentiated products and services at a much lower price is a powerful value proposition for its target customers (midsize hospitals).

But how does Mindray simultaneously pursue differentiation and lead the market on cost while enjoying a decent profit margin (about 25 percent)? Xu Hang, founder and chairman of Mindray, provides an explanation similar to that of Sany Heavy Industries: "The primary reason is that we are based in China with access to an abundant supply of low-cost, smart, and hardworking engineers. Though our engineers can only reach 80 percent capacity in comparison with Western engineers after three years of work due to our disconnected educational curriculum, the cost of our engineers is only one-fifth or one-sixth of their Western counterparts. Since we can afford to hire many more R&D engineers, we can offer products that are much more customized while selling them at a 20 to 30 percent lower price."[5] By leveraging such competitive advantages, Mindray is also successful in selling its products in more than 100 overseas markets, and more than 51 percent of Mindray's total revenue comes from outside China.

Sany and Mindray represent a new generation of Chinese firms that focus on the higher value-added activities of technological innovation, branding, and technical support rather than low-cost manufacturing. These firms have also built a much stronger foundation upon which to compete head-to-head with global giants both inside and outside the Chinese market. Other prominent Chinese firms that leverage Chinese knowledge workers for global competitiveness include Huawei, ZTE, Lenovo, Alibaba, and Tencent. Talent is a critical source of all of these companies' competitiveness.

Innovative HR Practices to Overcome the Talent Shortage

Although many Chinese firms recognize their need for Chinese knowledge workers to help them become globally competitive and move into higher value-adding activities, the kind of talent that Sany or Mindray requires is not readily available in China. China does produce five million to six million university graduates every year, but most of them lack relevant knowledge, experience, and maturity because the educational curriculum at Chinese universities focuses heavily on abstract theories and concepts. As a result, while it is not difficult for firms to pick and choose top graduates among the large number of students entering the job market every year, attracting and retaining skilled and experienced talent for midlevel and senior positions quickly becomes challenging.

Building Talent Internally to Overcome the Talent Shortage

Innovative companies address such challenges by picking the best university graduates early on and aggressively developing them internally to ensure a steady supply of high-quality talent with the right skills, experience, values, and levels of commitment to the company.

- Mindray needs employees who are talented across a range of disciplines, including biotechnology, software engineering, hardware engineering, electric control, and mechanical engineering. Such talent is not readily available in China. Mindray recruits heavily from university campuses by sending out a large number of managers and executives who spend more than 20 days every year on the road in efforts to hire the best graduates they can find. Once an offer is made, Mindray immediately involves the prospective employee in a program designed to help understand the company culture and products. Mindray puts prospects into Regional Learning Networks, where they meet regularly in many cities on weekends to go through basic training, to network with one another, and to meet their mentors, who are assigned by the company four to six months before graduation. A graduate who formally joins the company will go through a six-month probation period and then two years of systematic training and job rotation. The smart but inexperienced graduates who join Mindray quickly learn the ropes through projects and mentorship; they can be promoted to project manager within two years and even to vice president by their early thirties.

- Neusoft, the largest IT developer in China, needs to hire more than 3,000 software engineers and other employees every year to fuel its remarkable growth. To accelerate the transition of university hires from theoretical training to productive work, Neusoft hires students in their third year rather than their fourth. These students spend much of their last year of university as interns at Neusoft, participating in various kinds of projects and training.

- Suning, the largest electronic retailer in China, has committed to hiring more than 1,000 university management trainees every year since 2002 (and it reached 8,000 graduates in 2010). These graduates go through systematic training and job rotations so that they can quickly grow to take on leadership positions as store managers or general managers of branch companies within about five years. The university graduates of a few years ago now provide the middle management that is critical in supporting the rapid growth of Suning.

Energizing Talent for Long-Term Commitment

To retain critical talent for the long term, which is difficult in a tight talent market, innovative companies invest heavily in people not only through development opportunities but also through generous equity sharing via stock options or stock grants. As talent, not capital, is the most critical resource for the many increasingly knowledge-intensive and service-based Chinese firms, the ability to keep key technical staff or leadership talent is vital to the sustainable growth of a company.

Huawei, one of the leading telecom equipment manufacturers in the world, is very generous in sharing its long-term wealth and prosperity with its employees. In 2009, about 65 percent of the company's 95,000 employees held 98.58 percent of the company's stock equity; its founding president, Ren Zhengfei, owns the remaining 1.42 percent.[6] All Chinese employees are eligible for a certain amount of stock purchasing rights every year after having worked at Huawei for a year with satisfactory results. This allows employees to enjoy the return on the company's stock as part of the Huawei family. As Huawei is still a privately owned enterprise, employees are not allowed to trade stock with one another, and they must sell their stock back to the company when they resign. As all critical talent shares equally in the success or failure of the company, all employees strive to work hard and stay at the company for the long term. This is critical in emerging economies like China's, where demand for critical talent still far exceeds supply.

Although to a lesser extent than at Huawei, other high-profile companies—including Sany Heavy Industries, Mindray, Alibaba (a leading e-commerce company), and Tencent (a leading Internet service company)—have adopted similarly generous stock option and granting schemes for critical talent. As a result, many millionaires are made in these companies.

Companies such as Alibaba, Haidilao (HDL), and Vanke (the leading real estate developer) retain and motivate talent by offering a fair and transparent work environment. At Alibaba, the Top 300 Conferences (called Zuzhibu Conferences) are broadcast in real time to all employees so that they can understand what issues are being discussed and what decisions are being made at the senior management level. This fosters trust and transparency in all decision making. At HDL and Vanke, promotions are based on fair rules and meritocracy. Personal relationships and other nonwork-related factors are minimized in reward and promotion decisions. As a result, unlike other service industries, where employees must comply with a thick book of standard operating procedures, HDL motivates employees to serve customers based on the ultimate objective of delighting them with personalized service.

Required Changes in HR Roles and Competencies

To help Chinese firms progress into higher value-added activities and become globally competitive, we believe that HR functions and HR professionals need to excel in three major roles and competencies:

- Capability builder
- Change champion
- Talent manager and developer

Capability Builder

HR needs to rebuild and realign the organizational capabilities of Chinese firms to help them move from the traditional focus on aggressive cost management (being the low-cost provider of products or services) to being more innovative in product development and more creative in marketing and branding activities. Going from reducing costs to creating value requires a radical shift in company culture; the company needs less rigid organizational boundaries, changes in employees' skill sets, more empowered employees, and increased tolerance for failure and ambiguity. HR leaders need to redesign the company's culture, practices, behaviors, and work environment systematically for such major organizational changes to take hold.

The reality is that such changes in organizational capability are more easily announced than accomplished. Such deep change requires a conscious effort from the leadership team, starting from the very top, and this points to the second major role in which the HR function needs to excel—that of change champion.

Change Champion

To change how people (beginning with top leaders) think and behave in daily decisions and activities is never easy. It requires a conscious effort to unlearn and relearn over a sustained period of time. As most Chinese firms are led by strong CEOs with tremendous personal influence on how the companies are being run, HR leaders need to work closely with the top leaders to focus their attention on the agreed-upon change initiatives and to remind them if they fail to follow through on changes in the midst of competing business priorities.

To be effective, HR leaders must have tremendous courage and credibility. Once the top leaders are focused on change initiatives, the HR function can make use of different HR tools such as communication, recognition, performance review, promotion, training, recruitment, and separation to consistently send cues to people at various levels about what kind of behavior the company is looking for and rewarding. This is important if companies want to sustain change and institutionalize new behaviors and values.

Talent Manager and Developer

Last but not least, HR leaders need to help business leaders identify, develop, retain, and promote the talent that is required to support the new direction of the business. Talent management (part of the HR innovator and integrator domain) is of paramount importance in emerging economies where high-caliber talent is in short supply and subject to constant poaching. Failure to build a pipeline that can ensure bench strength is a common weakness in many Chinese firms, partly because of the speed of their growth and partly because of the lack of long-term planning and commitment to talent development. Innovative companies—Suning, Mindray, and Neusoft, for example—have become more successful than their peers in sustaining growth due to their investments in talent.

Implications

HR leaders and functions are, unfortunately, not ready to take on these extensive responsibilities in many Chinese firms. Instead, we observe that HR roles such as capability building, becoming a change champion, and talent management are actually driven by the founders and CEOs in many well-run companies (including Haidilao, Huawei, Sany, Mindray, Alibaba, Neusoft, and Tencent) as cited in this chapter. Founders and CEOs take on (or at least oversee) many roles that are assumed by HR leaders in other developed countries. The good news in this situation is that the top leaders are deeply convinced of the strategic relevance of HRM in sustainable business success. They can set the right organizational tone so that HR leaders and professionals can more easily implement the required HR tools. The bad news is that these business leaders often don't have enough time to think through HR roles and issues thoroughly because of the many pressing business issues they are facing. As a result, the capabilities of the HR function are not persistently and systematically improved.

Most HR professionals in China (including those in both multinational firms and local Chinese firms) excel in execution. They can implement HR tools and systems with great enthusiasm and professionalism. However, they generally lack the experience, capability, and credibility to design innovative HR tools in a systematic way. As many Chinese firms aspire to become global players in the coming decade, we believe that HR professionals need to upgrade their expertise quickly to support business growth and transformation. The bottom line is that HR professionals should avoid becoming bottlenecks in business growth even if they are not yet catalysts for change and transformation.

Review and Discussion of the 2012 HRCS China Findings

Drawing upon approximately 1,400 respondents in China, the 2012 round of the Human Resource Competency Study (HRCS) produced a few interesting findings related to the roles of the HR function and the competencies of HR professionals. In many ways, such findings illustrate the current state of the profession and the challenges and opportunities confronting the field of HR in China.

First, compared with the global sample, HR professionals in China have received less formal education. In the Chinese sample, 58 percent of participants had received only a four-year degree, while 28 percent had received a graduate degree. In contrast, 38 percent of participants in the global sample had earned only a four-year degree, while 50 percent had received a graduate degree. HR professionals in China also have less experience in the profession. Forty-two percent have fewer than 5 years' experience and only 10 percent have more than 15 years' experience. In contrast, only 24 percent of HR professionals in the global sample have fewer than 5 years of HR experience, and 36 percent have more than 15 years of HR experience. These findings reflect the fact that China is still an emerging economy.

Business-oriented enterprises have not been popular until the past few decades. HR as a profession also has a relatively short history, having been introduced to China through multinational firms in the late 1980s. Before that, the personnel function in state-owned enterprises primarily exercised administrative control. Because of their recent development, the HR function and HR profession in China are still in the learning and development stages. Nonetheless, given the rapid growth in business scale and complexity as well as the radical transformations many businesses are undergoing, many HR professionals are successfully facing organizational and HR challenges they have never faced before.

Second, in terms of the competencies of HR professionals, the average scores of Chinese HR professionals in five of the six domains—strategic positioner, credible activist, capability builder, change champion, and HR innovator and integrator—are lower than the scores in the global sample. (Scores in the sixth domain, technology proponent, are equally low in China and the global sample.) The lower scores are partly related to the educational and professional backgrounds of the HR professionals and partly to the demanding HR tasks required to cope with the rapid growth and transformation of the corporations they are supporting.

However, the scores don't necessarily mean that Chinese corporations are not paying attention to HR management, as founders or CEOs are often filling such roles themselves. In a sense, many CEOs are also CHROs, even though they don't have the title. Among the six HR competencies, HR professionals score highest as credible activists (mean score: 4.18), which is fundamental to being an effective HR professional. Without credibility, HR professionals will not be able to influence senior leaders and other line managers. Chinese HR professionals score relatively well on capability builder (mean score: 3.87), change champion (mean score: 3.84), and HR innovator and integrator (mean score: 3.82). These three competencies are critical to the HR roles required in the current Chinese business situation.

Realigning organizational capability from the traditional focus on lowering costs to an emphasis on innovation and creativity is vital to the growth and transformation of many Chinese firms. It is also essential for HR professionals in China to facilitate and sustain changes with the help of top leaders and HR tools, and to manage talent through integrated HR tools in recruitment, training and development, retention, and succession planning. Chinese HR professionals score relatively low on the last two HR competencies, strategic positioner (mean score: 3.78) and technology proponent (mean score: 3.74), as they represent competencies that are removed from their current day-to-day work or reflect more recent developments in the HR field.

In terms of the relative impact of the six HR competencies on individual performance, credible activist (19 percent impact) and HR innovator and integrator (19 percent impact) turn out to be the two highest-impact competencies, while the other four are quite similar in their impact on the perceived performance of HR professionals. While being a credible activist is the foundation of personal influence, being an HR innovator and integrator is perceived to be at the core of HR professionals' responsibilities, and HR professionals consequently need to demonstrate proficiency in this area. The other four competencies (15 to 16 percent impact) may be perceived as adding value, but they will be considered desirable rather than essential.

In terms of the impact of the six HR competencies on business results, credible activist (14 percent impact) once again turns out to be the least important. This finding may suggest that while being a credible activist can earn HR professionals the ability to influence senior executives and line managers, ultimately, the ability to add value to the business depends on other, more substantive skills and competencies. HR integrator and technology proponent (both at 19 percent impact) turn out to be the most important competencies. HR integrator is the only competency that matters to both individual performance and business performance. Clearly, HR professionals need to pay attention to this.

We were surprised to see that technology proponent is the competency on which Chinese HR professionals score the lowest (mean score: 3.74) but have the highest impact on business results. Although new to many HR professionals, this is a competency that needs to be embraced. Making use of e-HR to improve operational efficiency, leveraging social media to connect with employees internally and related stakeholders externally, and building an employer brand online are new areas that HR professionals need to become familiar with. The remaining three competencies—capability builder, change champion, and strategic positioner—have the same impact (16 percent) on business performance. These are competencies that HR professionals need to continuously improve.

In short, the key findings and insights of the 2012 HRCS can be summarized as follows:

- HR professionals in China receive less formal education and have less HR experience than their counterparts in the global sample.
- Chinese participants score relatively well on credible activist, capability builder, change champion, and HR innovator and integrator, but they score lower on strategic positioner and technology proponent.
- In terms of both individual and business performance, HR innovator and integrator is the competency with the highest impact.
- Being a credible activist is perceived as important to individual performance but not to business performance. It is necessary for creating value for the business, but it is not sufficient on its own.
- Being a technology proponent is critical to business performance, but is the domain on which Chinese HR professionals (like their colleagues elsewhere in the world) rated lowest out of the current competencies.
- Capability builder, change champion, and strategic positioner are three competencies that Chinese HR professionals need to continue to learn and improve upon as Chinese businesses go through rapid growth and transformation.

Suggestions for Improving HR Competencies in China

How can HR professionals in China improve on these competencies and increase their contributions to the businesses? We have the following suggestions:

- Learn about the businesses and design the HR functions accordingly.
- Learn and master systematic thinking.
- Learn about and embrace information technology.

Business Knowledge and HR Design

Most HR professionals in China tend to be execution-oriented and risk-averse. More often than not, they immerse themselves in operational and technical details while losing sight of the bigger strategic picture. They also have strong tendencies to adhere to prevalent HR practices. *Benchmarking* and *best practices* are big buzzwords in HR circles in China. As a result, HR professionals tend to design or copy HR tools based on industry standards (or best practices) rather than on business needs.

In addition, many Western HR tools need quite a lot of adaptation before they can be applied in a Chinese corporate environment. Our observation is that HR tools that work well in the West tend to be too sophisticated (or too complex) and too structured for Chinese firms, which usually emphasize flexibility, entrepreneurship, and risk taking. When designing or introducing tools, Chinese HR professionals need to consider not only sociocultural differences in their business environments but also the unique situations their companies face, including the rate of environmental change, the rate of business growth, and the nature of Chinese business. Compared with Western firms, Chinese firms are apt to be dealing with more radical and faster-paced changes, an annual growth rate 10 times as great, and established practices designed for labor-intensive and cost-driven business rather than knowledge-intensive and service-based business. All these differences need to be fully taken into account to avoid blindly copying best practices that fail to live up to their sponsors' hopes.

To develop a deep knowledge about the unique nature of their businesses, we strongly suggest that HR professionals seek opportunities to rotate out of the HR function and into different line functions, especially sales and operations, so that they can understand firsthand how HR tools can be used to solve business problems. Alternatively, the HR function should welcome the opportunity to have people from outside HR join the team and bring in new perspectives. If job rotation across HR and line functions is not feasible in a corporate setting, corporate and back-end HR professionals should at least rotate working as business partners, to get more HR employees close to frontline actions. Shadowing and project teams provide other opportunities to expose HR professionals to real business needs so that they can design HR tools with a deep understanding of their businesses.

Systematic Thinking

To excel as HR innovators and integrators and as capability builders, HR professionals need to think about and design HR tools in integrated, systematic ways. Our experience tells us that such systematic thinking can be enhanced with a few tips:

- Learn and master a diagnostic framework like 7S, Star Model, organizational architecture, or Yeung's Triangle that you consider to be useful and comprehensive.[7] Any framework will do; the key is to have something systematic that you can trust and understand well.
- Audit or diagnose the current situation based on your chosen framework to systematically identify current strengths and gaps for improvement.
- Design and deploy relevant HR tools to bridge the gaps in a holistic manner rather than piece by piece.
- Roll out the relevant HR tools at a reasonable pace to avoid inflicting too much work at a time and to enable quick wins to help sustain the change effort.

HR professionals can master these skills and thought processes by working closely with seasoned HR executives or external consultants. Participating in complex HR projects from the early stages of diagnosis and design all the way to implementation is the best way to learn and master systematic skills.

Information Technology

While e-HR has been promoted in the United States and Western Europe since the early 1990s, many Chinese firms are still lagging behind in its application.[8] HR databases in compensation and benefits, recruitment, training, and employee relations are often fragmented and unable to talk to one another. A lot of manual work is required to compile and analyze data from different databases to provide a complete picture. This results in many HR functions being preoccupied with low-value-added HR activities. We feel that Chinese firms are just beginning to make use of e-HR systems to upgrade their HR efficiency and have a lot of opportunity for improvement.

At the same time, the latest developments in social media networks like Weibo, Weixin, and LinkedIn are rapidly changing how people network and communicate with one another. Such social media can be used internally to reduce communication barriers between employees and senior management. They can also be used externally to reach targeted groups of prospective employees through alumni networks or interest groups. Finally, these social media networks can be used to build the employer's brand by regularly sharing successful or unique HR practices with external stakeholders.

To learn about and embrace social media, HR professionals should set up accounts of their own and play around with them. This is the best way to learn, explore, and think about how to make use of social media for HR applications.

Conclusion

HR professionals in China are working in an exciting era when their firms are undergoing major transformations for higher value-added output and global operations. In the process, the HR function can make huge contributions as capability builder, change champion, or talent manager and developer. To fulfill these roles, HR professionals need to learn fast and upgrade their competencies accordingly, especially given the brief history of HRM in China and the swift pace of growth there.

CHAPTER 6

EUROPE

6

ALLAN FREED, CHRISTINE CLEEMANN, EVEN BOLSTAD, AND HÅVARD BERNTZEN

HR professionals in Europe operate in a unique and exciting context. With a combined population above 500 million, the 27 member states of the European Union (EU) have 23 official languages and more than 150 others that are used regionally—all in an area approximately the same size as the United States.[1] As we attempt to identify trends and practices that are helpful to HR professionals across Europe, we are keenly aware of cultural, ethnic, and economic heterogeneity and an increasing tendency toward high levels of institutional and political homogeneity.

In this chapter, we explore two crucial questions that go beyond national boundaries and that prevail in many European HR functions:

- How do HR professionals establish reputations for personal effectiveness?
- What HR competencies matter most for value creation and for driving business performance in Europe?

The ability to understand the external environment is always crucial for building internal capabilities that lead to improved business results, and nowhere more so than in Europe. This outside-in approach is central to HR's ability to function as full partner in the business and to create substantive value. HR professionals require specific competencies to respond to this business environment in a way that drives performance, and the 2012 HRCS results allow us to offer suggestions and insights for HR professionals in the region as they seek to develop the right competencies.

European Context

A number of economic, political, social, and demographic trends can be observed in the complex European environment. The following sections identify the ones with regional impacts. These trends do not have equal significance in each nation of Europe; the implications for organizations in the different countries of the region will vary, but it is nonetheless useful to take a high-level overview.

Economic Trend: Growth

The current map of EU economic growth displays huge regional variation. A number of countries in the east still have a comparatively low GDP per person employed—Ukraine at US$9,564 or Romania at US$11,019, for example—whereas in the more developed economies of the west the rates are significantly higher. France enjoys US$55,033, the United Kingdom is at US$51,604, and Sweden at US$49,778.[2]

Rates of economic growth in European states in recent years also generally differentiate the growing economies in the east from the more developed economies of the west. Bulgaria (21.2 percent), the Czech Republic (21.1 percent), Poland (30.2 percent), Romania (17.5 percent), and Slovakia (34 percent) experienced staggering GDP growth during the 2005 to 2010 period. Growth in the United Kingdom (3.9 percent), Denmark (2.5 percent), and Germany (6.7 percent) over the same period has been conservative by comparison.[3] Although the combined GDP of the member states of Europe is on the increase, the region's percentage of gross world product is decreasing, due largely to the substantial growth experienced in China, India, Brazil, and other fast-developing nations.

HR Implications

The organizational implications of stagnant growth in Europe's largest markets and decreased percentage of world production throughout the region are clear. Large European organizations and multinationals are increasingly looking to invest outside Europe to build market share and to access economies of scale in areas delivering significantly higher growth rates. HR professionals need to help organizations build the talent pool and organization capabilities required to be effective in new high-growth markets—while at the same time finding ways to increase profitability and productivity in their developed markets.

For example, Damco is a global freight forwarder that has expanded rapidly in emerging markets from a European base. Its HR VP, Karsten Breum, reports that business and HR leaders have learned important lessons in the process. "When markets and customers change, we have learned that HR work has to change accordingly," he says, adding, "increasingly the growing markets need to be fueled by local talents, and local solutions need to be developed for business problems that are somewhat unique to these geographies. Building skills that establish relationships with local partners, customers, and in some cases competitors to further define business opportunities and attract local talent has helped our colleagues in HR to add competitive business edge."[4]

As HR professionals endeavor to support growth in overseas markets and improve profitability in mature markets, they have to reconsider approaches to strategic workforce planning, leadership development, HRIS, and recruitment, development, and retention practices.

Economic Trend: Unemployment and Economic Uncertainty

The combined unemployment rate across EU member nations in the first quarter of 2012 was 10.9 percent.[5] Some member states enjoy very low levels of unemployment: Austria (4 percent), the Netherlands (5 percent), Luxembourg (5.2 percent), and Germany (5.6 percent). In the aftermath of one of the worst economic recessions in generations, however, many member states continue to fight endemic unemployment rooted in deep economic uncertainty. In Spain and Greece, with unemployment at 24.1 percent and 21.7 percent respectively, the problems are particularly challenging. Rampant speculation about the stability of the euro in the wake of the recession has had a negative impact on business conditions throughout Europe. Many analysts believe that the root causes of the economic problems faced by European member states remain unresolved and that tight market conditions and limited prospects for growth appear likely to remain for the foreseeable future.

HR Implications

During times of economic uncertainty, organizations generally become more conservative and risk averse. They tend to have more disciplined focus on managing costs and living up to promises that they make to shareholders and customers. HR professionals contribute by focusing HR practices to reinforce efforts to keep stakeholder promises—identifying and reinforcing high-performance employees who create value for key stakeholders, for example. HR professionals also add competitive value as they look outside their firms to develop relationships with target customers and build practices and competencies that drive employees to behave in ways that increase the likelihood of those target customers engaging with the companies.

In addition, HR professionals ensure that organizations do not become too risk averse when it comes to attracting, training, and retaining talented employees. In the midst of economic uncertainty, the absence of convincing data may mean that crucial hiring and development decisions are delayed or cancelled. HR staff may spend so much time looking for a perfect profile that they fail to fill roles responsively and take appropriate risks when making hiring decisions. Other firms may choose to delay employee development opportunities to conserve resources without realizing that they may be losing opportunities for accelerated growth at a later date.

During the recession, a global management consulting firm with a major presence in Europe excelled in developing leaders.[6] The firm highlighted the following practices as a key to success:

- "We never stopped screening and hiring service-oriented employees. If you pick up a phone and call another company associate anywhere in the world for help, they will not only take your call but do everything they can to help you. And you know you are getting the best because we hire consistently across the globe."

- "We did not become afraid of recruiting diamonds in the rough—those who weren't taught critical thinking skills in their educations and those who normally would not qualify for the firms given their current skill set. They have persevered through hard situations, not Ivy League educations. We mentor and develop them to succeed in our organization . . . working with them beforehand so they succeed in their interviews. They are inspiring."

Economic Trend: Labor Cost Variation

Hourly labor costs differ significantly across Europe. In 2011 the highest hourly labor costs were found in Belgium (US$50.22), Sweden (US$49.96), Denmark (US$49.33), and France (US$43.70). The lowest costs were found in Bulgaria (US$4.47), Romania (US$5.37), and Lithuania (US$7.03).[7]

HR Implications

Such wide variance in labor costs has altered the nature of work for European organizations. Many firms have shifted labor-intensive operations to cheaper markets in the east, accounting in part for the stellar GDP growth some of these countries have experienced. HR professionals have contributed to business performance by transferring capabilities to new centers of operation while maintaining service or product quality. They have also created value by engaging with business leaders to retain crucial technical skills and organizational capabilities and to relocate or outsource the right work.

Political Trend: The European Union

The EU has played an instrumental role in integrating formerly sovereign states into a more coherent, interdependent union. EU legislation has created a unified legal context in which European organizations and HR professionals operate. The political institutions of the EU have succeeded in creating four accepted freedoms with significant implications for organizations and HR professionals in Europe:

- Freedom of movement of goods
- Freedom of movement of services
- Freedom of movement of persons
- Freedom of movement of capital

The ongoing efforts of the EU political institutions are designed to increase the establishment of a clearer and more meaningful European identity. We can reasonably expect increased convergence in the future as legal systems, economic policies, and other frameworks are created at the European rather than at the national level.

HR Implications

The ability to move goods and services across borders to reach a market of over 500 million people relatively seamlessly has increased business transactions among EU member states. HR professionals help drive business results when they source, train, reward, and retain talents capable of creating and supplying demand in a variety of markets. They do this effectively when they innovate HR practices across geographies to adapt to local conditions while keeping these adapted practices integrated with business strategies and aligned to practices in other regions.

The freedom of movement of persons has had a profound and lasting impact among member states. Many Eastern Europeans have migrated to the developed economies of Western Europe in search of improved career opportunities and higher salaries. This has led to some shortages of talent in the east and an oversupply of lower-skilled talent in the west. Political parties on the extreme right have polarized public opinion and campaigned to reduce levels of immigration in the western member states.[8] In the midst of an economic recession, such parties have become increasingly popular.[9]

Social Trend: Globalization

Technology continues to enable the transfer of knowledge across boundaries, driving the pace of globalization and changing the way people think and behave. In today's global environment, virtually everyone has access to similar sources of information. Firms that manage to translate data into consumer insight and products or services will enjoy increasingly important market advantages. For many years Europe has been a major destination for products manufactured in Asia. Now European knowledge workers increasingly have to compete with their low-cost counterparts from these nations. If European companies and their workers are unable to respond to these challenges, we will see even more transfer of work and wealth to the emerging Asian countries.

HR Implications

Developing the competence of employees to think and act globally will become increasingly crucial to the success of European organizations, as will developing the technological capacity to mine data in ways that lead to new insights and closer connections to customers. Generating new ideas and translating them into products and services will allow European firms to continue to grow in developed and emerging markets. However, global competition will punish firms that are unable to provide best-in-class products and services on a global scale with best-in-class knowledge and skills. HR professionals must quickly develop practices that communicate and develop world-class standards to employees so that organizations can continually refine their capacities to design and manufacture globally competitive products and services.

Social Trend: Diversity

In recent years the workforce of most European companies has become more diverse in terms of gender, ethnicity, age, physical ability, religion, and sexual orientation.[10] Legislation has been passed and enforced at the EU level and also within member states to encourage increased diversity. For example, since 2008, the boards of all publicly traded companies in Norway have had to have at least 40 percent female representation. Companies that fail to comply can be shut down. Meeting this standard took a major effort; in 2002 barely 6 percent of Norway's corporate directors were women and 70 percent of the top companies in the country did not have a single female representative on their executive boards.[11]

HR Implications

HR professionals are increasingly responsible for driving the diversity agenda and for ensuring that increased diversity translates into competitive edge. HR professionals who recruit and develop diversity in all of its forms create value when they ensure that diversity is encouraged where it matters—in strategy formulation and in anticipating consumer trends. However, they must also ensure that unity of purpose and direction prevails when it comes to strategy execution. A 2011 internal study analyzing employee engagement data at A.P. Møller-Mærsk Group demonstrated that teams with higher levels of gender diversity had higher engagement and stronger managerial effectiveness. Besides being linked to higher performance and customer satisfaction, gender-diverse teams at the firm are proven to lead to better financial results and increased retention of employees.[12]

Social Trend: Work-Life Balance

Employees across Europe continue to search for the right balance between work and personal life. The Organisation for Economic Co-operation and Development (OECD) applies three criteria when defining and measuring work–life balance:[13]

- Proportion of the labor force working very long hours (more than 50 per week)
- Time devoted to "leisure and personal care" (spending time with friends, going to the movies, pursuing hobbies, sleeping, eating, and so on)
- Employment rates for women who have children

European countries generally score well in these dimensions—that is, low on proportion of workers putting in long hours and high on personal time and proportion of working mothers. This is especially true in Scandinavia where Denmark, Sweden, and Norway finished in the top seven of all OECD countries.

HR Implications

Undoubtedly, European nations perform well in this area largely because of the high level of government regulation designed to protect employees and the rights they enjoy in their employment. As in all regions, some firms go above and beyond what is required by law to provide additional benefits in an effort to drive performance and improve engagement. The creation and adoption of innovative work practices and policies that promote work–life balance is now seen by many companies as crucial in the attraction and retention of talent.

Companies that build solid reputations for promoting work–life balance seriously engage in HR practices such as these:

- *Re-recruitment of top performers.* Good companies regularly re-recruit key talents by highlighting their own unique value proposition and reinforcing why they are great places to work.
- *Well-defined career paths and transparent succession planning.* When talented employees have ways to channel their aspirations and goals within career structures of their present employer, they are more likely to stay with the firm, be more productive, and enjoy a healthier work–life balance.
- *Self-leadership practices.* Improving the ability of employees to manage themselves has been pioneered by several Scandinavian firms, including Volvo.[14]
- *Flexible working policies.* Measures to increase the amount of flexibility for key talent to improve their work–life balance and levels of engagement and satisfaction are now common in many European organizations. Flexible policies encourage competent individuals to return to the workplace or to enter the job market. This has been particularly helpful for mothers with children.

- *Effective use of technology.* Companies that connect employees to one another using technology such as webinars, social media, and videoconferencing are more able to implement policies that minimize business travel, reduce costs, improve flexibility, and drive work–life balance than those that do not use technology in this way.

- *Mentoring and reverse mentoring.* Traditional mentoring and coaching programs continue to prove helpful in encouraging and monitoring effective change. In addition, several companies have implemented reverse mentoring programs where senior executives and key managerial talents are mentored by newer recruits on ways to achieve work–life balance.

Demographic Trend: An Aging Continent

A century ago, Europe was home to 25 percent of the world's population. It is currently home to approximately 12 percent; if demographic trends continue along current projections, Europe's share may fall to around 7 percent by 2050. It's clear that the EU faces challenges in its demographic future. In many countries across Europe, the rate of reproduction falls well below the required figure for maintaining population stability (that is, an average of 2.1 children per woman). Statistics for 2009 indicate that only three member nations of the EU have a rate near this mark (Ireland at 2.07, France at 2.0, and Iceland at 2.23). Germany (1.36), Portugal (1.32), and Hungary (1.32) fall well below the EU average of 1.59.[15] Declining birth rates and increased life expectancy lead to aging populations with fewer active workers supporting retirees.

HR Implications

These demographic trends have wide-ranging implications for HR professionals and organizations in Europe. Some European governments have already increased the age at which people can retire, and other countries are considering similar action. The adoption of workplace policies more suited to an aging population will increasingly become a source of competitive advantage for European firms. HR professionals will have to adapt recruitment policies, learning and development programs, reward systems, and flexible benefits and retention strategies to account for these changes.

In sum, understanding the trends that bear on European organizations is the starting point for innovating and adapting HR practices in ways that help organizations respond to their external environment. Business conditions in Europe are increasingly volatile and uncertain. Complexity and ambiguity are increasing, and the business environment continues to change rapidly. When HR professionals are able to clearly see the external challenges faced by their organizations, they are much more likely to build human capital infrastructures that help firms respond to external challenges effectively and well.

Europe's leading organizations are evolving and changing as they come to terms with the current set of social, economic, political, and demographic trends. HR professionals who engage fully in the creation of value help position their organizations well for the future by ensuring HR practices deliver the talent, the leadership, and the capabilities required to respond effectively to the changing marketplace and the changing needs of consumers and stakeholders.

Embracing the Environment at Volvo

At Volvo, HR VP Geoff Glover has been at the forefront of the drive to understand the external environment and help prepare the company for the challenges of tomorrow. The Volvo Cars leadership team understands that the talent and organizational capabilities required to build cars desirable to consumers in important markets tomorrow are different from those required today. Consumer insights suggest that cars of tomorrow will not only have to be elegant and well designed, they will also have to use innovative technology to enhance performance. The successful car manufacturers will be those that develop technologies that engage and delight drivers—features likely to shape the industry include Internet connectivity, technologically advanced safety features, smart-sensing technology, gesture recognition, and improved communication between the vehicle and the driver.

These insights have helped Volvo start preparing for tomorrow. Its leaders no longer consider traditional competitors as their only rivals. They have identified a whole range of new companies with the potential to be game changers in the industry. The majority of these firms are based in Asia, giving them easier access to the markets that will be growing fastest.

Volvo is recruiting and developing talent with new core technical profiles and competency frameworks that drive employee development. The HR professionals are recruiting talent today who have expertise in working with lightweight materials, integrating technologies, human augmentation, electrification, and connectivity—skills that have not been core to date but that will be increasingly critical to business success. They are also building levels of competence to ensure that high performers work together virtually, develop global perspectives, prioritize sustainability, manage knowledge effectively, and transfer knowledge across sectors. As HR professionals have worked to align practices to secure, develop, retain, and unleash the talent required for strategy execution, they have contributed significantly to a transformation that is driving the creation of value. Their investment of time and energy in understanding the outside world is helping them shape the HR practices and processes inside the organization.

Review and Discussion of the 2012 HRCS Europe Findings

In the 2012 HRCS, 13 percent of the 20,000-plus responses were from companies and professionals based in Europe. Analysis of the European data has led to a series of interesting insights that cast light on the state of the profession in the region and help professionals identify strengths and areas for improvement.

First, compared with the global sample, HR professionals in Europe are more likely to have a graduate degree (58 versus 50 percent) and have more years of experience in the profession than colleagues in the emerging markets. Thirty-two percent of the European HR professionals have more than 15 years' experience in the field. In China and India this figure is 10 and 22 percent respectively. This is clearly a reflection of the maturity of the profession in Europe and the wide availability of academic programs and social conditions that support adult learning. Europe continues to be an exciting place to practice and study HR. Organizations there continue to be at the forefront of pushing HR boundaries, and demand for thought leadership in the functions are high. These efforts are supported by a number of well-respected journals and professional organizations.

Looking at the mean scores of HR professionals from the different regions of Europe, it's noticeable that the scores of the European contingent in all of the six competency domains are lower than the scores in the global sample. The message is clear and suggests that HR professionals in Europe must do a better job at responding to the trends facing businesses in their regions today.

The volatility and fast-changing nature of the European business environment require HR professionals to be agile enough to develop competence in all six of the domains identified in the latest round of research. However, it is also the case developing competency in some domains will have greater impact on individual effectiveness and business performance than in others (see Table 6.1).

These data show that to be seen as personally effective, HR professionals in Europe need to continue to focus time and energy developing and mastering

Table 6.1   Impact of HR Competencies on Perception of HR Effectiveness and Business Performance

	Mean European score on this competency domain	Impact on perception of HR effectiveness (Beta weights scaled to 100%)	Impact on business performance (Beta weights scaled to 100%)
Credible Activist	4.19	23%	8%
Strategic Positioner	3.82	17%	11%
Capability Builder	3.90	16%	23%
Change Champion	3.85	16%	16%
HR Innovator & Integrator	3.81	17%	21%
Technology Proponent	3.61	11%	21%
Multiple R²		42.9%	6.2%

the credible activist domain. They do this by building relationships of trust and by demonstrating a strong business and HR point of view. They also need to have a good mix of the next four competencies. The domain that has the least influence on perceived personal effectiveness is technology proponent, and it is done least well. Collectively, the competencies explain 42.9 percent of the effectiveness of an HR professional in the region.

These HR competencies also explain 6.2 percent of a business's success in Europe. It is noteworthy that the competencies that predict personal effectiveness differ from those that predict business success. At the domain level, HR professionals who build organization capabilities have greatest impact on business performance, and they do it at a medium level of effectiveness. This provides an opportunity for competitive advantage. The most counterintuitive finding for European HR professionals is that competency as a technology proponent has by far the least effect on perceived individual effectiveness but is close to the top in its impact on business performance. Insights on technology, HR integration, and capability building share high levels of business impact. This is hardly surprising, given that these competencies allow HR professionals to translate the external environment into internal activity that affects a whole organization. While personal effectiveness continues to be driven by the credible activist domain, the competencies that drive business results require teams of HR professionals collaborating and collectively building and executing practices that help shape organizational responses to the external context.

These conclusions are further refined in Table 6.2, which shows the factors within the six domains and how they affect individual effectiveness and business performance.

For HR professionals who are striving for a significant impact on business results, four key areas of focus will have most effect:

- *Technology proponent*: Connecting people through technology
- *Capability builder*: Aligning strategy, culture, practices, and behavior
- *HR innovator and integrator*: The domain as a whole
- *Change champion*: Sustaining change

Table 6.2 Factors for HR Competence on Individual Effectiveness and Business Success

Factor	European Mean (1–5)	Individual Effectiveness (100%)	Business Success (100%)
Credible Activist			
Earning trust through results	4.27	6.9	4.0
Influencing and relating to others	4.15	7.0	4.1
Improving through self-awareness	3.95	6.5	4.7
Shaping the HR profession	4.09	4.4	2.9
Strategic Positioner			
Interpreting global business context	3.79	4.4	4.2
Decoding customer expectations	3.74	4.4	5.2
Cocrafting a strategic agenda	3.88	6.3	4.6
Capability Builder			
Capitalizing organization capability	3.95	5.4	5.3
Aligning strategy, culture, practices, and behavior	3.85	5.3	6.1
Creating a meaningful work environment	3.89	4.1	5.2
Change Champion			
Initiating change	3.88	5.4	4.8
Sustaining change	3.79	4.7	5.7
HR Innovator and Integrator			
Optimizing human capital through workforce planning and analytics	3.86	5.5	5.6
Developing talent	3.74	4.0	5.3
Shaping organization and communication practices	3.86	5.8	5.6
Driving performance	3.76	4.7	5.2
Building leadership brand	3.78	4.9	5.4
Technology Proponent			
Improving utility of HR operations	3.58	2.9	5.0
Connecting people through technology	3.65	4.6	6.3
Leveraging social media tools	3.52	2.7	4.7
Overall R^2		.431	.108

Technology Proponent

The factor that has the single biggest impact on driving business performance for HR professionals in Europe is connecting people through technology, which is part of the technology proponent domain. This domain has the lowest mean scores for HR professionals in the region—and the message seems to be clear. This is a primary opportunity through which European HR professionals can create competitive advantage. As European companies struggle to grow in a difficult economic environment, HR professionals need to be skilled in using technology to drive down costs, streamline operations, and generate insights that lead to product or service innovations resulting in consumer impact. The HR function should also be at the forefront of pioneering technological solutions that keep talented employees well connected to one another inside the firm and to consumers outside the firm.

Remaining unskilled in this particular domain has the potential of contributing to competitive disadvantage. Firms that are unable to drive down or aggressively manage costs, keep talents connected to important stakeholders, and generate ideas and innovations from knowledge workers will lose serious competitive advantage when faced by competitors who do this well. HR professionals who excel in this domain should do the following:

- Facilitate the design of internal communication processes that connect employees and align them to the business strategy.
- Facilitate the design and dissemination of external communication processes.
- Align HR practices with external customer criteria.
- Remove low-value-adding or bureaucratic work.

Capability Builder

The specific competency factor that has the next greatest impact on business performance is in the capability builder domain: aligning strategy, culture, practices, and behavior. European HR professionals who master the skills and knowledge in this factor will set themselves at a competitive advantage relative to those who do not. The steps for making this alignment happen are straightforward:

- Define a business strategy that reflects customer reality as clearly and specifically as possible.
- Specify the collective ways of thinking and behaving that are most central to designing and delivering products or services that are most required by your firm's best customers.
- Ensure that all HR practices are constructed and implemented to create and sustain the desired culture.

As this alignment occurs, the collective capabilities of the unified organization become focused on meeting the requirements of the marketplace more quickly and accurately than the competition.

HR Innovator and Integrator

The message of the HR innovator and integrator domain is likewise important and interesting. At the domain level, this competency set has the greatest impact. Even though none of the individual factors are in the top group, the domain itself has more impact on business results than any other. Thus, to have impact on business success, all the individual factors must come together and focus on a few critical business issues and organizational capabilities:

- HR professionals must have clear lines of sight to the business strategy and to customer requirements.
- They must audit their organizations to ensure that the collective HR practices are consistent in their design and focus.
- They must also audit and align leadership behaviors that drive and sustain culture and ensure that leadership and HR practices mutually reinforce each other.

It will come as little surprise that such HR professionals are more closely connected to customers and other key external stakeholders when they design and deliver HR practices that create and sustain human talent and organizational capacities that align with market requirements.

Change Champion

HR professionals should be able to initiate and sustain change. However, although initiating change has greater impact on individual performance, sustaining change has a greater effect on business success. Furthermore, HR professionals might be seduced into thinking that the glamour of initiating change is more important than the daily discipline of sustaining change, even though the latter is what gives them real impact on business performance. To excel in this competency, HR professionals do the following:

- They make change happen at the individual, initiative, and institutional levels, and help people learn and sustain new behaviors.
- They learn how to engage others in the process of change.
- They break larger changes into simple steps as needed.
- They ensure that desired changes show up in behaviors, HR processes, and metrics.
- They hold people accountable for doing what they say they will do.
- They learn from both successes and failures in change.
- They help people find personal passion and emotion from their changes.

In sum, the HRCS research is important for HR professionals in Europe because it defines what they need to focus on to enhance their personal effectiveness and the success of their businesses. Being an effective HR professional requires more than mastery of HR technical expertise. It is necessary to apply knowledge and insight to business challenges in ways that drive performance.

Increasing Business Impact at AXA

AXA is a good example of a company working to enact collective HR competencies. Headquartered in Paris, AXA is one of the largest insurance companies in the world. For the past several years, its HR leaders have invested significantly to ensure that their functions are at the forefront of thought in the field and contributes to growth in a changing and intensely competitive environment. HR professionals at AXA focus on aligning their practices in managing talent, building leadership, and developing organization capabilities that support business priorities. These priorities have been shaped around the goal of connecting customers into the fabric and culture of the firm.

HR professionals have created a leadership learning agenda that reinforces this organization capability by focusing on building competencies that include inclusiveness, diversity, empowerment, collaboration, and straight talk among the firm's leaders. Recruitment criteria have also evolved to focus on providing talent who are most comfortable and able to live the brand promise of being available, reliable, and attentive. HR professionals at AXA continue to contribute to evolving the culture and positioning the group for ongoing success as they align their efforts to build talent, leadership, and organization capabilities to the objectives of their businesses. Despite the negative impact of the recent financial downturn, AXA continued to invest in its community of HR professionals. Company leaders have learned that aligning HR activities to business objectives yields a rich return on investment.

Conclusion

Developing competence in the six domains identified by the latest round of the HRCS research will help HR professionals in Europe respond to business conditions in ways that improve personal effectiveness and business results.

In the strategic positioner domain, HR professionals in Europe must turn outside business trends and stakeholder expectations into internal actions. Many professionals in the region continue to work from the inside out, building technical HR competence without developing the skills to apply that knowledge to real-life business challenges. If HR professionals in the region continue to develop technical skills without improving their abilities to apply those skills to the external environment and the challenges faced by the organizations they work in, they run the risk of losing their hard-earned seats at the table. The skills of the strategic positioner enable the HR professional to work from the outside in effectively.

In the credible activist domain, HR professionals must focus on both immediate business results and long-term talent development. European traditions and history often deter HR professionals from developing a deep understanding of the mechanics of the businesses in which they operate. Many HR professionals entered the profession because they enjoy working with people. Tomorrow they will need an even greater passion for business results. Value must be created for customers on the outside or it cannot be created for employees on the inside.

In the capability builder domain, HR professionals should target both individual abilities and organization capabilities. Establishing and aligning HR practices that reinforce the capabilities required for organizational success is a crucial skill for HR professionals. Developing the skills of the capability builder helps HR professionals assess current capabilities, build them, and identify the capability requirements needed for ongoing success tomorrow.

In the HR innovator and integrator domain, HR professionals need to realize that their work is not an isolated activity or practice; it requires sustainable and integrated solutions. HR professionals who are innovators and integrators align systems and create patterns to build and reinforce behaviors that targeted customers appreciate and value. They fundamentally understand the importance of making the HR whole more valuable than the sum of its parts.

In the change champion domain, HR professionals should respect the heritage of the firms they work in without being afraid to shape the future. They help create value as they build patterns of activity that reinforce the behaviors that customers value today and desire to see tomorrow. These behaviors help shape the future, and thus, they are more important than the ones that helped the firms succeed in the past. The change champion domain helps HR professionals to initiate—and sustain—patterns of change in an organization.

In the technology proponent domain, HR professionals must attend to both day-to-day administrative processes and long-term strategic practices. Managing the trade-off between administrative and strategic tasks is a crucial skill. It is also essential to design departments, roles, and workflow to ensure important work is prioritized and business partners have space and time to think and participate in the running of the enterprise. Embracing the use of technology to drive down the amount of time spent on administrative tasks is a major part of work in this domain. At the same time, effective HR professionals will play more active roles in harnessing technology to access, filter, bundle, share, and use information as competitive advantages.

We are optimistic about the present and the future of the HR profession globally and in Europe. And we have empirical reasons for our optimism. We now have specific insights on what HR professionals need to know and do to improve their own work and deliver value to employees, organizations, customers, investors, and communities. The mean scores of the six competencies in Europe suggest that professionals may need to focus more time and energy on working collectively to drive results rather than on securing individual reputations.

Throughout this chapter, we have evaluated the context in which HR work is done in Europe today. It is clear from that evaluation that organizations need effective HR professionals who can help chart tempestuous conditions. This is an exciting time to be an HR professional in Europe. Opportunities to influence decisions and contribute to value creation exist now more than ever.

CHAPTER 7

INDIA

Wayne Brockbank and L. Prabhakar

India is emerging as one of the world's most dynamic economies—and one of the most dynamic locations for the innovation of value-adding HR practices. It is currently the ninth largest country by nominal gross domestic product and second among the fastest-growing major economies.[1] Emerging from a controlled economy in 1992, it has become a powerhouse of competitiveness, innovation, and aspiration. In many ways, it is setting the global standard for HR practices that accelerate growth while balancing the complex challenges of a large developing country.

ICICI Bank: Excellence in Action

ICICI Bank was founded in 1955 to promote the industrial development of newly independent India. Since the liberalization of the Indian economy in 1992, ICICI has turned itself into a universal financial services group that includes the largest private-sector bank (only the government-owned State Bank of India is larger), the largest private-sector life insurance company, the largest private-sector general insurance company, and one of the largest asset management companies in the country.

It has ushered in the retail banking revolution in India, making consumer credit available and affordable to tens of millions of people. It has also taken banking beyond physical branches by rolling out the nation's first ATM network and Internet and mobile-banking platforms.[2]

As their bank has grown through business-line diversification and globalization, ICICI Chairman, N. Vaghul, and CEO, K.V. Kamath, have recognized the need to access financial, technological, and human capital. They have given K. Ramkumar (executive director responsible for HR) a clear strategic mandate concerning people and organization, and fulfilling that has required Ramkumar and his team to move away from their traditional focus on administrative processes and transactions. In the late 1990s, they repositioned HR as a driver of growth with three major initiatives:

- Making sure that the right number of people with the right knowledge and skills are assigned to the right businesses in the right locations.
- Integrating these people into a cohesive organization with a shared identity, culture, ethos, values, and business orientation.
- Ensuring the availability of high-quality leaders to carry the culture and build other organization capabilities.

As the new century emerged, these three challenges grew more formidable. In 2001, 110 people were hired; in 2007, the number was 15,000. Getting the HR and organization agendas correct were the keys to ICICI's ability to achieve its vision to serve India and beyond.

To accomplish this vision, the first challenge was to have a clear definition of the kinds of ICICI people needed for success. Quality standards had to be maintained even while stretching to achieve challenging quantitative goals. The quality challenge was framed not only in terms of technical requirements but also in terms of the needed organization culture. As Ramkumar says, "How do we create a flexible, customer-focused, and innovative organization? We had to hire people who have our cultural DNA. We wanted people who shared our vision of what India's banking future would look like in terms of growth, capabilities, and aspiration. We wanted people who had the same future vision as our most senior leaders."[3] ICICI HR began looking for people who envisioned great growth in the financial sectors, who wanted to be on the road with customers instead of in their air-conditioned offices, who were savvy with new technology, and who were comfortable being self-starters in the midst of high ambiguity.

With these criteria in place, ICICI had to create a fast pipeline of talent. It needed people to come into the bank who were "shop ready"—able to add value upon arrival. To address this challenge, ICICI helped establish the Institute of Finance, Banking, and Insurance (IFBI). Beginning in 2007, carefully selected college graduates were put into a rigorous six-month program of technical and cultural training that included intense evaluation and feedback, and concluded with a postgraduate certificate in banking. Now they were shop-ready. Out of 18,000 graduates over four years, ICICI hired 12,000. In spite of having provided much of the financial support for this school in its start-up phase, the ICICI leadership made the decision to allow other banks to be involved in this initiative. Thereby, ICICI contributes to India's larger financial ecosystem.

To further enhance the trajectory of leadership development, ICICI established the ICICI Manipal Academy for Banking and Insurance, which focuses on the training of people from poor families in smaller cities, as well as the ICICI Business Leadership Programme with NIIT, which results in an MBA in finance and banking and a specialized postgraduate certificate in securities markets with the National Institute of Securities Markets.

To accelerate trained leaders through the pipeline, ICICI has gone beyond the traditional leadership development tools of 360-degree evaluations, feedback, coaching, and mentoring.

- It provides intensive on-the-job development opportunities. "If you don't take risks with people, you will never build leaders. If you want generals, give them an army."[4]
- It assumes that "treating everyone as a diamond," pleasant as it is as an aspiration, will not get you where you need to be quickly enough from a leadership standpoint. Instead, some people who aspire to be leaders will end up being disappointed. ICICI is willing to live with its disappointments. Those who do not make the cut are given financial and nonfinancial acknowledgement but are not placed in leadership positions.
- It focuses leadership selection on identifying and building on strengths, and not on absence of weaknesses. "If you look for gods among the people, you will not find them. Therefore, emphasize what people can do, not what they cannot do."

This orientation to recruit, train, and promote leaders through HR activities is supported by the strong involvement at the most senior levels. ICICI's norm for scanning the organization for upcoming talent—talent scouting—is an intense way of life. For example, ICICI's current CEO, Chanda Kochhar, expects to meet 20 high potentials every month. These individuals frequently come from deep in the organization. She spends an hour to an hour and a half with each candidate. She looks for their strengths, weaknesses, and aspirations. She compares her perceptions against their formal evaluations. She also learns what is going on in the organization. This requires Ramkumar to spend two days per month traveling to meet people, identify talent, and stay in touch with the business. As a result, HR and senior leadership co-own the HR and organization agenda and are fully aligned in crafting ICICI's future.

Contextual Trends: Economic and Political, Social and Talent, and Business

In the past 60 years, India has gone through dramatic and occasionally traumatic changes. Beginning with its independence in 1947, India entered a new phase of development with optimism but with challenges.

Economic and Political Trends

With India's drive for domestic autonomy on the international stage, the period from 1947 to 1992 was marked by several developments that Western observers find unfortunate. The country moved toward Soviet-style central administration of the economy, complete with five-year planning and its accompanying slow, expensive, nonresponsive, and occasionally corrupt bureaucratic control infrastructure. To do business in India on any meaningful scale, business licenses had to be obtained from Delhi's central bureaucracy—the "License Raj." This licensing process tended to favor large, established companies that could afford to pay for the privilege and that could thereby control the level of competition from overseas and from Indian start-ups.

The combination of central planning and minimization of competition led to substantial disincentives for innovation in large companies and for entrepreneurial initiative in small start-ups. A result was chronic oversupply in some goods and serious shortages in others. Concurrently, government policy strongly encouraged economic isolation from the rest of the world. The trend toward isolationism was reinforced by stringent limitations on the inflow of foreign capital and the outflow of Indian capital. Under these circumstances, the only growth option for established companies was radical unrelated diversification. For example, in the early 1990s, the RPG Group diversified into financial services, foods, automotive supplies, business machines, entertainment, and energy.

With the economic liberalization of 1992, reforms reduced tariffs, interest rates, and income taxes and diminished the License Raj. Several public monopolies were broken up or disbanded, allowing greater competition; the flow of foreign capital into the country was encouraged; and obstacles to overseas Indian investment were reduced. In this new environment, active companies such as Wipro, Dr. Reddy's, and Axis Bank have come into existence and prospered.

India's intellectual capability and entrepreneurial instincts have driven a remarkable economic transformation on the bases of these reforms. In the 20-plus years since liberalization, India's economic growth rate has continued strong. Current GDP is US$1.3 trillion, and economic growth for 2012 to 2013 is projected to be 6.5 percent—and 7.5 percent for 2013 to 2014.[5] Service sector growth (driven by outsourced IT functions from the USA and Europe) is expected to continue to outpace the industrial sector, and both of these will substantially surpass the agriculture sector. Thus, globalization will continue as a way of economic life. Net capital inflows in 1990 were US$7.1 billion; in 2008 they were US$428.7 billion. The share of merchandise exports relative to GDP increased from 5.8 percent in 1990 to 15.1 percent in 2009. During the same time period, merchandise imports increased from 8.8 percent to 25.5 percent. Per capita income grew from 1.1 percent between 1951 and 1980 to 5.4 percent between 2000 and 2009.[6] India's middle class is expected to grow 1,000 percent between 2005 and 2025, while the total population will increase 30 percent.[7] This will make India's middle class one of the world's most formidable purchasing blocs.

Social and Talent Trends

Even in this dynamic economy, India's population continues to face paradoxes and challenges. The Human Development Index (HDI) provides comparative measures of life expectancy, literacy, education, and standard of living. In 2006, India placed 132 out of 179 countries in the world—11 places below its 1990 ranking of 121. Against the absolute standard, India's HDI score is increasing, but relative to global standards, it is diminishing. India continues to struggle with high poverty rates. Even with a 7 to 8 percent decrease in its poverty rate between 1993 and 2005, it continues to be the poorest among G-20 countries. Per capita consumption expenditure is less than US$0.38 per day—in a country that has more than a 100,000 millionaires whose lifestyles put a lot of upward pressure on the average.

Education is a high priority in Indian families. Children from wealthy families are expected to uphold the family tradition of economic success, and children from poor families are encouraged to study their way out of poverty. Considerable progress has been made in the availability of public education, with 91.1 percent of children aged 6 to 14 actively attending school. This has contributed to India's increased literacy rate—from 52.2 percent in 1991 to 74 percent in 2011. Even with this increase, however, India's literacy rate remains lower than the worldwide average.[8] Teacher and student absenteeism remains a major challenge. The shining star is the advances that are being made at the college and university undergraduate and graduate levels, where the relatively strict meritocracy helps make sure that the brightest and the most capable individuals have access to higher education.

India is becoming healthier.[9] Infant mortality is down, and life expectancy is increasing at a pace of 4.5 years per decade. As a result, India's population is growing; it is expected to be the largest in the world by 2030. Furthermore, compared with many industrialized countries and China, India's population is remaining relatively young.

Prior to 1992, corruption was institutionally enabled through the License Raj. Despite substantial cutbacks in that system, however, the culture of corruption has unfortunately continued. In 2005, a study by Transparency International found that more than half of the individuals surveyed had found it necessary to pay bribes to get work done through public officials.[10]

Women in India have among the highest levels of ambition for personal professional progress in the world—85 percent, compared with 65 percent in China and 36 percent in the United States.[11] A noticeable attribute of India's professional women is their tendency toward degrees in mathematics and the hard sciences. Additionally, 68 percent of Indian women in a national survey of employed professionals indicated that they were very or extremely loyal to their employers—a rate that was notably higher than that of their male counterparts. Indian women are increasingly having highly visible role models in CEO or chair positions: Chanda Kochhar at ICICI, Kiran Mazumdar-Shaw at BIOCON, Kalpana Morparia at J. P. Morgan, Shobhana Bhartia at Hindustan Times Group, and Shikha Sharma at AXIS Bank, to name just a few.

In its medieval origins, India's caste system provided division of labor (amounting to serfdom for some), as well as guild structures and training.[12] In the modern era, the caste system continues to segment the population vertically through job categories and horizontally through levels of authority, responsibility, and upward mobility. Besides undermining human dignity, the caste system has three negative outcomes:

- It creates unquestioned compliance with requests from hierarchical seniors, thereby limiting upward feedback from those who are frequently closest to operational reality.
- It limits society's capacity to apply the skills and abilities of much of its population.
- It places psychological dampers on the lower castes' aspirations to innovate and contribute.

Several leading companies—including Tata, ICICI, Aditya Birla Group, RPG Group, ITC, and Mahindra and Mahindra—are working to reduce these social inequities as a way to enhance India's competitiveness.

Business Trends

Indian businesses are responding to these economic, political, and social trends by skillfully balancing a set of paradoxes:

- Scale versus quality
- Home markets versus external markets
- Diversification versus free information flow

India's companies are shifting from competition based on scale and low cost to competition based on innovation and quality. Because of the country's size, it is possible to quickly turn scale and costs to competitive advantage. C.K. Prahalad recognized this in his groundbreaking *Fortune at the Bottom of the Pyramid*; he argues that by radically reconfiguring cost structures, firms will be able to leverage scale and thereby be able to provide products and services to the low-income masses.[13] Frugality in every aspect of business is instinctive to Indian employees and executives alike. It is no accident that the US$2,500 car, Tata's Nano, originated in India. That same innovative instinct is now focused on improving features and quality as sources of competitive advantage. Examples include designer watches from Titan, new airport designs by Larsen and Toubro, and new consumer product packaging by Marico.

Until 20 years ago, Indian companies had little to do with the outside world. Indian markets were sufficiently large to use up state-regulated-production capacity. Deregulation provided an opening for Indian companies to compete abroad, and it also provided an opening for the best companies in the world to compete in India. To expand abroad and to protect local market share, India had to develop the organization capability and cultural mindset to meet world-class standards. Its success in so doing is exemplified by Suzlon's accomplishments in wind power, Tata's acquisition of Jaguar and Land Rover, Aditya Birla's acquisition of Novellis, Mahindra and Mahindra's overseas sales of tractors, Bharat Forge's competitiveness in automotive supplies, and Larsen and Toubro's large-scale infrastructure projects.

Because of the historical limits on investment outside India, Indian firms entered new businesses or bought other players in order to grow. This led to some of the world's most diversified conglomerates. Many of the large groups are now seeking to find commonalities and to leverage them across group companies so as to make the corporate whole more valuable than the sum of the individual businesses. As an example, the Godrej Group competes in 21 different product and service categories. Even with such a diversified portfolio, the Godrej Group seeks to find points of interbusiness learning and to deploy them for individual and collective competitive advantage.

Review and Discussion of the 2012 HRCS India Findings

In this economic, governmental, and social context, HR departments and line executives in India, as elsewhere in the world, have had to radically transform their visions, and expectations of HR. There are probably few places on earth where HR professionals and their line executives are working with greater intensity to build and blend the human and organizational sides of business for competitive advantage. This is evidenced by several statistics. Infosys spends US$65 on training for every US$1,000 in revenues; this compares to the US$6.17 spent by IBM.[14] HR job openings are increasing compared with other regions.[15] Our global experience suggests an excitement and urgency about getting HR right as noticeable as anywhere on earth. While underlying business drivers push this trend, deeper values of care, concern, and service appear to be in play in India. In Hinduism, members of the higher castes have a moral obligation to care for those in the lower castes. When this moral obligation becomes linked with competitive necessity, the human agenda takes on vibrancy in India that is seldom duplicated in other parts of the world.

In 2012, 1,800 respondents participated in the HRCS survey in India. This was the highest response rate that India had experienced in its four iterations of involvement since 1997. This successful involvement of the HR community in India was made possible by the efforts of the National HRD Network, with support by the Ross School of Business at the University of Michigan and the RBL group.

The six HR competency domains have their own impact on individual and business performance in India.[16] Table 7.1 shows how they play out.

Table 7.1   HR Competency Domains in India

HR Competency Domain	Mean Score (High 5, Low1)	Impact on Perception of Individual Effectiveness	Impact on Business Performance
Credible Activist	4.19	21%	15%
Capability Builder	3.96	16%	17%
Change Champion	3.92	16%	15%
HR Innovator and Integrator	3.89	17%	18%
Strategic Positioner	3.83	16%	15%
Technology Proponent	3.82	14%	21%
Multiple R²		.483	0.138

Credible Activist

The results-based integrity of the credible activist serves as the foundation of personal trust that, in turn, translates into professional credibility with internal and external stakeholders. With an average score of 4.19, HR professionals in India are most adept in this domain. Their effectiveness in exhibiting the specific competencies of the credible activist is what has greatest influence on their personal effectiveness as perceived by their HR and non-HR associates (21 percent). This provides a solid foundation for their involvement in other activities that are more centrally related to the business. However, as in other parts of the world, the influence of this competency on business performance is substantially lower, at 15 percent. There is a potential danger here. HR professionals excel at being credible activists, but competence in this domain has relatively little influence on business performance. Thus, they must be careful not to believe that the respect of their associates means they are actually improving business performance.

Coromandel International Limited is a fertilizer, specialty nutrients, and crop-protection company within the Murugappa Group, and its 2010 to 2011 revenues were US$1.7 billion. Its HR professionals have been highly effective as credible activists.[17] In 2009 to 2010, Coromandel leadership was involved in intense discussions about the feasibility of keeping its Technical Crop Protection manufacturing unit at a location that was being converted into a business office center. HR at Coromandel was convinced that the traditional, well-accepted pattern of paying compensation and easing people out in this type of situation was not beneficial for either employees or the company. Instead, HR proposed that the workers be retained and moved to other plants, thereby remaining gainfully employed. HR faced several challenges. Management wanted to relocate the unit quickly, and layoffs with compensation was the fastest means of doing so. Employees wanted short-term severance payouts and did not want to be relocated 700 miles from their homes and families. Union leaders were suspicious of the company's motives.

Coromandel's HR department confronted these obstacles in a highly effective manner. First, HR secured the buy-in of management by making a strong case on the basis of business, legal, and ethical logic. It then took unprecedented steps to convince the union and employees to buy into the approach. Through a program called Go Kiss the World, HR presented empirical research on the results of the traditional layoff schemes. These studies showed that no matter how attractive the initial separation compensation, after a few years the vast majority of former employees were found to be in poor health, physically or financially—or both. HR professionals convinced the company to fund educational opportunities for each employee who moved to a new location. They showcased the technology, scale, and size of the new plants to which people were being transferred. They facilitated meetings between senior managers and the families of the workers to explain how families would benefit from the transfers. They sponsored employee trips to the new manufacturing locations. In six months, the company had successfully moved 70 percent of its Technical Crop Protection employees to its other manufacturing locations. The external union leader, a veteran in the field, commented during the interactions: "I have never seen or heard of any company taking so much effort in terms of time and resources not to send out its employees." As a result of Coromandel's HR professionals striving to be credible activists, all stakeholders benefitted. Coromandel is now ranked by *Business Today* as one of the top 20 best companies to work for in India.

Capability Builder

HR professionals in India score at a reasonably high level of 3.96 out of 5.00 on the capability builder competency domain. This domain has roughly equal influence on individual effectiveness (at 16 percent) and on business performance (at 17 percent) in India.

Marico is a leading consumer product and service company.[18] With revenues of US$695 million in 2010 to 2011, Marico is present in 25 countries. One out of three Indians uses Marico products, from cooking oil to skin products and hair oil. Marico maintains that it excels at working "outside the box, to bring innovation to customers through the careful creation of continuous and sustainable change."

Marico believes that every employee from the top of the organization to the bottom should innovate, constantly try to improve things, and think differently. These capabilities are at the heart of Marico. As the custodian as well as the facilitator of Marico's values and culture, HR defines people processes, policies, and practices that drive results and enable profitable growth. Its annual strategic business planning process articulates future imperatives and capability needs for the company. These are translated into individual actions and outcomes through a management-by-results process that requires employees to clearly define the outcomes that they will strive to achieve over the next year. Performance rewards are directly linked to achievement of these goals by the company, its businesses, and individual employees. This has helped focus people on critical business issues and promote the right behaviors needed by Marico in the long term for sustained profitable growth. The process is integrated into the personal development planning process, which is designed to identify and build individuals' development needs, career aspirations, and future potential consistent with Marico's key organizational capability requirements.

Seventy-five-year-old Larsen & Toubro (L&T) is a professionally managed technology, engineering, construction, and manufacturing company.[19] L&T has successfully built and sustained capabilities in technology and service solution development. These are implemented through collaborative relationships with leading companies and governments in more than 30 countries, resulting in sales of US$11.7 billion in 2010 to 2011. These key organizational capabilities have been translated into specific output and behavioral criteria that serve as the basis of talent acquisition that balances the potential growth of internal talent with the need to continually identify and access top-class business leaders from the rest of the world. L&T's capabilities are reinforced through its Framework for Linking Appraisals with Incentive and Rewards, integrated with ICONS (Immense Contribution of Noteworthy Significance)—an individual and team recognition program. Its succession planning process emphasizes promotions based on performance and contributions to L&T's organizational capabilities. Finally, its management leadership program and its leadership development program focus on helping present and future leaders acquire the skills and knowledge to build and sustain L&T's capabilities. These, in turn, serve as the basis of its competitive advantage throughout the world.

Change Champion

HR professionals in India confront the challenges of change at a high level, 3.92 out of 5.00. Their abilities to do so have equal impact on both individual effectiveness (16 percent) and business performance (15 percent). Excellent examples of HR professionals acting as change champions are found at HCL Technologies and Maruti Suzuki India Limited.

HCL Technologies is a US$4 billion global company (present in 26 countries) that brings IT and engineering service expertise together to solve complex business problems.[20] Its services are provided in such industries as healthcare, manufacturing, consumer services, public services, and financial services. In 2005, the company line leadership (together with senior HR professionals) envisioned an organization that would recognize employees as the primary value creators in the customer-employee relationship. They sought to give "confident and capable" employees the right tools and ownership to serve customers quickly and accurately outside the command-and-control structure. HR was charged with creating a framework in which employees could focus their ingenuity and motivation on solving customer challenges instead of continually looking to management for solutions.

The overall philosophy was called Employees First, Customers Second. It consisted of several initiatives. Among the most dramatic was Destroy the Office of the CEO. Employees were encouraged to focus on their customers instead of on their managers. They were told "Managers are your resources; you are not theirs." Management was to be accessible to employees, but not allow employees to delegate upward. Customer-focused problem solving remained on the shoulders of employees. The responsibility and accountability was with the employee to create extraordinary levels of customer satisfaction.

This philosophy is reinforced by several specific practices. Accountability is facilitated by 360-degree evaluations. Outstanding performers (those who reach the top 5 percent and remain so for two years in a row) become members of the 02 Club. They are fast-tracked, honored with their families, presented with trophies, and given the opportunity to represent the company in public forums, including meetings and webinars. They are also given the opportunity to confront difficult and challenging work. Young people are surprised by the level of responsibility they receive, given their ages. Compensation is market-driven with incentives based on individual and, in some cases, group performance. In addition, HR has instituted the Extra-Mile Program, which is modeled after airlines' frequent flier programs. Each employee receives 300 miles per year to give to others. Employees can allocate those miles to others who have helped them by providing information, giving useful coaching, or writing insightful and useful white papers. Different numbers of miles qualify recipients for different club levels: silver, gold, platinum, and CEO. Each of these levels is recognized online, and they come with escalating award levels including travel opportunities, personal visits with the CEO, and purchase vouchers.

By serving as change champions so effectively, the HR department has had impact. Employees are doing what they want to do with their work and their careers; they are solving challenging problems for their valued customers. As a result, customer satisfaction has increased 75 percent over the past six years, and employee satisfaction is at an all-time high.

Maruti Suzuki India Limited, a subsidiary of Suzuki Motor Corporation of Japan, is India's largest passenger car company; it has a turnover of US$6.8 billion and employs more than 9,000 people.[21] It is largely credited with having brought an automobile revolution into India. In its history, Maruti has gone through several major changes. The most challenging of these occurred in the years following the liberalization of India's economy. When the Indian government pulled out its equity, Suzuki Japan became the primary owner, with 54 percent equity. Maruti had to convert itself from government appendage to private-sector company—while facing tough competition from the likes of Tata Motors, Hyundai, Ford, GM, Toyota, and Honda. This required dropping its monopolistic mindset and developing a customer-centric business culture. With these challenges clearly identified, the HR department set out to transform its labor relations orientation to a more progressive and people-centric approach that aligned HR with the business.

Maruti HR formulated a three-year HR plan that aligned people policies, systems, and processes with the three-year strategic business plan of the company. One of the first initiatives focused on leadership development interventions at the top and senior management levels followed by middle management. The goal was to enhance change-leadership skills among senior team members and expose these people to best global business processes and to trends in successful global companies. These programs were supported by a 360-degree feedback process for all division general managers and above, including directors and managing directors. The process included the formulation of individual development plans. Totals of 5 days of annual training per employee at the supervisory level and 10 days per employee at the managerial level have been achieved. HR now also partners with more than 220 dealer and 80 vendor companies to enhance HR capabilities across the value chain. Thus HR's change capability has been on the forefront of preparing Maruti to face the challenges of the increasingly competitive Indian automotive market.

HR Innovator and Integrator

Indian HR professionals function as HR innovators and integrators at a reasonably high level (3.89 out of 5.0). Through this competency domain, HR professionals in India influence their individual effectiveness and business performance at approximately the same levels: 17 and 18 percent, respectively.

HR professionals at Bharti Airtel (Airtel) are effective examples of how to add value as HR innovators and integrators.[22] With more than 243 million customers across 20 countries, Airtel is the world's third-largest telecom operator. It is the largest cellular service provider in India, with more than 181 million subscribers. In Airtel's fastest growth years (in the 1990s), HR focused on staffing and other basic administrative functions. In the mid–2000s, it focused on streamlining transactional processes including shared services, competency models, performance management, and talent management. These helped to standardize practices across businesses and to tap synergies of scale for HR operations. Over the past few years, the department has adopted the HR innovator and integrator role by strengthening and integrating innovative practices in talent acquisition, rewards, benefits, talent management, and talent development.

HR professionals at Airtel have clearly outlined a leadership competency framework that forms the bedrock of its people management systems. Its Promoting Entrepreneurship policy provides financial and managerial assistance to budding entrepreneurs within the company by allowing them to take charge of specific business opportunities. The "Jobs Never Done Before" initiative encourages Airtel's employer brand proposition to be "future-facing and consumer-oriented" and to "give scale to those who have entrepreneurial DNA, to charter the unchartered." A recognition policy and process called Kudos creates online visibility and incentives for employees to demonstrate Airtel values and competencies. BLeAP and ELeAP are programs for high potentials in middle management through which they are groomed for business leadership roles in an integrated set of structured interventions, including classroom learning, on-the-job training, special projects, and career movements spanning two to three years. These initiatives are supported by the high involvement of Airtel's senior leadership and its management board in mentoring high potentials.

Finally, the One Airtel initiative has created panels to evaluate select people for critical organizational roles. It provides greater visibility for internal talent, encourages growth and movement across businesses, and has introduced rigor and transparency in selection of candidates for critical positions.

As a result of these innovative and integrated practices, HR at Airtel is building unique, winning capabilities for the business by "consistently delivering trend-setting solutions to its business and people." By so doing, HR has helped to define Airtel's culture and translate business strategy into positive business outcomes.

Strategic Positioner

In India, HR professionals function as strategic positioners at a level slightly below their scores in the preceding domains (3.83); however, the impact of this domain on individual and business performance remains about constant at 16 and 15 percent, respectively. Thus, this may be an area for targeted improvement.

Two companies in India stand out as exceptional examples of HR professionals as strategic positioners: Dr. Reddy's Laboratories and Mahindra and Mahindra.

Dr. Reddy's is an integrated global pharmaceutical company.[23] It offers a wide range of products and services including active pharmaceutical ingredients, custom pharmaceutical services, generics, differentiated formulations, and new chemical entities.

Dr. Reddy's focuses on industry-leading science and technology, product offerings, and customer service through excellence in execution. In the medium to long term, it seeks to become a proprietary drug company through a patient-focused and low-risk innovation strategy. It recently crossed the US$2 billion threshold in annual revenues.

Increasing competition, commoditization in generics markets, and pricing pressures are changing the business scenario for the pharmaceutical industry. This has forced Dr. Reddy's to revamp its business strategy in alignment with the changing business needs. The two pillars of the organization's strategic framework are its strategy and management principles and its HR philosophies. As facilitated by HR with the involvement of senior line executives, its values and culture are designed and implemented to serve as the foundation for the future organization.

Aligning HR strategy to business and customer requirements has been a key differentiator for the organization. Strategic HR themes have been integrated under three focus areas:

- *Alignment.* Organization design, cross-business collaboration, harmonized practices, and employee engagement
- *Accountability.* Performance metrics, robust reviews, and total rewards
- *Ability.* Talent management, functional expertise, and leadership development

Through HR's involvement in strategy formulation and through business-focused HR practices, HR professionals add strategic value to the present and future success of Dr. Reddy's.

Mahindra and Mahindra is a US$14.4 billion multinational group that spans the automotive, aerospace, aftermarket, financial services, logistics, real estate, retail, and two-wheeler industries.[24] At the core of its business success is a strategy development process in which each business sector develops a strategy in line with group aspirations, core purposes, and BHAGs (big, hairy, audacious goals). These strategies are formulated and discussed in the "War Room" with the vice chairman and managing director (Anand Mahindra), respective sector presidents, and other key members who either contribute to or challenge business assumptions. As integral contributors to the strategy creation process, the HR heads help formulate company vision and values, business requirements, rules for success, required assets, and key capabilities.

In this context, HR strategies are developed to be "strategically proactive." HR professionals at Mahindra and Mahindra begin by understanding key customer requirements, macroeconomic trends, business performance, key business metrics, and targeted outcomes. From this, they identify key customer-related business imperatives and articulate HR implications, with key deliverables and measurables. HR deliverables are divided into three categories:

- *Capacity.* HR interventions such as roles, structures, and processes for supporting the development of business capabilities
- *Capability.* Building individual capability through exposure, experience, and education with a view to keeping a strong leadership pipeline

- *Connection*. Building cultural capability in alignment with group philosophy and business requirements (such as customer sensitivity)

By being centrally involved in the group's strategy formulation processes and by building individual, leadership, and cultural capabilities that implement business strategy, HR contributes fundamentally to one of India's most successful organizations.

Technology Proponent

As in the rest of the world, HR professionals in India are least skilled in the technology proponent domain. The domain factors also have the least impact on individual effectiveness. However, they do have the highest impact of any competency domain on business performance. This provides a remarkable source of potential competitive advantage.

Wipro Limited is a significant example of a company in which HR professionals are serving as role models of the technology proponent domain.[25] Wipro is India's second-largest IT services company. Its 135,920 people worldwide generated US$7.37 billion in 2010 to 2011. Its business lines include outsourced R&D, infrastructure outsourcing, and business consulting services. These are delivered in three dominant segments: IT services, IT products, and consumer care and lighting. In 2012, Wipro ranked as India's most valuable brand.

Wipro was an early driver in applying technology to HR. It has automated a wide range of transactions including payroll processing, taxation, employee data management, hiring and on-boarding, off-boarding and exits, salary and wage, incentive and commission processing, step administration, benefits administration, performance management, learning administration, leave-of-absence administration, time and attendance monitoring, employee records management, and contingent worker data management.

Over the past few years, the role of technology as applied to HR has morphed from being a tool for efficiency and cost reduction into being a primary mechanism through which people inside and outside the firm use social networks to cocreate solutions for business and personal applications.

At Wipro, technology has changed the role of HR and redefined how employees can be enlisted to build solutions for business and customers alike.

Wipro's spirit of collaboration is born out of a cultural aspiration to make business a win-win. Winning does not come at all costs and should not be pursued at the expense of others. Instead, winning is about increasing synergies by defining individual success in terms of team success—and team success in terms of customer success. In this cultural context, Wipro's HR department set out to create an ecosystem where people collaborate, socialize, and create apps for the benefit of the entire community. They wanted to crowd-source innovative ideas and draw on the whole technical talent base of the company's employees.

One outcome of this way of thinking on the part of HR was the creation of the AppLife platform. AppLife invites employees to develop ideas that can improve the lives of others, and employees refine their ideas by socializing about them in the Wipro AppLife "idea space." Employees from the Wipro's AppLife developers' community bring the ideas to life by creating mobile apps for successful ideas on Android, iOS, BlackBerry, or Windows. Once an app is available, other Wiproites rate it and use it to make their lives simpler. AppLife recognizes both the app developer and the employee who had the idea. Apps that have been developed include Super Hero, which connects employees to emergency services; WiFi Remote, which lets employees use a phone as a gesture-based, no-button remote to their Smart TVs; Wipro Locator, which helps employees find Wipro offices throughout the world, along with nearby community services; and Automator, which sets automatic activities for employees as they desire.

Just a few years back, the role of HR in innovation was to test new ideas by running a few focus groups and then rolling the results out to employees. Now HR at Wipro uses technology to be far more inclusive. HR leaders no longer merely engage employees with a few focus groups; now they use technology to connect and empower a talented community of thousands of employees distributed across 54 countries. The apps help empower employees to solve their own problems. The role of HR is to provide platforms for idea creation through the talent and passion of Wipro employees.

Conclusion

As noted at the beginning of this chapter, India is emerging as one of the world's most dynamic and exciting locations. Business growth and the drive for competitiveness have placed HR at the center of the agenda in many of India's leading companies. With pressures from these business dynamics and with an understanding of the required competencies, HR professionals in India are positioned to continue their substantive contributions to their individual careers, their companies, and their country as a whole.

CHAPTER 8

LATIN AMERICA

8

MICHEL HERMANS AND ALEJANDRO SIOLI

Upon acquiring McDonald's Latin American operations in August 2007, Arcos Dorados became its largest franchisee in the world. The company is building on the region's economic expansion, exhibiting a strong growth strategy that has led it to open 232 new McDonald's restaurants, 124 McCafé locations, and 430 Dessert Centers; and to remodel 308 existing restaurants. By the end of 2011, Arcos Dorados operated 1,755 McDonald's restaurants, 267 McCafés, and 1,300 Dessert Centers in 20 countries throughout Latin America and the Caribbean. Moreover, it has committed to open at least another 250 restaurants from 2011 to 2013. The company employs approximately 86,000 people, has its corporate headquarters in Buenos Aires, Argentina, and has been listed on the New York Stock Exchange (as ARCO) since April 2011.

Finding effective solutions to HR challenges has been critical to sustaining the company's growth. Although Arcos Dorados had its own franchised restaurants in several Spanish-speaking South American countries, expanding to the entire region presented challenges in integrating operations regionally and developing an organization culture that would overcome intraregional differences and the legacy of individually operating franchises. Simultaneously, turnover rates in the fast-food industry are typically high; annual turnover above 100 percent is not exceptional. Talented and motivated employees are critical to delivering good service, but attracting and keeping them is particularly difficult in Latin America. Restaurant staff members are typically young and have moderate levels of education. While the number of potential candidates is high, attracting talented candidates to jobs with moderate pay levels and limited career prospects requires the development of a strong employer brand, nonfinancial incentives, communication, and supervisor skills.

Headed by Pablo Rodriguez de la Torre, Arcos Dorados's HR team has responded effectively to these challenges. In 2011, the company was ranked fourth in the Great Place to Work Institute's list of large employers in Latin America. One of the numerous initiatives Arcos Dorados has undertaken is developing a My First Job employer brand that appeals to candidates' future aspirations. The company organizes internal contests in which employees can share their artistic talents with colleagues and holds large-scale events in which achievements of both the company and individual employees are celebrated. Recently, the company has been invited to collaborate with the Inter-American Development Bank and the International Labor Organization to create skill development projects aimed at preparing younger people to enter the formal workforce.

The Latin American Business Context

Although the region includes 20 independent countries, Latin America is often seen as a fairly homogeneous business context. A shared history of colonization by Spain and Portugal, the predominance of Roman Catholicism, and early immigration waves from similar countries have contributed to the development of a singular Latin American cultural profile. Likewise, the region has a uniform economic profile, that is based on the exploitation of natural resources. Exports of minerals, agricultural products, and oil and gas are more economically significant than the activities of a handful of companies in industries such as IT, aircraft manufacturing, entertainment, and professional services.

Latin America has a history of economic turbulence. The combination of governments' centrality in the region's economies, frequent shifts of power among ruling elites, military coups, and emerging social movements has caused profound crises in the region's economies. Examples include the foreign debt crises during the 1980s, during which bonds of several Latin American countries were classified as junk bonds. Similarly, the radical adoption of market-based policies and opening of economies to free trade between the late 1980s and early 2000s required profound structural adjustments. As most countries were unable to make these changes, governments used public debt to compensate for lack of competitiveness, leading countries such as Mexico, Brazil, and Argentina to strong devaluations and renegotiation of public debt.

Another shared characteristic of Latin American countries is the uneven distribution of income. While governments use different policies to help people make the transition out of poverty, bringing historically marginalized segments of the population into the workforce as a means to distribute income more evenly remains an important challenge that affects organizations in several ways. For example, in Peru, Chile, and Argentina, the populations of villages located close to mining operations increasingly protest and obstruct operations by blocking access to mines and demanding a share of the profits, more local employment, and support in the development of infrastructure and educational facilities. Likewise, the uneven distribution of income is related to high urban crime rates. Drug trafficking and organized crime have become important businesses on their own. Companies may find that employees are unwilling to relocate to cities known for outbursts of violence and crime.

Most Latin American countries suffer from corruption in economic and public life. Although corporate scandals around the globe suggest that delinquent management is not confined to Latin America, corruption in the region takes many forms and occurs at all organizational levels. Of the 182 countries audited by Transparency International, a nongovernmental organization (NGO), most Latin American countries occupied positions in the lower half of the ranking, suggesting lack of transparency.[1] Companies that operate in the region need to enforce administrative compliance and codes of conduct to avoid becoming involved in dubious transactions.

Notwithstanding these intraregional similarities, Latin American economies have diverged since the early 2000s, particularly in their orientation toward the world economy. Countries can be grouped into two broad categories. The first, composed of countries such as Venezuela, Ecuador, Argentina, and Bolivia, is characterized by anti-free-market and nationalistic economic policies and populist support. Public policies in these countries have created employment and opportunities for local or less risk-averse investors to build or expand their businesses. However, government intervention in these economies has grown ever stronger, affecting companies in areas such as collective bargaining, price setting, transferring profits from subsidiaries to corporate headquarters, and supply-chain management (through restrictions on imports). In extreme cases, governments have even expropriated businesses. In Venezuela, for example, Hugo Chavez's government nationalized assets of Exxon Mobil and acquired Banco de Venezuela from Spanish Banco Santander after repeated threats of expropriation. One of the main challenges in these countries, for both national firms and multinationals, is to maintain a sound relationship with the government while operating a business in a context of uncertainty and continuous change.

The second group includes countries such as Brazil, Peru, Chile, Mexico, and Colombia that are working to create government policies that foster integration with global markets while also attending to the social needs of their populations. Brazil's internal, market-driven economic growth and the international expansion of Brazilian companies have drawn much attention. Chile, Mexico, and more recently, Peru and Colombia have had more export-driven economic growth; and companies from these countries are expanding rapidly throughout the region and beyond. For example, Mexico's América Movil has become the world's third-largest mobile telecommunications operator by integrating national operators under its Claro brand over the past several years.[2] Challenges for companies that operate in these economies are mainly related to growth: securing access to finance and talent, integrating existing and new operations, and—especially in the case of multinationals—controlling the risk of excess exposure to overheated economies.

Regional Organization Trends

Three distinct but complementary forms of business organization occur in Latin America. First, multinational companies have historically played an important role in integrating the region into the international economy through investment, transfers of technology, and international trade. Second, national economic groups, also called *grupos*, are a conglomerate organizational form that allows local investor groups—often families—to control diversified business interests. Third, as in most countries, small- and medium-size companies are responsible for the largest share of formal employment. Additionally, Latin America has a large informal economy, estimated to represent up to 70 percent of employment in countries such as Bolivia or El Salvador. However, as the HRCS focused on formal employment, HRM in the region's informal economy may reward future research.

Multinational Companies

Following the trend of integration of the Latin American region, many multinationals have abandoned the practice of naming country managers. Instead, they create regional or subregional offices that allow for the deployment of common strategies. The scope of regional integration varies among companies. While some group together all countries from Mexico in the north to Argentina in the south, others use criteria such as language or market size to define subregions (for example, Andean countries, River Plate, or Brazil). The establishment of regional offices has been accompanied by the creation of shared services organizations, in particular for staff functions such as HR, procurement, IT, and finance.

Multinationals have long viewed Latin America as a secondary market that adapts to product offerings. However, travel and the Internet allow affluent customers to acquire high-end products offered in companies' home markets, thus limiting the ability to delay product launches and charge a premium for the same products in Latin America. Simultaneously, historically ignored lower-income segments represent new opportunities, particularly in the market for consumer goods. Bottom-of-pyramid business models require corporations to develop an understanding of less-affluent customers' needs and their ability to pay for the products and services offered.

Finally, some multinationals find their opportunities to benefit from the region's economic growth constrained by headcount limits imposed by corporate headquarters. Subsidiaries tend to circumvent such limitations by hiring temporary staff, subcontracting, and outsourcing. Such practices provide multinationals with considerable flexibility but come at both an economic and managerial cost. Particularly for organization-specific processes, using temporary personnel or subcontractors involves additional costs for training, adaptation periods, operational monitoring, and drafting and revising contracts.

Latin American National Economic Groups

Originating from local investors' diversification strategies in volatile econo-mies, most *grupos* compete with multinationals but face different challenges. The grupos typically benefitted from their social and political relationships with national governments, obtaining concessions during privatization pro-cesses, privileged access to financing, and access to the state as a client. During the past decade, some grupos have moved beyond their national borders, focusing on a specific industry or niche to internationalize their activities. In so doing, they have become Latin American multinationals, or "multi-Latinas." Examples include CEMEX, Grupo Bimbo, and América Movil from Mexico; Embraer, Camargo Correa, and Petrobras from Brazil; LAN, Masisa, and Falabella from Chile; Alicorp from Peru; and Tenaris and Arcor from Argentina.

Most *grupos* and multi-Latinas have grown significantly during the past decade. Expansion, particularly beyond national borders, has required organi-zations to stretch themselves as they expatriate managers and key employees, redefine resource allocation and control mechanisms, adapt to cross-cultural management challenges, and overcome challenges related to new acquisitions. These changes are often eased by having visible owners who are actively involved in day-to-day management and who allow for different attitudes toward the risks associated with growing an organization in Latin America. Because they are accustomed to the volatility of the region's economies, local owners are more willing to assume risks and apply a longer-term perspective than managers of multinationals, who are focused on quarterly results. On the other hand, the vis-ible presence of owners in daily operations puts additional pressure on senior and middle managers, especially in decisions involving capital expenditure.

Small- and Medium-Size Enterprises

The Latin American landscape of small- and medium-size firms is large and diverse. However, some common trends may be identified. First, Latin American SMEs are increasingly required to professionalize their opera-tions, particularly their management, to assure their survival. Although pro-tectionist measures have eased competition with imported products in some countries, competition within countries and incorporation into the value chains of multinationals or grupos is forcing SMEs to upgrade technologically, solidify their financial management, and enhance their human capital. Second, many SMEs are part of the supply structures of multinationals or grupos. As second-tier players, SMEs absorb fluctuations in the operation of larger organizations, which requires them to be flexible in their capacities. Third, unlike their counterparts in Italy and Germany, Latin American SMEs seem disinclined to form clusters. Explanations for this vary and include a lack of institutional support, different entrepreneurial preferences, and a lack of transparency in accounting practices.

Talent Trends in Latin America

Notwithstanding a large number of unemployed or underemployed people, one of the principal constraints on economic growth in Latin America is the lack of talent. The Latin American workforce contains a large group of low- to medium-skilled people who are typically employed in low-wage jobs or in the informal economy. A smaller, more skilled group is employed in the formal sector or runs its own companies. The lack of talent is likely to grow because the quality of education in Latin America is comparatively low. In the OECD's Program for International Student Assessment (PISA) ranking of 2009, Chile had the highest achievement of any Latin American country—occupying the forty-fourth position out of 65 participating countries worldwide.[3] Although several countries have initiated educational reforms, even in the best-case scenario, these reforms need time to take effect.

Over the past 20 years, many talented Latin Americans have emigrated, leading to a brain drain. Some countries have initiated programs to repatriate talented individuals, and the current crisis in Southern Europe has reversed the flow of migration. However, the prospect of careers with multinational companies and better job markets outside Latin America still encourages top talent to leave.

Finally, women's participation in higher education and the workforce has been increasing. However, while the examples of Maria das Gracas Foster at Petrobras, Ivonne Monteagudo of Sam's Club in Mexico, and Isela Costantini at General Motors Argentina suggest increased participation of women at the most senior level in corporations, such examples remain rare.[4] Latin America's cultural heritage places women at a disadvantage in the pursuit of both educations and careers. As a result, women are particularly likely to fall into low-wage jobs and informal employment.

Companies that operate in Latin America are increasingly aware of Latin America's contradictory combination of labor surplus and talent shortage. Most continue to rely on short-term solutions, such as competitive entry-level salaries, fast-track career promises, retaining older workers with specific skills, and enhancing their employer brand to fulfill talent needs. These strategies are unlikely to be sufficient in the long run.

General Implications for Regional HR practices

Compared with more liberal market economies, the Latin American region is characterized by government intervention and participation in the economy. Such intervention limits companies' abilities to implement HRM practices that are aligned with their business strategies. While countries such as Chile, Peru, and Mexico allow firms more leeway, either because of flexible labor laws or laissez-faire government attitudes, Brazil, Argentina, and Venezuela stress workers' rights with their employment regulations. In countries where popular political parties maintain close relationships with large unions, HR is even further limited as unions represent employees in collective bargaining and sometimes provide training, suggest or obstruct changes in job design, negotiate hiring decisions, and offer benefits such as health services and tourism. Moreover, unions can exert indirect influence through government policies related to minimum wages, maternity leave, or the use of temporary workers and subcontractors.

Notwithstanding these constraints, companies increasingly seek to involve unions to develop human-capital-based competitive advantage. For example, Volkswagen Argentina's expansion of its production facility required hiring 400 new employees. Together with SMATA (the Argentine union for auto-workers) and the Argentine Ministry of Labor, three- and six-month training programs were designed to develop job candidates' functional competencies for different positions along the assembly line (such as body shop, assembly, and painting). More than 620 candidates were selected for the program, which included classroom instruction and paid internships. Of the 420 candidates who completed the program and had their functional competencies certified by the Ministry of Labor, 380 were hired by Volkswagen Argentina and became members of SMATA. The program was also intended to have a spillover effect as candidates who were not hired had developed skills that improved their chances for employment at other car manufacturers or at Volkswagen in the future.

The incorporation of more sophisticated technology in the workplace and integration with global markets has implications for HRM practices as well. Companies engage in bidding wars to attract the small group of technologically literate people who are capable of interacting in international contexts. As a result, HRM practices for this segment need to be focused on attraction and retention. Companies that train lower-skilled employees face different challenges. Instruction that allows employees to develop basic skills, such as foreign languages or computer literacy, contributes little to the development of specific skills that allow for competitive advantage. At a more sophisticated level, once effectively trained, employees become targets for poaching by other organizations. This makes it difficult to retain talent.

The impact of social changes on HRM practices can be observed in career models. The increasing participation of women in the workforce, both in operational and managerial positions, presses companies to deal with dual careers, maternity or paternity leave, and other care responsibilities. Alternative career paths have broader implications for staffing, training, and performance evaluations, which need to be tailored to the particular career stage and aspirations of each individual.

More generally, HRM practices in Latin America used to be imported by multinationals and adapted to local realities. Because of work done by consultancies, benchmark projects, and human resource professional associations, Latin American companies are being run according to ever more sophisticated and global standards. Rapid economic growth, social changes, and institutional uncertainty, however, have created a need for alternative HRM practices. Instead of importing best practices from multinational headquarters, organizations benefit from locally responsive practices that can be adapted quickly to shifting conditions and that address the specific challenges faced in each country.

Review and Discussion of the 2012 HRCS Latin America Findings

As regional partners for Latin America, IAE Business School from Argentina collaborated with IPADE Business School from Mexico, the Universidad del Pacífico from Peru, the Latin American branch of the RBL Group, and the Federación Interamericana de Asociaciones de Gestión Humana (FIDAGH). The regional sample contains 2,949 completed evaluations of HR participants distributed across the Latin American region. Most worked at organizations with 1,000 to 5,000 employees (45 percent). Business units with more than 10,000 employees represented 11 percent of the sample, and small- to medium-size firms (1 to 1,000 employees) made up 34 percent. The distribution by industry was similar to that of the global sample. Service industries made up 29 percent of the sample, followed by companies in manufacturing (14 percent), financial services (14 percent), and mining (9 percent). Unlike past rounds of the study, not a single organization from the public sector participated.

Results

As illustrated by Figure 8.1, the average Latin American scores on the competency domains are in line with global trends.

Figure 8.1   *Competency Mean Scores for Global and Latin America Samples*

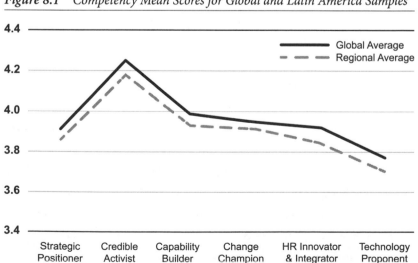

As in past rounds, Latin American HR professionals scored highest on the items comprising the credible activist domain. The people-centered cultures of the region create a strong focus on relationships inside and outside work, which are facilitated by HR. Moreover, HR is often considered a caring function, putting HR professionals in a position to talk with employees and management about their professional and personal needs. In contrast, scores on strategic positioner and technology proponent were considerably lower. Considering the evolution of the HR profession globally and particularly in Latin America, these results are not surprising. HR departments in Latin America generally initiated the shift from being merely an administrative function to becoming a strategic business partner later than their counterparts in other regions. Building on thought leadership and experience imported mainly from North America, multinationals were among the first to introduce business partner roles and to centralize or outsource transactional HR work. While many organizations are still in this transitional phase, the complexity and volatility of the Latin American business context often limits HR departments to reactive behavior, leaving less space for longer-term strategic decision making. HR's role in facilitating and guiding technology within the organization is limited at best. As many HR departments are still in the process of integrating technology into HR operations, they typically rely on IT and operations departments to propose and introduce technology into the organization.

Competency Domains and Individual Performance

The six competency domains are weighted relatively equally in their correlation to Latin American HR professionals' individual effectiveness. As in previous rounds and other regions, personal credibility was the most significant domain (22 percent). We interpret competency in the credible activist domain to be a sine qua non for becoming an effective HR professional. Credibility seems especially important in Latin America, where interpersonal relationships are critical to intraorganizational functioning.

Next in importance were the HR innovator and integrator domain and the capability builder domain (18 and 17 percent, respectively). This suggests that in order to become an effective HR professional, it is critical to have knowledge of HR practices and the ability to innovate and combine practices to build organization capabilities in an ever-changing environment. Surprisingly, the strategic positioner and change champion domains were less significant in explaining variance in individual HR professionals' performance (16 percent each). We interpret this to mean that non-HR colleagues may not necessarily think of HR professionals as being able to discuss challenges related to the business context and required organizational change. While senior managers can often make sense of the Latin American business context, HR executives seem to focus more on pointing out the constraints imposed on the organization by unions and regulators than on articulating new strategic options. In a region characterized by volatility, change initiatives are increasingly facilitated by managers themselves or by external consultants. This leaves fewer opportunities for HR professionals to contribute in the change champion domain. Additionally, these relative weights refer to the extent to which a domain differentiates more effective HR professionals from less effective colleagues. When HR professionals have similar competency levels—either high or low—in a domain, that particular domain's contribution to explaining differences in effectiveness will be limited.

Finally, the technology proponent domain had the lowest relative weight (12 percent). This suggests that HR's role in the use of technology in the organization is not critical to perceptions of individual effectiveness. We have met several technologically literate HR professionals who make extensive use of videoconferencing, develop strategic reports based on data extracted from HRIS, and have redesigned HR processes to incorporate social media. Technological skill, however, tends to be attributed to personal preference and is not perceived as an essential characteristic of strong HR professionals. Again, we found limited variance in evaluations of Latin American HR professionals on this domain, while the absolute score was low. We interpret this to mean that only a few organizations have begun to redefine the way they organize work. The expectations business leaders have of HR as an enabler of technology-mediated work are increasing but are currently of limited importance in explaining the individual effectiveness of HR professionals.

Notwithstanding the relative weights of the competency domains, the overall model explained considerably less of the variance in perceptions of individual

HR professionals' effectiveness in Latin America than in other regions. Whereas the regression coefficient for the global sample was 0.42 (42 percent of the variance explained) and was even higher in North America (0.48) and Australia (0.56), the Latin American coefficient was only 0.27. This means that although HR professionals in the region obtained similar scores on the domains of the competency model, these domains explain less of their effectiveness as perceived by their colleagues. We attribute this to the diverse needs of organizations in different industries and to differences observed across countries. Two examples of HR professionals we regard as successful and have had the pleasure of knowing more closely may illustrate this difference.

In her role as HR Head Latin America South at Syngenta, Cristina Franichevich played a leading role in bringing HR closer to the company and contributed to business results by initiating a number of changes both within and outside the organization. Examples include her help in facilitating growth strategies that aimed to decommoditize Syngenta's seeds and crop-protection products, strengthening and aligning distributors, and leading programs for external top farmers to help them manage the growth challenge they were facing. A mix of personal credibility, understanding of the business, cross-cultural management skills, and the introduction of new HRM practices allowed the HR team to effectively overcome these challenges. Because of the positive impact of her change initiatives on business results, Franichevich was promoted to a global HR business partner role at Syngenta's headquarters in Switzerland.

Alejandro Melamed is currently VP of HR for Coca-Cola's South Latin Business Unit (SLBU). During his career at Coca-Cola, Melamed has been able to capitalize his previous experience in consultancy and his vast knowledge of training and development, culture, and change management. Promoted to his current position after a short-term assignment in Belgium, his main challenge is to maintain the organization's high performance, balancing employee motivation and effectiveness. Building on the contributions of the regional HR team and drawing upon technical HR skill, Coca-Cola SLBU has implemented award-winning employee well-being and work-culture programs. Employee motivation remains high, and workers are actively engaged in finding ways to perform their jobs more efficiently. In 2010 and 2011, Coca-Cola SLBU obtained the top position in the Great Place to Work Institute ranking. Melamed is often invited by universities to give lectures, and by companies to share his knowledge and experience. Moreover, he is about to publish his third book.

These examples show how HR professionals can be equally effective as individuals but draw on different competency domains to win their colleagues' appreciation. Because of the wide range of challenges that Latin American organizations face and the fact that individual HR professionals have different strengths, the key to individual effectiveness in Latin America is arguably more a matter of finding how to apply one's strengths than strictly following global or regional standards.

Competency Domains and Business Performance

While perceptions of individual effectiveness determine, to a large extent, the conversations HR professionals share, they do not necessarily explain the contribution of HR professionals to business performance. Indeed, a regression analysis shows that in Latin America, only 1 percent of the variance in business performance is explained by variation in individual effectiveness.

In Latin America, as in most other emerging markets, the competency domains have a considerable impact on business performance. Whereas in North America or Europe the regression coefficients were 0.07 and 0.06, the Latin American coefficient was 0.11. More interestingly, the weights of individual domains in explaining variance in business performance differed from the weights of the same domains in explaining variance in personal effectiveness. The capability builder and HR innovator and integrator domains had the strongest impact (19 and 18 percent, respectively), suggesting that HR's contribution to the business is based on the effective use of HRM practices to develop organization capabilities. In volatile business contexts such as Latin America, understanding the business and facilitating adaptation to ever-changing challenges is necessary to build the required capabilities. The effect of the corresponding strategic positioner and change champion domains is somewhat lower (16 percent each), however, given that HR professionals in the region typically collaborate with line managers in articulating strategy and changing the organization.

Implications of the HRCS Results

International HRM scholars tend to attribute differences in practices and the approaches of individual professionals to cultural differences. The findings of the HRCS suggest that while Latin American culture influences HR management to some extent, numerous other factors come into play as well. First of all, individual HR professionals may have different levels of competency in each domain, which affects both perceptions of their individual performance and the impact of their actions on outcomes related to the business. Second, the contextual characteristics that shape the organizational needs that HR professionals respond to are not necessarily cultural—they can be economic, political, technological, and demographic. Third, while culture is stable, the results of the HRCS suggest that HR competencies are most relevant in the context of change that requires organizations to redefine their organization capabilities. Because of the characteristics of the Latin American business context and the different effects of the HR competency domains on perceptions of individual HR professionals' effectiveness and their impact on business performance, we can conclude that for HR to have an impact, a basic understanding of Latin American cultures is insufficient.

HR Adding Value Through Competent HR Professionals

As the social and economic landscape in Latin America shifts, HR professionals have the opportunity to make unique contributions to their organizations and to the societies they operate in. Volkswagen's training of large numbers of job candidates before hiring or Arcos Dorados's active role in helping younger workers enter the formal workforce, as mentioned earlier, show that the ideas of HR professionals who understand the context and the capabilities of their organizations add value from economic and social perspectives. Adding value, however, is defined differently based on the characteristics and strategy of an organization. Two examples will help illustrate this.

Repsol, a Spanish oil company, increasingly collaborates with nontraditional players such as Malaysian Petronas and the India Oil and Natural Gas

Corporation in its Venezuelan operations.[5] Compared with traditional partners such as local PDVSA or Italian ENI, these new partners have different practices related to work hours, employee empowerment, security policies, and housing and recreational facilities at exploration sites. As conflicts regarding these issues may obstruct operations, HR professionals have a strategic role in managing developing mutual understanding and assuring the provision of basic services.

A different challenge is faced by Unilever's Rio de la Plata HR team. In an attempt to develop a better understanding of consumption at the bottom of the economic pyramid, the organization started recruiting from nontraditional sources. Instead of limiting recruitment efforts to elite private universities, the HR team brought in talent from public universities in areas where the company's targeted consumers live. This helped build capabilities in logistics and sales that are aligned with the target consumers.

These examples illustrate different ways in which Latin American HR professionals add value to their organizations, while drawing on the six HRCS domains. Both require a thorough understanding of the relevant business environment and the social context in which organizations operate. Building on an understanding of the business strategy, HR professionals apply new and existing HRM practices to build organization capabilities—which often require further change in the organization. When necessary, HR initiatives incorporate technology or help employees use technology to become more effective. Finally, HR professionals must have sufficient credibility in the eyes of their colleagues to be able to diverge from the usual HR approaches.

Stakeholder for HR's Influence on Business Performance

Managing stakeholder relationships effectively is critical to business success in Latin America. As in other regions, we found that almost 26 percent of the variance in business performance is explained by the extent to which organizations focus on stakeholders as they develop new capabilities. However, the importance of stakeholders is not equally distributed in every region. Historically, Latin American HR professionals focused on employees needs as a means to develop capabilities; employees' motivation to put their skills to work was sufficient to drive business performance. Regional results suggest that employees' needs continue to be important (22 percent), as motivated employees deliver better service, and good labor relations help companies avoid obstruction by unions or governmental interventions.

The importance of other stakeholders has grown. Increased competition among firms in Latin America and more sophisticated business models have made line managers and investors (22 percent each) more relevant stakeholders. Line managers must integrate and coordinate actions and communicate strategies within regional organizations. In a context of fast-paced change and uncertainty, these capabilities are critical to business success. In a similar vein, integration with global capital markets has made shareholder value a mantra at many companies. This is particularly true at multinationals and companies that obtain capital through stock listings or from venture capital funds, where the pressure to deliver returns to investors is high. Latin American HR professionals seem to have adopted this line of thinking as well. In their desire to be recognized as strategic business partners, HR executives have shifted their focus from representing employee interests to representing the interests of senior management and investors.

Two stakeholder groups affect, to a lesser extent, the development of capabilities that drive business performance. First, consideration of external customers' interests when defining and implementing HRM practices is uncommon in Latin America or not always possible, which explains the weaker relationship with business performance (18 percent). Many firms in the sample were multinationals whose offerings and required capabilities are determined at the regional or corporate level. Likewise, organizations in the mining, oil and gas, and agriculture industries commercialize commodities and do not have visible external customers that can be involved in the articulation of HRM practices.

Second, relations with communities have a weaker effect (17 percent) on the development of capabilities, given that most companies act in similar ways. In interventionist economies, relations with communities are often replaced by relations with government agencies. As regulation applies to all firms, consideration of these agencies in the development of HRM practices does not differentiate one firm from another. Also, companies in Latin America respond to social needs through corporate social responsibility programs that tend to be coordinated by the HRM department. Examples of these programs include volunteer programs, coordinating donations, and training programs aimed at building NGOs or helping people into the labor force. Except for particular industries, such as mining, where maintaining sound relationships with neighboring communities is critical, relationships with communities are based more on solidarity than on interest in driving business results.

Beyond Individual Action: The HR Department

Latin American HR professionals' individual competency scores predicted business success. However, the effectiveness of the HR department as a whole predicts business success even better (regression coefficient 0.40). Compared with other regions, interaction with the board of directors had little effect on the department's contribution (6.3 percent). This may be due to the large number of multinational subsidiaries in the Latin American sample. At these organizations, the HR strategy is often defined at corporate headquarters.

HR departments in Latin America have experimented with numerous organization designs. Adopting shared services structures and centers of expertise is common but has not led to the expected outcomes. Differences between individual countries and business units, the lack of people prepared to assume business partner roles, and gaps between functions in the typical organization design are some of the potential explanations for the low impact of having well-defined roles in the HR department (6.3 percent) and of matching the HR department structure with the structure of the business (7.3 percent). While designing the HR organization is a necessary step, achieving effective collaboration between specific functions within the department to provide integrated HR solutions has a stronger impact (8.6 percent).

The need for motivated employees and the retention of critical talent has led many organizations to train line managers in people management skills. In Latin America, such investments seem to pay off; the impact of line managers serving as agents of the HR department is considerable (9.0 percent).

Latin American HR departments have a stronger impact on business results when they are able to align HR initiatives with strategic priorities (10.6 percent), link HRM practices to the business strategy (9.3 percent), and measure the impact of HR initiatives (8.1 percent). HR departments in Latin America often operate within regional organizations and changing contexts, which tends to dilute change initiatives. Also, only a few HR departments have sufficient strategically oriented talent to fill all the positions involved in implementing these initiatives. This leads to poor execution of HR initiatives at lower levels in the organization. The use of HR scoreboards with the right indicators is often seen as difficult, but it allows for the detection and correction of misaligned HR initiatives.

The lack of reliable regional providers of outsourced HR services and the low cost of keeping administrative work in-house has led many HR executives to keep transactional work within the HR department. Particularly in regional HR departments, the problems associated with coordinating vendors for local service delivery reduces the impact of outsourced HR activities on business results (6.8 percent).

Opportunities for effective training of HR professionals in Latin America are limited at best. While several universities and business schools have programs for HR professionals, such programs are often oriented toward the use of standard HRM practices. The low impact on business performance of training and development of HR professionals (5.5 percent) is not really surprising.

HR's role in articulating and building the organization's culture is the single most important factor (11.5 percent) in explaining the HR department's contribution to business success in Latin America. Combined with the impact of connecting HR initiatives to external stakeholders (10.3 percent), it provides the organization with an identity that allows for the integration of functional areas (such as sales and operations) into organization capabilities. Given the volatility and fast pace of change in Latin America, managing culture and focusing the organization on its stakeholders represents stability and a long-term orientation.

Conclusion

A decade of economic growth driven by a mix of record commodity prices, structural reforms that are just beginning to show results, and a legacy of uneven training and contextual constraints represent a few of the challenges for HR in Latin America. Sustaining economic growth inevitably implies further technological improvement, which requires more skilled workers.

While companies currently rely on short-term HR practices to compete for talent in limited pools, eventually they will have to develop practices that help enlarge the talent pool. Especially in countries where educational systems do not allow for the acquisition of advanced or specialized skills, HR will need to find ways to move talent from other markets and to develop talent locally. However, this does not mean that HR should replace public policies. As they develop innovative HR practices, firms will simultaneously need to position themselves to maximize the return on their investments and to attract the best human capital available from growing pools of talent. The example of Volkswagen Argentina's training of more people than needed for immediate hiring illustrates how companies can create spillover effects that enlarge a talent pool while appropriating the benefits of the investments made.

Latin America's economic volatility and widely divergent needs in terms of HR management have both required and allowed companies to articulate innovative HRM practices. While historically multinationals were able to leverage sophisticated HR practices developed at global headquarters, global standardization of practices and a loss of decision-making power in Latin American subsidiaries have eroded that advantage. In contrast, a deep understanding of the region's peculiarities and the involvement of owners in day-to-day management have allowed multi-Latinas to develop HRM practices that both fit their business needs and contribute to the development of human capital in a broader sense. To paraphrase our colleagues and friends Dave Ulrich and Wayne Brockbank, "Now is an exciting time to be in HR." We would add, "Especially in Latin America."

CHAPTER 9

THE MIDDLE EAST

9

Adam Rampton, Fouzi Abdulrahman Bubshait, and Andrew Lindsay Cox

The 2012 HR Competency Study 6 was conducted during a period of significant social and economic change in the Middle East as a whole, including the region covered in this chapter: the Gulf Cooperative Council (GCC) countries— Qatar, Bahrain, Saudi Arabia, Kuwait, the United Arab Emirates (UAE), and Oman.[1] Political observers point to an undercurrent of cultural change driven largely by unrestrained sharing of information through easier access to global media, the Internet, and various forms of social networking, such as Twitter and Facebook.[2] The expectation is that the GCC will see increasing demands for social reform and a more rapid move toward democratic forms of government.

If the transition follows historical norms, these countries will struggle through a learning curve and experience periods of political unrest before their socioeconomic systems stabilize.[3] The challenge confronting their leaders is to anticipate these changes and initiate gradual reforms to avoid political instability and economic problems.[4] The effects of the global financial crisis, the ongoing European debt situation, and the slowdown in global growth have all been felt in the GCC countries. Despite these outside influences, the region has been experiencing high growth in real GDP compared with global averages. Unfortunately, the weaker global economy is expected to pull this growth down at a time when the region is experiencing high underutilization of its human capital, leading to increasing demands on governments to spend more on fiscal stimulus, boost salaries in the public sector, and support a greater number of social programs.[5]

Spending by governments across the GCC is expected to increase as leaders focus their attention on the regional events collectively referred to as the Arab Spring. Unrest in Bahrain and to a lesser extent in Oman has led to measures that have been introduced to increase public-sector employment and spending on social issues, housing, and infrastructure.[6]

Economic Trends Affecting GCC Countries

The International Monetary Fund lists the GDP per capita for the GCC countries in the following order: Qatar, US$74,901; UAE, US$57,884; Kuwait, US$37,009; Bahrain, US$20,475; Oman, US$19,405; and Saudi Arabia, US$16,267.[7] Differences across the region are vivid enough to make it desirable to review each country in turn.

Qatar

Qatar's stellar growth (18 percent in recent years) was largely bolstered by huge increases in liquefied natural gas (LNG) production and exports, accounting for a total 50 percent in 2010. Government services make up about 11 percent of GDP, the construction sector accounts for about 10 percent, and manufacturing makes up 5 percent. The private sector has limited scope to drive growth. Infrastructure and diversification spending will be key over the next five years. Winning the World Cup hosting bid for 2022 is likely to boost Qatar's economy and its standing in the world. Qatar is one of the few countries where the government is the main driver behind economic growth, as opposed to the private sector.

United Arab Emirates

Dubai is experiencing a revival of growth in its trade and service economy. Continuing weaknesses in the real estate industry will tend to increase UAE deficit levels, but these are offset to some extent by Abu Dhabi's increased revenues from oil production, which represents about 60 percent of the GDP. The net effect has been a slowing down or cancellation of major projects.

Med Jones, president of the International Institute of Management and one of the few experts who predicted the U.S. financial and economic crises of 2008, argues that efforts to deal with the situation have been unproductive, noting, "Experimentation with labor and business laws and the rising cost of doing business in Dubai does not help the real estate sector or Dubai's economic recovery."[8] He suggests that Dubai should implement a bundle of strategies that includes reducing restrictions on foreign labor and movement, reducing the start-up cost for doing business, granting investors and rich expats permanent residence cards, and relaxing student and tourist visa requirements. He also recommends improving governance standards and transparency of financial institutions, and ensuring compliance, and resisting involvement in regional arguments that could lead to hostilities that would threaten the real estate investments, trade, logistics, and tourism that are at the heart of Dubai's economy.

Kuwait

Oil constitutes more than 90 percent of the country's total revenue, so it plays a big role in Kuwait, but its government also understands the need to consider diversification of revenue sources.[9] The $100 billion plan approved in February 2010 under the Kuwait Vision 2035 program includes a number of aims in support of "transforming Kuwait into a financial and trade hub for investment, in which the private sector leads economic activity."[10]

The Kuwait Vision 2035 strategic plan calls for a range of changes.[11] These include reducing red tape to encourage and facilitate start-ups; creating fair and equal opportunities to reduce government intervention and encourage foreign investment; promoting a sound and sustainable fiscal position to stop the rapid growth in public-sector employment and salaries; increase privatization, reduce government expenditure on infrastructure, and diversify government revenues; and expand and empower the energy sector, so as to isolate it from politics and allow it to become more open to international expertise. The strategic plan also includes education reforms intended to improve the effectiveness and quality of education outputs by linking education output to labor market demand.

Labor market reforms in Kuwait aim to encourage Kuwaitis to work in the private sector. This involves raising professionalism and tightening working conditions in the public sector, as well as preparing Kuwaitis for the private sector through training and matching skills to needs while improving working conditions there. Relevant legislation relating to immigration and nationalization of selected job categories in the private sector will also be revisited.

Bahrain

Bahrain, like Dubai, has limited oil reserves and is focusing on diversification of its economic development. The private sector is expected to drive much of the recovery from the global financial crisis as Bahrain continues to position itself as a regional financial, business, and tourism hub. However, it needs to invest more if it is to compete with the likes of Dubai. The financial sector contributes about 25 percent of GDP and is still some way off from a full recovery.

About 15 to 20 percent of private-sector jobs and about 80 percent of public-sector jobs are held by Bahraini nationals, and this imbalance is expected to persist amid continuing mismatches in skills and types or qualities of labor. The government is hoping to improve the country's socioeconomic stability by growing the economy and lifting the standard of living for its population through an education policy that focuses on developing entrepreneurship and small business enterprises. These policies aim to promote Bahrain as a business-friendly destination that allows workers to accept job offers and transfer without their prior employer's consent, thereby improving its position as a competitive regional-services hub.

Oman

Oman's unrest and protests in early 2011 and continuing high levels of unemployment see a continuation of demands for political reform. The government's strategies have been to increase public-sector jobs, raise salaries and pensions, and spend more on the social sector and infrastructure. A consequence of this approach is an increasing gap between salaries, benefits, and tenure of jobs in the public sector compared with the private sector. Growth in GDP is being maintained by high oil prices coupled with increases in oil and gas production, along with investments in diversification.

Saudi Arabia

Saudi Arabia's growth is expected to ease because of reductions in government stimulus spending.[12] Continuing high oil prices will help support confidence, although the government's ability to fund its programs is exposed to any sudden reversal in export price brought on by declining global demand. The significant growth in domestic consumption is also putting pressure on export capacity. Population growth and development are causing water supply shortages across the entire region.[13] Saudi Arabia's desalinated water production, principally powered by oil energy (although natural gas is rapidly being introduced), is expected to nearly double to almost six million cubic meters per day by the end of 2015 (annual growth of 14.5 percent).[14] This, together with an annual 8 percent increase in demand for electricity, plus the highly subsidized "price at the pump" of about 16 cents per liter of gas, is increasing pressure on real growth in revenue from external crude sales.

Demographic Trends in GCC Countries

The supply-and-demand equation for human capital in the region was discussed at ASHRM2012—the 11th Arabian Society for Human Resource Management International Conference and Exhibition, which was held in Abu Dhabi from March 25 to 28, 2012. This conference highlighted underutilization of the region's human capital as one of the most important current issues there and discussed the roles of the three major stakeholder groups that influence the issue: business, academia, and government.

Keynote speakers at ASHRM2012, all of whom were leaders of large organizations from the region, spoke about the increasing investment in learning and development of the workforce. Saudi Aramco, for example, is now spending more than US$1 billion a year on developing its workforce.[15]

The issue with figures such as this, however, is that they measure activity rather than success. Another major concern relates to the matching of aspirations of people with appropriate job opportunities. This seems to be the escape clause, in that it is always possible to claim the lack of available "suitable" jobs, thereby raising questions concerning what constitutes a worthy job and who instills work ethics. All of this suggests that staffing considerations begin with family considerations.

Population

Of significant importance to all leading organizations in the region are the rapidly changing demographics of the workforce. Many organizations—including Saudi Aramco—expect 60 percent of their workforce to be under age 30 within three to five years. This could be seen as the crisis required for organizations to start changing from the top while they can direct the change, before they are changed from the bottom by sheer weight of numbers.

Because of shortages of supply from national human capital pools, the GCC's booming economy in recent years has created substantial demand for expatriate workers and caused rapid growth in the region's population. However, population growth rates now seem to be moderating. In part, this could be due to the delay or cancellation of some major projects in the region and a slowdown in construction, particularly in Dubai, or it could simply mean that improving job availability at home is making the expat labor route less attractive.

GCC population reached an estimated 46.8 million in 2011, up sharply from 33.2 million in 2004, and is forecast to rise to 49.8 million in 2013.[16] Current estimates and forecasts show the rate slowing to 3.2 percent for the period 2009 to 2013, which is still high compared with the 1.2 percent yearly growth in the global population. The growth rate for the population of GCC nationals is forecast at 2.4 percent for the period 2009 to 2013, down only slightly from 2.5 percent in the preceding five years. This is double the global average, driven by a youthful population, high birth rates, and the improving life spans that result from investment in healthcare. Although its growth did slow, the expatriate population is forecast to continue to grow at a steadier rate of 4.0 percent for the period 2009 to 2013, down from the rate of 10.8 percent in 2004 to 2008, which was a period of rapid development in the nonoil sector and required large numbers of construction workers.

As a result of the slowdown in immigration, the expatriate share of the GCC population is only forecast to rise marginally to 48.4 percent in 2013, up from 47.8 percent in 2011, compared with 37.8 percent in 2004.

Education

When debating whether academic institutions possess the appropriate skills, methods, and tools to train and develop the workforce of the future, less than 1 percent of attendees at ASHRM2012 agreed that universities in the region do a good job at producing high-quality graduates.[17] One plausible explanation for this is that academia is not agile enough; the security of tenure eliminates academics' motivation to adjust to changing demands for skills. The demographic profile in the region is changing faster than the abilities of academia to adjust. It is claimed that in many cases, academia simply finds it too hard to plan for the future.

The ASHRM2012 panel also suggested that assessment processes used in academia don't seem to accommodate the skills being demanded by industry for the future. One comment from the panel: "Not sure whether industry has informed universities of what they expect from graduates." Universities also often fail to help students manage their expectations for the future—many new graduates expect to become CEOs within five years.

Regional HR Trends

Regional demand for specific skills is expanding; the airline industry needs to fill 35,000 jobs, while the hospitality industry will require an additional 1,500,000 workers. But where will these workers come from? Currently, most employees in the hospitality industry come from outside the region. Some suggest that knowledge transfer from expats to nationals is not happening in the GCC countries.

The HR field in the region has no professional standards and thus lacks one of the nine important characteristics of a profession.[18] The discussion during the ASHRM2012 conference focused on the need to develop a regional standard rather than adopting one from somewhere else. Part of this discussion includes the question of what should be contained in a regional body of knowledge. It is difficult to draw a conclusive and comprehensive picture of HR in GCC countries. Organizations typically use a whole range of HR policies and practices, and the HR profession itself is at different stages in different countries.[19] As a result, it's very hard to say with any degree of confidence that there is a single HRM model with distinct GCC characteristics.

Reliance on Expatriate Workers

The six GCC countries are the largest recipients of temporary migrants in the world.[20] According to Fargues and Shah, the percentage of nationals in the population has fallen from about 90 percent in 1975 to about 57 percent in 2010 (see Table 9.1[21]); in Qatar and the UAE, more than 80 percent of the population consists of non-nationals, and policies that make it impossible for non-nationals to become citizens continue to persist across the GCC.

Various scholars of global migration note the following as some of the characteristics of migration to the region:[22]

- An upward trend in the proportion of foreigners has persisted during the past two decades despite concerted policies and efforts to reduce the number of non-nationals in the population and workforce through localization.
- A consistent shift from Arab to Asian workers has taken place over time, with the result that a majority of all foreign workers in most GCC countries are now Asian.
- About two-thirds of migrant workers are men.
- Among men, more than half are engaged in low-skilled occupations in the production and labor category, or in the service sector.
- Reliance on foreign workers results from shortages of indigenous workers to fulfill the ambitious development plans, coupled with the preference among nationals for public-sector jobs and the relatively low labor-force participation of indigenous women.

Table 9.1 National and Foreign Populations in the GCC Countries, 1975 to 2010

Year	Absolute Numbers			Percentage		Annual Rate of Growth	
	Total	National	Foreign	National	Foreign	National	Foreign
1975	9,731,259	8,790,223	941,036	90.3%	9.7%	3.2%	14.5%
1990	22,522,620	14,281,239	8,241,381	63.4%	36.6%	3.3%	5.0%
2010	41,093,624	23,536,409	17,557,215	57.3%	42.7%		

Many economists suggest that the current situation in the GCC is not likely to change much over the next 10 years, arguing that the impacts of large investments by GCC governments in their education systems and in promoting workforce participation will not address the cost gap that currently encourages employers to recruit expatriate workers.

Workforce Localization

Each of the GCC countries has some form of localization program intended to foster the inclusion of nationals in its workforce, particularly in the private sector, and usually in preference to expatriates.

Localization in the context of the GCC could benefit from in-depth studies into the gaps between educational expectations and reality. Evidence supports the view that most graduates in the region have inflated expectations of what jobs they are suited to upon graduation. As a consequence, *wasta* ("influence") through friends and families becomes increasingly important for many graduates to obtain employment that meets their expectations.

The Saudi localization program is labeled Nitaqat, an Arabic word meaning "boundary" or "range." We can only speculate that the use of this term is meant to imply that the boundary provides a form of control to the number of expatriates joining the Saudi workforce; in other words, a protective boundary around the Saudi population.

The Nitaqat program has four categories that measure organizations' compliance with the government's nationalization quotas: Premium, Green, Yellow, and Red. Each code determines incentives or punitive measures relating to a company's flexibility to hire expatriates, renew work and residency permits of its expatriate staff, and to hire foreign workers from firms in other categories without permission from their current employers. The quotas are determined by a number of organizational characteristics, including size and industry.

Women's Participation in the Workforce

The World Economic Forum—Global Gender Gap Index examines differences between men and women in four fundamental categories: economic participation and opportunity, educational attainment, health and survival, and political empowerment.[23] The GCC countries all rank very low in this index, with the UAE consistently ranking first among the GCC countries—at 103 overall.[24] The participation rate of women in the UAE workforce has increased in 2010 from 41 to 43 percent and the wage gap narrows relative to the US$40,000 maximum value for men. Literacy rates for women are now higher than those for men, the enrollment of women in primary, secondary, and tertiary educational institutions is improving, and the proportion of women holding ministerial-level positions has increased.

After gaining six places in 2010 because of higher-than-average performances on educational attainment and despite a small overall gain in its score (to 110), Bahrain's ranking remains unchanged; other countries are moving ahead faster. Bahrain's improvements are mainly driven by significant increases in the proportion of women legislators, senior officials, and managers, and the proportion of women holding ministerial-level positions.

Qatar (at 111) boosted its overall ranking in 2011 by six places through gains in labor force participation and wage equality. Its strength lies in education, especially secondary and tertiary education, and in reductions in wage gaps over the past year.

Between 2009 and 2010, Saudi women's workforce participation rate has climbed from 20 to 22 percent, the perceived wage gap for similar work has improved, literacy rates have improved, and women's enrollment in tertiary education has increased from 35 to 37 percent.[25]

The highest-ranking economies of the region have invested heavily in increasing women's education levels; in many, the tertiary education enrollment rates of women are higher than those of men. The next step for these countries will be to better integrate these women into the economy so as to reap the benefits of this investment.

Retirement Bulge

According to the ASHRM2012 keynote address by Amin Nasser, a senior vice president of Saudi Aramco, GCC countries are "undergoing a huge generational shift." Besides the increasing youth of the population noted earlier

(60 percent of the workforce below age 30 in three to five years), it seems likely that almost half the current workforce will have retired within that time frame. For example, approximately 30,000 Saudis were hired by Saudi Aramco during the period from 1978 to1984. These employees are all rapidly approaching their eligible retirement date, with the peak expected in 2014.

Demographic changes of this nature are typical throughout the GCC, with large numbers of young people either entering the workforce or still looking for productive roles. This generational shift is often referred to as the Great Crew Change, and is probably the biggest challenge confronting organizations like Saudi Aramco. A massive undertaking is required to transfer knowledge across the experience gap to accelerate the readiness and ability of young talent; even though knowledge and experience have some overlap, they are far from identical.

The Public Sector—Private Sector Gulf

A 2009 Silatech-Gallup poll of *shabab* (a popular word in Arabic, meaning "youth") indicated a 60 to 80 percent preference for working in the public sector rather than working in the private sector or starting a new business. In the case of OECD countries, public-sector employment's share of total employment is about 21 percent; it is about 40 percent in countries in transition to a market economy.[26] The reality is that the public sector continues to attract young people with higher wage and benefit packages and better job security than the private sector. Historically, the public sector has always been the engine of job creation for nationals and culturally is seen as part of a social contract, dating back decades, that rewards higher educational attainment with access to low-productivity and high-pay government jobs.

Whereas in other countries SMEs are typically the engine for creating jobs, the GCC has a significant gap between the huge enterprises at the top, which are typically state owned, and the very small one- or two-man operations at the bottom. The middle layer, which one would normally expect to generate employment opportunities for youth, has traditionally consisted of family businesses that hire migrant workers for low-pay and low-skill jobs because they generally have lower wage expectations, require less training, and are subject to more flexible labor market regulations. In effect, the workforce is segmented, with the public sector dominated by nationals and the private sector by foreign workers, which contradicts government efforts to localize the workforce.

Review and Discussion of the 2012 HRCS Middle East Findings

The challenges facing HR professionals in the Middle East are great. As a result, HR professionals need to know what contributions will deliver the greatest value to their businesses. The 2012 HRCS provides guidance for HR leaders in the Middle East to know where to focus their growth and development efforts so as to be effective and create significant impact for stakeholders.

Table 9.2 identifies the effect of HR competencies on perception of HR effectiveness and business performance in the Middle East.

The table shows that the domains of credible activist, capability builder, and strategic positioner have the highest impact on the perceived effectiveness of individual HR professionals in the region. By contrast, the domains of HR innovator and integrator, technology proponent, and change champion are what have the most effect on business success.

Table 9.2   Competency Domain Impact in the Middle East

	Mean Score on This Domain (1 to 5)	Impact on Perception of HR Effectiveness (Scaled to 100%)	Impact on Business Success (Scaled to 100%)
Credible Activist	4.19	18%	14%
Strategic Positioner	3.84	17%	14%
Capability Builder	3.92	18%	15%
Change Champion	3.87	17%	17%
HR Innovator and Integrator	3.82	17%	22%
Technology Proponent	3.72	14%	18%

Impact on Individual Effectiveness

As in the rest of the world, HR professionals need to be credible activists who earn trust through delivering results and establishing strong relationships whereby they relate well with and are able to influence others in the business. The domain of credible activist serves as a catalyst for the HR profession in the region as it continues its evolution from administrative function to strategic business partner.

This is just as important for expatriate HR professionals in the region as it is for nationals, particularly as they seek to influence business leaders and build local HR talent. To be perceived as effective, HR professionals must also help their organizations identify and build the key capabilities that will enable business strategy. Many companies in the region are recognizing the need to build capability in the areas of leadership and talent in order to achieve growth targets as well as address an overreliance on expatriates and promote development of national talent.

A telecommunications company based in the region was expanding into Saudi Arabia and sought rapid market-share growth. To achieve its targets, the company identified a three-pronged strategy for the new business focused on growth, achieving efficiencies, and a differentiated customer and employee experience. HR leaders recognized that having a strong leadership capability would be key to the company's ability to achieve success.

With CEO sponsorship, the CHRO engaged an external consulting firm to help develop a clear leadership brand and competency model tied to the company strategy. This was then used to assess approximately 200 senior leaders in the organization, and a robust leadership development program was designed for top leaders consistent with company strategy. Further, and in order to develop local leaders, the first two cohorts—approximately 60 leaders—were comprised primarily of Saudi nationals.

The yearlong leadership development program challenged participants through a series of assessments, workshops, executive coaching, action learning, and individual development plans, all tied to helping the leaders achieve their specific business objectives. This initial investment in building leadership capability for the company resulted in 86 percent of the leaders achieving higher levels of competency as determined through a post-program 360-degree assessment. Further, 76 percent of the participants had progressed beyond being strong technical experts and individual contributors; others now viewed them as effective leaders characterized by their abilities to connect individual and team agendas, build overall competence of the group, and coordinate and direct the work of the team or department. These leaders helped the company deliver record growth in 2011.

Capability builders align strategy, culture, practices, and behavior to enable their businesses to achieve their objectives and deliver stakeholder value. HR's focus on building leadership capability helps a company to succeed, and it also addresses a challenge facing the region—development of local talent and an ability in the long term to overcome an overreliance on expatriates.

The domain that has the highest impact on perceived effectiveness of HR professionals is strategic positioner, characterized by interpreting the global business context, decoding customer expectations, and cocrafting a strategic agenda. These HR professionals connect the needs of stakeholders outside the business to the actions of leaders inside the business.

At Saudi Aramco, HR is working side by side with business transformation teams to cocraft the strategic priorities for the business to achieve an aggressive transformation program over the next 8 to 10 years. This program is based on the changing needs of stakeholders and the implications of external trends for these stakeholders and the business. HR is leading a major element of the transformation program to define and develop the leadership competencies and specific behaviors that are required for successful business transformation. Additionally, HR is aligning leadership identification, selection, development, and incentives to strategically position the business for success.

Impact on Business Results

It is interesting to note that although the credible activist and capability builder domains increase perception of an HR professional's effectiveness, they have less impact on overall business performance than HR innovator and integrator, technology proponent, and change champion.

HR professionals must be able to improve their practices through innovation and integration. Having innovative solutions means finding the best ideas in HR and adapting them in a way that drives business success. Saudi Aramco's billion-dollar-a-year investment in the development of its talent may be unique, but it illustrates the abilities of many organizations throughout the region to invest heavily in world-class HR systems and partnerships with elite providers and consultants in the areas of talent management, organization design, compensation and benefits, recruiting and staffing, and workforce planning. As HR professionals use these investments to identify innovative solutions and then adapt those solutions to their organizations' specific needs, they will drive business impact.

Being innovative is not enough, however. HR professionals must also integrate the various solutions, systems, and practices around talent, leadership, and culture specific to their organizations so that business strategies are achieved and real business problems are solved. This presents a great opportunity for HR professionals in the region to impact business results.

Established in 1995, EQUATE Petrochemical Company is the single operator of a fully integrated world-class manufacturing facility producing over five million tons of high-quality petrochemical products annually. EQUATE represents Kuwait's first international petrochemical joint venture, which is a collaboration of the country's state-owned Petrochemical Industries Company, Dow Chemical Company, and Boubyan Petrochemical Company and Qurain Petrochemical Industries Company from the Kuwaiti private sector.

Achieving sustained growth, maximizing revenue and profit by extending globally, creating an environment where people thrive and excel, and achieving a corporate reputation and brand of operational and business excellence worldwide were among the core drivers for HR transformation and integration with the business.

Over the past two years, EQUATE has embarked on a significant HR transformation to align HR structure and practices to drive successful business performance as well as embed and sustain EQUATE's cultural capabilities across its operations. Through innovation and integration, HR is creating significant impact on the organization and enabling the business to deliver increased value to stakeholders.

To begin this journey, HR engaged business leaders, HR professionals, employees, and other key stakeholders to identify the business case for HR transformation. Once the why of transformation was defined, HR continued to work with stakeholders to craft the HR strategy and define the specific desired outcomes—the what of HR transformation. "If we are successful," they asked, "what will be the impact on the business and stakeholders?"

Through this process, three critical outcomes of HR transformation were identified: developing core technical competencies, building EQUATE's unique cultural capabilities (focused responsiveness, disciplined and efficient teamwork, and proactive innovation), and building leadership brand aligned with the business need. The involvement of line leaders and non-HR stakeholders was critical to ensuring that HR strategy and transformation outcomes would address business challenges and enable the business to carry out its strategy.

Once the HR transformation outcomes were identified and agreed upon by the business and HR, EQUATE HR leaders set about aligning HR practices to achieve the desired outcomes. Based on input from 63 line leaders and the entire HR department, eight focus areas were identified as HR transformation projects. These projects were led by Six Sigma transformation teams and focused on the following areas: measurement, rewards, promotions, outplacement, leadership, organization structure, work design, and reality checks (focused on bringing internal and external realities of EQUATE's customers and market dynamics to employees as a whole—ensuring communication from the outside in to enhance decision making and ensure responsiveness).

After building a strong business case for HR transformation (the why) and clearly identifying and agreeing with the business on the desired outcomes of HR transformation (the what), HR then moved to the how of transformation by integrating its people, performance, communication, and work practices to deliver maximum value to the business and help EQUATE deliver on its promises to customers and stakeholders.

To fully integrate these activities and build the required organization capabilities, the transformation teams focused on three areas: ensuring alignment of the HR strategy, creating the right structure for the HR organization, and upgrading the HR staff. The HR transformation team started this journey by setting a new HR strategy with input from the business that supports the dynamic business requirements. This project had an implementation plan of 18 to 24 months and resulted in an outside-in strategy for HR that was aligned with the goals of the business.

To create the right structure for the HR organization to deliver on its new strategy, criteria and input were gathered from HR's business stakeholders. The team arrived at a structure that permitted the following:

- Improve execution of business-focused HR strategy
- Ensure greater expertise in each category of HR activity
- Enhance the functioning of HR as a cohesive lateral unit
- Expand the concept of business partner and HR generalist to all departments at EQUATE

In addition to the structural changes, HR was able to help employees quickly get behind the strategic growth priorities as defined in the 2020 corporate strategy through a series of business-alignment sessions. HR also partnered with the business to identify leadership practices that promoted the desired cultural capabilities. This enabled HR and the organization to drive focused plans by prioritizing improvements and therefore building the desired culture that would sustain and further grow world-class performance.

EQUATE is a prime example of how HR can add significant value to the business through the domain of HR innovator and integrator. As EQUATE continues its journey of integrating HR strategy, structure, and development, its HR department is well on its way to contributing to business success.

The second domain that has great impact on overall business performance is technology proponent. HR professionals can use technology in two primary ways: to deliver the administrative aspects of HR, and to connect people both inside and outside the organization in meaningful ways. Social media tools such as Twitter, Facebook, and LinkedIn enable organizations to communicate and connect with stakeholders in new and direct ways.

Mobily, a telecommunications company based in Saudi Arabia, launched a first-of-its-kind service by integrating Twitter user names with its internal system for customer-care CRM. Mobily's customers add their Twitter user names to their information in Mobily's customer-care database—and then receive instant responses to their complaints or inquiries easily through Twitter.[27]

As the communication experts in many organizations, HR professionals should follow this type of example in order to play integral roles in building positive social relationships inside and outside their companies. Social media can be used to engage employees, customers, investors, potential hires, and other stakeholders to create goodwill, increase transparency, build networks, foster a positive firm identity, demonstrate the company's culture, and showcase investments in leadership development and talent management.

As mentioned earlier, a 2009 Silatech-Gallup poll of Arab youth indicated a 60 to 80 percent preference for working in the public sector rather than working in the private sector or starting a new business. As HR professionals help their organizations reach out to Arab youth through social media, they can help shape positive corporate identities, engage in meaningful dialogue to understand perceptions, and influence young talent toward employment in the private sector.

Finally, the third domain impacting overall business performance is change champion. As businesses respond and adapt to the economic, political, and social trends noted earlier in this chapter, HR should play a leading role in helping businesses initiate and sustain the necessary change initiatives. This can be done through integration of HR programs and practices to ensure alignment with the desired outcomes of the change efforts. As the steward of company culture, HR is uniquely positioned to drive needed change so that the company can adapt, develop, and meet stakeholder needs.

Conclusion

To prepare their leaders, talent, and organizations for success in the face of the dramatic changes the region was facing during the 2012 HRCS, HR leaders must build greater competency across the six domains. HR professionals in the region will have the greatest impact on their overall business performance by improving HR practices through innovation and integration so as to solve future challenges and by using technology both to deliver the administrative components of HR and to connect people inside the company with external stakeholders. This is an exciting time for the HR profession in the Middle East and we are confident that HR professionals—individually and collectively as a function—are uniquely positioned to contribute significant value to their organizations and the region.

CHAPTER 10

NORTH AMERICA

KEITH LAWRENCE

10

The role of HR professionals has evolved and is evolving in large part because our businesses are changing and being affected by both external trends and internal factors. We have the opportunity to embrace these changes by redefining our roles and asking questions of ourselves that can help us do so.

Regional Trends

Businesses in North America have experienced dramatic changes, especially during the past five years, based on trends in five key areas:

- *Economics.* Steep declines in the stock market and housing values resulting in lower consumer spending and increasing pressure to pay for the escalating costs of healthcare and social entitlements
- *Politics.* Changing levels of regulation and uncertainty because of record levels of government debt and gridlock in Washington, D.C.
- *Society.* Issues of sustainability, ethics, and equity
- *Business.* Significant layoffs and offshoring of jobs to increase global competitiveness and to build new multinational capabilities, coupled with adoption of rapidly evolving technologies to speed communication and collaboration and to increase employee productivity
- *Demographics.* A seismic shift in the composition (diversity, union membership, and skill level) of the workforce and in the needs of individuals at work

These trends are but a part of what has been affecting the roles and requirements of HR professionals. Internal forces are also having a profound impact on the focus and critical capabilities required of HR people in North America:

- Pressure for continuously decreasing employee costs for factors such as head count, pay, benefits, and training
- Expectations of lowering the expense of providing HR support through factors such as shared services, outsourcing, and employee self-service
- Attention shifting away from labor relations and personnel activities to employee engagement
- Necessity of recruiting, training, retaining, and fully engaging a more diverse and challenged workforce
- Importance of pioneering new ways of organizing work (through social media or strategic partnerships, for example), of leading organizations to further unleash innovation and employee potential, and of supporting new industries

As an example, consider Procter & Gamble (P&G), one of the world's largest consumer products companies, which has its global headquarters in the Midwest. One of the keys to the success of this 175-year-old company has been its willingness to constantly renew itself. In the book *Built to Last: Successful Habits of Visionary Companies,* coauthor Jim Collins describes its basic premise as, "Preserve the core and be willing to reinvent everything else." Virtually every aspect of this company (including HR) has been changed in its efforts to remain highly competitive in a dynamic world.

Over 90 percent of U.S. households have at least one P&G product. Trends affecting consumers (that is, the economic trends) thus meaningfully affect the company and how it thinks about developing and marketing its products. Globalization has also had an impact; more than half of the company's business now comes from outside North America. Organizing globally has been a must, and the company has radically changed its structure and has been continuously refining that structure as new learning emerges on how to operate across geographies. Later in the chapter, we discuss the specific HR practices and capabilities that were instrumental in enabling this new design to be so successful.

Economic Trends

The bursting of the U.S. housing bubble in 2007 caused the values of securities tied to real estate to plummet, damaging financial institutions globally. This led to a 53 percent decline in the U.S. stock market in 2008, a phenomenon often called the Great Recession. Consumers (who drive 65 percent of U.S. GDP) dramatically reduced their spending, and weaker sales forced companies to retrench and similarly cut back. The official jobless rate went from 5.3 percent in January 2008 to a peak of 9.9 percent in April 2010. The underemployment rate (which takes into account people who hold temporary or part-time jobs but would prefer permanent full-time work) remains problematic, with nearly one out of five people seeking additional employment. These issues compound the problem of the 5.8 million manufacturing positions that disappeared in the first decade of the twenty-first century. As a result, the average S&P 500 company generates $420,000 per employee in revenue today—compared with $378,000 in 2007.

Pay and benefits were also reduced in a number of firms and industries. Annual bonuses were trimmed. Contributions to retirement accounts were cut or eliminated, further aggravating the severe underfunding of workers' retirement savings. The median household headed by a person aged 60 to 62 with a 401(k) account has less than one-quarter of what is needed in that account to maintain its standard of living in retirement.[1]

Even public sector employees were affected as rising government budget deficits led to renegotiation of their pay and benefits. From 2007 to 2011, 112,800 U.S. government jobs were eliminated (most of them in the U.S. Postal Service).

These reductions, coupled with increased unemployment, place much heavier demands on people who do have jobs. These employees are being asked to do more with less, which subsequently raises their stress at work and limits the time spent at home and in other nonwork-related activities.

Healthcare costs in the United States are a major economic issue. The country now spends a record $2.6 trillion a year on health-related services, 10 times what it spent in 1980. This trend is predicted to extend well into the future. A key driver of this huge change is the dramatic increase in the prevalence and variety of chronic diseases: a third of America is obese, resulting in much higher rates of diabetes and heart disease. A major piece of federal legislation was passed in 2010 (called the Affordable Care Act) to address some of these issues. Its long-term impact on slowing the rate of healthcare inflation is uncertain from both a practical (if costs can really be lowered) and legal standpoint.

Americans have borrowed heavily to maintain their lifestyles. Over 40 percent of U.S. families spend more than they earn. Americans carry, on average, $8,400 in credit card debt. At the same time, 56 percent of families have no budget, and 30 percent have no savings. It seems probable that 96 percent of all Americans will be financially dependent on their families, government, or charities at retirement.[2]

The cumulative effect of these fiscal factors has had a major impact on public confidence in the soundness of the U.S. economic system and its various institutions. Increasingly, families rely on the government for support, as evidenced by the fact that one out of seven people receives food stamps to purchase basic sustenance (up 59 percent in just three years).

Canada has fared a bit better during this period because its economy is not as heavily leveraged with debt. Canadian unemployment peaked at 8.5 percent and currently stands at 7.2 percent (compared with 8.2 percent in the United States). However, given the close ties between the two countries, the health of the Canadian economy is tightly connected to the state of business in the United States.

Political Trends

The Great Recession caused the U.S. federal government to pump trillions of dollars into the economy beginning in 2007. That, combined with the sustained wars in Iraq and Afghanistan, has led to a budget deficit of more than $15 trillion (up from $9 trillion in 2007). Currently, 41 cents of every dollar spent by the U.S. government is borrowed (creating $4 billion per day of additional debt). The U.S. Congress and president have been unable to find common ground on how to address this looming fiscal crisis. These political divisions were partially responsible for the loss of the U.S. AAA credit rating, which has added to the cost of borrowing money.

As a result of this gridlock, companies are hesitant to invest in new equipment or significant numbers of new employees. It is a vicious circle of uncertainty, stagnation, and lack of economic growth.

Social Trends

A number of prominent issues and concerns for North Americans have been influencing businesses.

Sustainability has become a major priority for many businesses, as the threat of climate change continues to grow more pervasive and energy costs are rising. Leading-edge companies are finding innovative ways to reduce their carbon footprints and provide products and services of equal quality to consumers while lowering costs and reducing their environmental impact. For example, P&G is pioneering new detergents to clean clothes in cold water, saving the average household $63 per year and requiring 33 million fewer megawatt-hours of electricity generation nationally.

Ethics has emerged as an area of keen interest following the questionable actions of several companies, such as Enron, MCI, and Lehman Brothers. Choices made by leaders of these companies had a significant negative impact on the lives of thousands of their employees and customers, leading to a broad distrust of corporations.

Equity (fairness) is increasingly a topic of conversation and public demonstrations. The earnings and assets of the "top 1 percent" are under closer scrutiny. For example, the average CEO in the United States today makes 325 times what the average rank-and-file employee does—and the ratio was 263 to 1 just three years ago. Among the nation's top firms, the S&P 500, CEO pay in 2010 averaged $10,762,304, up 27.8 percent from 2009. The average worker's pay was $33,121, up just 3.3 percent over the year before.[3] The belief that the economic success of the wealthy trickles down to the rest of the population is being challenged because the wealth of the upper class has grown at a much faster rate than the wealth of those at lower income levels.

Business Trends

While many companies in North America have been shedding jobs through layoffs and offshoring work to strengthen their global competitiveness, others have been rapidly adopting new technologies to improve productivity and innovation. Social media, including web-based and mobile technologies, have transformed many aspects of how people do their work. Through innovations introduced by companies based in Silicon Valley and other technology parks across the United States, most employees can more readily access information or connect with colleagues than in the past.

Another key trend has been the pursuit of a greater number of partnerships among companies looking to take advantage of one another's respective strengths. A noteworthy example of this is P&G's Connect & Develop initiative. From 2000 to 2007, it increased the proportion of new products with outside partners from 15 percent of its total offering to 50 percent.[4] The Mr. Clean Magic Eraser, for example, was launched after spotting a revolutionary new household sponge in Japan. In fact, the company is even working with its competitors to develop new business. For example, P&G shared breakthrough bagging technology it had pioneered with Clorox to launch its very successful Press'n Seal food wrap.

The Rise of Multinational and Global Companies

With the North American economy slowing, future growth for companies based in the region lies in expanding their businesses into developing markets elsewhere. Increasingly, leaders' time and attention are focused on growing operations into new white space. This requires a whole new set of skills and capabilities, many of which have been learned the hard way as companies tried to simply reapply what worked in North America.

Yum! Brands, headquartered in Lexington, Kentucky, provides an example of successful adaptation. It flexed its standard business model, particularly its menus, as it expanded into China. In 2011, Yum! Brands' 3,900 restaurants in China earned more revenue than all 19,000 U.S. Yum! Brands restaurants—including KFC, Pizza Hut, and Taco Bell. This expansion required a fundamentally different mindset and the development of a whole new range of competencies to operate successfully as a large global corporation.

The Decline of Unions

Since the advent of major corporate restructuring beginning in the 1980s, involving tactics such as reengineering, mergers and acquisitions, and offshoring jobs to lower-cost countries, the number of employees belonging to unions has declined dramatically in North America. Today, only 6.9 percent of employees in the U.S. private sector belong to a union, down from 23 percent in 1980, bringing union membership to its lowest level since 1932. However, unions continue to hold political influence and are strong advocates for new federal legislation, such as the card check, to make it easier to organize groups of employees. Many companies, particularly in the automobile industry, have shifted their investments to the southern parts of the U.S. where laws are less union-friendly, and these companies understandably have a higher nonunion workforce.

Demographic Trends

The United States and Canada are experiencing a significant graying of their populations and workforce. In 1990, 11.9 percent of the U.S. labor force was 55 years old or older. By 2010, that number had increased to 19.5 percent— and it is projected to surpass 25 percent by 2020.

A large part of this shift is being driven by the changing demographics of those entering and exiting the workforce. Ten years ago, 10 workers were entering the workplace for every person retiring. Today that ratio is one to one—and 10 years from now, 10 workers will be retiring for every new person hired. The end of World War II led to a large population boom, while typical families in recent years have had fewer children. This has led to a number of developments that affect the work of HR professionals.

A Multigenerational Workforce

For the first time, four different generations of employees are working alongside one another:

- Matures (mid-sixties and older)
- Baby Boomers (mid-forties to early sixties)
- Generation X (late twenties to early forties)
- Millennial or Gen Y (mid-twenties and younger)

Each group brings with it a distinct set of characteristics and needs, heavily influenced by the experiences its members had growing up. Understanding these differences is critical to grasp what everyone brings to the workforce and therefore avoid conflicts resulting from misunderstandings and unmet needs.

A Diverse Workforce

The number of women in the North American workforce has grown dramatically. Today 46 percent of the total U.S. labor pool is made up of women. However, the majority of them (59 percent) are in jobs paying less than $8 per hour. This disparity has put significant pressure on companies to have more flexible work arrangements and greater opportunities for women to have long-term careers and pay equal to men's.

Since 1980, the percentage of minorities among those of working age has risen from 18 to 37 percent in the United States—the result of large numbers of younger Americans being minorities and many of the older white working population retiring.

The increase in women and minorities in the workforce creates a new set of needs that many firms have not yet dealt with:

- Having a balanced life in the face of increasing workload demands and pressure to stay connected to work 24/7 through technology
- Finding meaning in the work and desiring to make a positive difference in the world
- Wrestling with the challenges of aging parents, dual careers, young families, rising healthcare costs, uncertainty about future layoffs and the country's ongoing economic woes
- Feeling a stronger connection to colleagues and a deeper sense of community

Implications of North American Trends on HR Practices

The challenges faced by the region over the past few decades have had significant implications for HR. Virtually every aspect of the function has been affected.

Challenging New Talent

The education system in North America is no longer among the best in the world. Today, 25 percent of students fail to graduate from high school. More alarmingly, only 40 percent of minorities earn a high school diploma. One in four young adults has a four-year degree. An increasing number of companies report experiencing difficulty in finding applicants that can pass their basic entrance exams. Finding experienced employees in skilled trades is nearly impossible in many parts of North America.

At the same time, institutional knowledge of "how things get done" is rapidly evaporating in many workplaces. Every day, 10,000 U.S. workers reach retirement age—and many of them retire—and this exodus will continue for the next 19 years. Many then return to work in some fashion in order to supplement their incomes, replenish depleted retirement accounts, or fill critical skill gaps back in their old companies. Firms like YourEncore have been created to match hundreds of experienced retirees with companies desperate for skilled help.

The Work of HR

In the 1970s, the work of HR in North America was primarily in the areas of personnel administration, labor relations, or other process-driven roles. HR professionals were highly skilled specialists focused on recruiting, developing, and retaining employees (primarily from a legal and cost perspective). A large part of the work was to help companies avoid unfair and unsafe employment practices, and keep pay practices competitive.

Over time, the work of HR has shifted to determining how to create competitive advantage through the workforce. For example, in the mid-1960s, companies such as General Foods and P&G began piloting high-commitment work systems in their manufacturing plants. These efforts were a significant shift away from traditional HR practices, as companies began to view employees as sustainable sources of competitive advantage. People were treated with respect, and significant investments were made to build their capabilities and to empower them to own the business. At Toyota, for example, hourly employees were expected to point out and resolve problems in the production process—even stopping the line if needed. This role—for both line workers and their leaders—was radically different from the industry norm.

Results from these early experiments were very promising, delivering 30 to 40 percent better business results (cost, quality, and customer service) than the traditional command-and-control approach. A few highly skilled organizational development thought leaders led this pioneering work, which is now the basis for how most best-in-class manufacturing plants operate around the world.

These successes demonstrated to business leaders the significant value that HR brings as an equal strategic partner. In addition to developing and maintaining highly effective HR systems, the work of HR has evolved to encompass a number of new areas:

- Working with leadership to develop new business strategies
- Developing new organization designs to support expansion beyond North America to other parts of the world
- Aiding in the success of mergers and acquisitions (the majority of which fail when there is poor employee and culture integration)
- Understanding the unique needs of each generation in the workplace and building the organization's capabilities to make the best use of workers in each age group
- Refining recruiting and on-boarding practices to get the very best talent into the company and to jump-start the new employees' successes

In many companies, the work of HR has responded to incredible pressures on costs by taking measures such as these:

- Closely managing employee head count and costs
- Orchestrating reductions-in-force and cutbacks in employee pay and benefits, as well as revamping incentives to tie greater proportions of pay to performance (80 percent of U.S. companies do this today)
- Optimizing investments made in training and development to get the most mileage from the investment
- Redesigning the HR department to be able to get more done with smaller amounts of dedicated resources

The Composition of HR

The makeup of HR departments has shifted in North America, largely to mirror the change in overall demographics. For example, in 2010, women held 42 percent of the top jobs, up from 27 percent just a decade before.

HR professionals in organizations today can come from such varied backgrounds as engineering, psychology, organization design, marketing, and IT, to name a few. This reflects the multifaceted mission of HR and the capabilities required to develop and deliver high-quality products and services across the organization.

We also find many different nationalities within HR teams in North America, a function of both the region's diverse society and the global nature of many businesses.

Review and Discussion of the 2012 HRCS North America Findings

Not surprisingly, the North American survey results largely mirror those of the rest of the world. The key competencies that the study identified are critically important to the successful delivery of HR's mission in the region. In fact, the regression analysis indicates that the six roles have a stronger correlation for North America (R^2 of .479) than the global average (R^2 of .425).

Where North America differs most from the rest of the world is in the relative experience level of the respondents. More than half indicated they had been in HR for longer than 15 years, versus 30 percent globally. That is not surprising: tenure of talent is typically higher in North America (and Europe) than it is in the developing markets. Despite the fact that HR leaders in North America have vast experience to share globally, they can also learn a lot from HR professionals in other parts of the world, who do amazing things with very limited resources.

In looking at the relative focus areas, North American HR professionals score higher in two key areas:

- *Effectively interacting with the board (8.8 versus 7.7).* Given the recent focus in the region on ensuring that boards execute their roles effectively, HR has played a more active role with board members, in particular concerning talent management and employee and organization health.

- *Tracking the impact of HR (9.3 versus 8.8).* The significant cost-cutting pressures in the region have led to intense questioning on the return of every dollar companies spend, including in HR. It is, in fact, harder to measure the impact of investments in the softer areas such as HR. With the advent of new analytical tools, HR is now able to demonstrate its impact on the bottom line with hard data.

The results of the HR competency study identify further opportunities for North American HR groups to learn from the rest of the world. The region scored lower than the rest of the world in five key areas:

- Focus on the local community as a key stakeholder (14 percent in North America versus 18 percent globally)
- Connecting HR activities with external stakeholders (8.2 versus 8.9)
- HR being a culture role model (7.7 versus 8.4)
- Having clear roles and responsibilities for each group in HR (7.0 versus 7.6)
- HR group providing integrated solutions to the rest of the organization (7.7 versus 8.2)

Great organizations not only play to their strengths but work to strengthen their weaknesses. This must be true of HR groups in every region, including North America.

Building on Strengths

North American HR needs to continue to do what it does really well today:

- *Change champion.* In this role, HR can continue to partner with line leaders to develop and successfully implement change at every level: for individuals, for initiatives, and across the organization. The HR teams in companies based in Silicon Valley (such as Google and Apple) are masters at facilitating change in an industry that changes virtually every day, thereby helping their firms sustain their success over time.

- *Technology proponent.* By leveraging social networks to foster a greater level of enterprise-wide collaboration and communication, HR can help employees meet a growing need for community at work. Intel, IBM, and Dell have been at the forefront of using blogs, websites, Facebook, LinkedIn, and other tools to more fully engage employees and their stakeholders.
- *Capability builder.* North American HR professionals have been among the leaders in envisioning new ways of doing work, such as high-performance work systems, global-matrix organizations, and HR shared-service organizations. Many of these concepts have been adopted and built upon by others around the world. North America must remain an engine of innovation.

Strengthening Relative Weaknesses

The competency domains also include improvement opportunities for North American HR, as highlighted in the survey:

- *Strategic positioner.* While HR leaders have increasingly played an important role in coaching leadership and developing new strategies, it is evident that there is room to grow. HR professionals need to become more externally focused. During challenging times, people and organizations tend to turn inward and become very focused on the short term. They can lose sight of why they exist: to serve their external stakeholders. North American HR can play a greater role, within both the HR function and the broader organization, to get more in touch with "what's out there", by listening to the voice of the customers to create a vision and plan that fully reflects their input and uniquely positions the firm to win. The HR strategic positioner should be asking:
  - Do I know, by name, who my firm's key external stakeholders are? When did I last I meet with them? What are their top five needs? How am I doing in meeting these needs?
  - What is my company's long-term vision? Does it represent a truly sustainable competitive advantage? Will it meet the needs of *all* our various stakeholders?
- *HR innovator and integrator.* While North American HR has generated many revolutionary new ideas, it has not always capitalized on its potential

through simple, integrated, high-touch products and services that wow its customers. Much of the work of HR today continues to be done in independent silos and shows up on the doorsteps of employees as complicated, disjointed, and, in some cases, nonvalue-adding work. The HR innovator and integrator should be asking:

- o Am I in touch with the latest best practices within the industry? How would I know? In which HR forums do I regularly participate and share? Who are the leading-edge HR practitioners that I am aggressively learning from? Am I attending conferences and training workshops?

- o What is my company's plan for an integrated set of HR products and services that meet the needs of our key stakeholders? How do stakeholders really rate the quality of what we are providing? Do I listen to and act upon their feedback?

- *Credible activist.* Unfortunately, the dirty work of downsizing, outsourcing, and reducing pay and benefits has tarnished the image of HR among employees in North America. In some companies, HR is seen as a barrier instead of an enabler or resource to be trusted and engaged. In addition, HR professionals' lack of deep knowledge about businesses and their current challenges can impact their credibility. The HR credible activist should be asking:

- o Where do my key relationships stand today? Are those relationships based on mutual trust and credibility? What am I doing to strengthen them and my reputation as a credible activist?

- o Am I in touch with what is really going on, both in the business and at all levels of the organization? Am I seeking and listening to candid, unfiltered insights?

- o What is my unique contribution to the business? What is my organization's unique contribution to the business? Am I delivering that contribution?

North American Best Practices

Innovation is a strength of many businesses in North America. Innovation is especially important for HR as it leads to developing breakthrough ways of doing work. Here are three compelling examples from North America:

New Product Innovation

Many of the world's leading users of social media are North American companies, particularly in Silicon Valley. Companies such as Google, Facebook, Pixar, and Apple have created cultures that enable employees to be highly creative, collaborative, nimble, and energized, including:

- *Sufficient discretionary time.* At Google, 20 percent of an employee's week is "free time" to create.
- *Direct access to resources.* The structure of Facebook enables weekly contact with the CEO to speed decision making.
- *Highly talented, creative teams.* Pixar has developed some of the biggest Hollywood hits through the use of small, fluid groups of creative geniuses who are given unique ways of working together to constantly challenge one another to be even better.
- *Compelling purpose.* Apple has totally reinvented seven different industries, and, as a result, has the highest market value of any company in the world.
- *Leveraging online technology.* In 2006, IBM piloted a worldwide brainstorming session called Values Jam to tap into the ideas of its 426,000 employees. This was such a success that it has evolved to encompass many other aspects of the business, such as how to uncover new and innovative ideas or how to improve customer service.

Talent Attraction and Development

Because of the need to build a strong bench of people to support global expansion, many firms have created rigorous, highly effective ways to attract and develop top talent.

Cirque du Soleil is world-famous for its highly creative performances. Founded in Quebec City, Canada, it has reinvented the circus and created a whole new genre of entertainment. Multiple shows circle the planet, with over a hundred million people having attended a production. Cirque du Soleil is every bit as serious about the performers as the performances.

It has developed a creative yet rigorous methodology for recruiting, screening, and on-boarding new talent. Like Disney, it is obsessed with making sure every new performer fully understands and embraces the essence of Cirque du Soleil. In doing so, it achieves a deep connection between the people it attracts and invites to join the team and the products it delivers.

Whole Foods Market is a $10 billion supplier of groceries and has the highest market multiple in its industry. Each of its stores is made up of carefully recruited associates organized into small teams. Each individual and team is empowered to feel like an owner of the store. They are responsible for the budget and all aspects of the operation. Most important, Whole Foods cultivates a strong culture of high quality, great service, and sustainability of the products it sells.

Zappos is a billion-dollar-a-year online shoe and apparel business based in Las Vegas. It is consistently ranked as one of the best places to work (number 11 in the latest Fortune ranking) and has a very loyal following. Its mission is to "create happiness," and it has one of the most flexible approaches to customer service in the industry. To support its goal of having the best service, it has a 365-day return policy and free shipping. Zappos employees are empowered to do whatever it takes to satisfy the customer. For example, a woman called to return a pair of boots for her husband, who had died in a car accident. The next day she received a delivery of flowers that the call center rep had sent to her.

Attracting the right kind of talent to fit into the self-proclaimed "zany" Zappos culture is a challenge. After recently visiting its headquarters, we can attest to how very different its people are. It looks for people who are unique and willing to continuously learn and change. In addition to having team members interview all applicants, it offers a $2,000 "quit" bonus to all new hires during their four-week introductory training—as a test to see if the values of that person fit with those of the company. Interestingly, only 2 to 3 percent of new hires take up the offer![5]

Google has transformed its HR function through a new approach to talent called Three Thirds. The HR team consists of one-third traditional HR people, one-third high-end strategy consultants, and one-third master's and doctorate-level analytical professionals. This mix of skills has created new capabilities and has transformed how HR is perceived. The strategy consultants bring business understanding and problem-solving skills. The HR scholars understand employees and how to motivate them. The analytical gurus prove that what they do makes a difference in the company's results.

Globalization

P&G touches the lives of more people every day than any other institution on the planet. Fully 4.4 billion people use one of its products regularly, and the goal is to increase this to five billion in just a few years. Being able to market 300 brands in more than a hundred countries requires a highly effective global organization. Achieving $2 billion in new growth is no small feat—as if creating a new Fortune 500 company every year.

In 1999, HR was a catalyst for building the case for change that led to the most significant restructuring in the company's history. A revolutionary four-pillar organizational structure was conceived and put into place in 2000. It enables P&G to take advantage of its size and scale globally while remaining responsive to the unique needs of its customers in the markets it serves. These are the four pillars of the new structure:

- Global Business Units (GBUs) are responsible for consumer understanding, brand equity, innovation and design, and new business development.
- Market Development Organizations collaborate with the GBUs to create winning brand plans for local markets. They are also responsible for the recruiting and development of organizations in each region.
- The Global Business Services unit provides a full range of innovative, low-cost business services, technology solutions, and work processes to P&G employees.
- The Corporate Functions unit designs cutting-edge expertise, leads corporate governance, and facilitates the development of future functional leadership.

This structure enables P&G to operate nimbly in a very complex world. P&G seeks to meet the needs of many diverse consumers while partnering with thousands of suppliers and staying one step ahead of competitors, who can emerge from anywhere.

To support this new structure, P&G made a number of changes in its operations:

- Redefining "important" and putting the "consumer is boss" at the center.[6] To better understand customers' needs, employees immersed themselves in the daily lives of women around the world, leading to breakthrough new products like Downy Single Rinse detergent for use in Mexico (where clean water is at a premium).
- Creating P&G Future Works, a corporate fund set aside to invest in promising new technologies.
- Establishing New Business Development Groups, embedded within existing product categories, with the sole mission of seeking out new growth opportunities.
- Launching Innovation Hot Zones, such as Clay Street, where business teams incubate and pressure-test breakthrough product and package concepts.
- Shifting the organization's culture by creating a new set of Success Drivers that spell out desired behaviors, and by revamping the rewards and recognition systems.[7]

As part of early efforts to strengthen its global footprint, GE, like many companies, moved jobs out of North America to other, lower-cost countries. Recently, however, it is "re-shoring" some of these positions back to the United States. For example, it has invested $1 billion in its appliance business based in Louisville, Kentucky, and is hiring 900 new employees there. A combination of rising energy costs, higher wages in China, reduced supply-chain responsiveness, and implementation of lean methodologies led to this reversal in job creation. HR has played a key role in this transformation through negotiation of new wage contracts, relocation of key functional resources, and improved manufacturing team effectiveness.

HR's Influence on Business Performance

The intense focus of HR teams in North America over the past several years has helped companies weather the worst business environment since the Great Depression. The impact of their hard work is seen in many areas:

- Dramatic reductions in total cost of the workforce due to curtailing head count, optimizing pay and benefits packages, and fine-tuning investments in development.
- Reengineering how HR work is done to reduce costs, improve customer service, and build the business. Many firms, such as P&G, Kellogg, and Staples, have realized these benefits through greater employee self-service, shared HR service centers, and the outsourcing of routine transactional HR work.
- Maintaining employee engagement despite challenging economic times. According to Aon Hewitt, although engagement in North America dropped 4 percent from 2009 to 2010, overall employee engagement in the region remains 6 percentage points higher than in the rest of the world (63 versus 57 percent). Companies such as Fifth Third Bank, Mars, and Bon Secours have aggressive efforts to create a "great place to work." Their outstanding business results clearly demonstrate the value of the full engagement of the workforce.

Key Needs Looking Forward

The rate of change and competitive pressures will, if anything, accelerate in the years ahead. The good old days of stability and certainty will not return. As a result, the demands being placed upon HR will continue to escalate, requiring the function to both maintain its current capabilities and create new ones. To be successful in the complex business environment in which we live and work, HR in North America will need to be in touch with the rapidly shifting external environment, such as new government regulations, and be able to foresee what companies must do to prepare. HR professionals will have to stay abreast of new technologies and understand how they can enhance employee collaboration, innovation, and engagement; they will need to seek new, creative techniques from across the world to deliver high-impact HR services at the lowest possible cost to both HR and the business. HR will also need to pioneer new approaches that enable leaders to unleash the full potential of their organizations, help every employee seize the change that tomorrow will undoubtedly bring, and fully embrace the possibilities within it.

Although many of the themes discussed in this chapter relate to challenges faced by organizations in North America, we wish to emphasize the importance and opportunity that HR will play in the years ahead. As the North American economy continues its transition from a manufacturing to a knowledge-based economy, the role of HR becomes only more vital to business success. And as people become more integrated with the strategic directives of an organization and become the products, not just the producers, it becomes ever more imperative to train, develop, recruit, and incorporate human capital throughout the business. North America has many of the most innovative and forward-thinking organizations and thought leaders in the world, and it is HR's duty to bring its knowledge and expertise to the rest of the world. The challenge is daunting, but it is overshadowed by the opportunities that come with being more intimately aligned and involved in the strategic aspects of our organizations.

CHAPTER 11

TURKEY

11

Pᴇʟɪɴ Uʀɢᴀɴᴄɪʟᴀʀ ᴀɴᴅ Mɪᴄʜᴀᴇʟ Pʜɪʟʟɪᴘs

"Our CEO has stated that HR is too important to be left in the hands of HR people," the HR manager of a leading bank in Turkey recently told us. "We initially felt resentful when he said this, but we eventually came to understand what he meant, and we know that he was right."

In another conversation, the HR director of a fast-growing conglomerate in Turkey said, "One of our general managers called and complained to me about his business unit HR partner, who is on my team. He said, 'She asks too many questions about the business. The business is not *her* business.' He had apparently told her this as well. When she came to me asking what to do, I recommended that she keep doing what she always does because the business *is* her business."

The contrast between these two perspectives captures the state of HR in Turkey. The bar is being raised for HR in the country, but while that may be true for some organizations, it is clearly not the case for all. The most prominent variable in HR practices in Turkey appears to be the attitude of top management and its recognition of the value that HR creates. In some settings, expectations for HR practices and HR professionals are high. Leaders in these companies view their HR professionals as business partners who they can turn to for advice. However, in most organizations, HR is still restricted to operational work and is not seen as an influential discipline when it comes to matters of strategy.

Case Study: HR Provides a Business Solution

To improve its customer service, a major bank in Turkey adopted the Net Promoter Score (NPS) to measure its performance through the eyes of its customers beginning in 2006. Random customers were asked how likely it was that they would recommend the bank to a friend or a colleague. On a scale of 0 to10, people who rated themselves at 9 or 10 were considered promoters and loyal enthusiasts who would keep buying, referring others, and fueling growth. Those who rated themselves at 7 or 8 were considered passives, customers who were satisfied but vulnerable to competitive offerings. And those answering between 0 and 6 were considered detractors, customers who were unhappy and could damage the bank's brand and impede growth through negative word-of-mouth.

The NPS was conducted every year until 2008, and the results were shared with the top management and regional managers. As the scores were reviewed at the regional level, they were not really affecting branch performance. However, after recognizing the downward trend in the scores, bank leadership decided to take action. Cross-function project groups were formed to look at the in-depth causes of the decrease in customer satisfaction scores; they were also asked to provide possible solutions. They found these main complaints:

- "When I walk into the branch, nobody seems to notice I am there; nobody looks at me."
- "I seek assistance in my investments, but nobody is willing to give this service."
- "Branch employees are not smiling."
- "People I work with change very frequently."

Equipped with this feedback, the HR department took the lead and talked with employees, especially from branches in the low-scoring regions. After completing the interviews, the HR team noted that rapid growth meant the bank had hired many new employees in the branches, most of whom were either recent graduates or people with only a few years of experience. "The average seniority in the branches had fallen below one year," recalls one of the HR leaders. Since the branch manager pipeline was not strong enough to fill the new positions, people who were not yet ready had been promoted into them. The newly appointed branch managers, who were already struggling with their leadership roles, were not in the positions to lead branch employees effectively.

Realizing that even the excellent theoretical training they gave new recruits was not enough for them to meet customer expectations, the HR team started to look at alternatives for bridging the gap between theory and practice. Their solution was to create a culture of coaching: if they train experienced employees to advise less-experienced ones, newcomers would have mentors to give them on-the-job instruction.

The HR team developed two approaches. The first was called On the Job Training, which addressed the needs of sales representatives, account managers, and tellers whose main task was executing transactions accurately and promptly. Certain people in certain branches were chosen to train other people on the job. These trainers initially participated in training themselves to learn how they could best help others become competent at their work. Sales representatives, account managers, and tellers new to the bank would be sent to these branches to start their on-the-job training after they completed their theoretical training. They would stay at those branches anywhere from 3 to 10 days, depending on their learning needs.

The second approach, called On the Job Coaching, addressed the needs of portfolio managers who had serious sales targets. Employees who were promoted to a portfolio manager role, portfolio managers who moved to another branch in another region, and new hires as portfolio managers were each given a coach. While the coaches' main responsibilities were to coach their assigned employees in the peer portfolio manager role, they could also coach in the sales representative, account manager, or teller roles if the need arose.

Coaches were assigned on a volunteer basis, and they were selected by the regional managers according to a list of predetermined criteria. After the branch managers also approved the appointments, potential coaches were asked to confirm their wishes to be trained as internal coaches. "People felt honored to be given such responsibilities, but it was very difficult to find qualifying coaches at the beginning," recalls one of the project managers. "When we started in 2009, we only had 6 coaches; today we have 310 coaches in 922 branches."

Today, the system has become fully institutionalized. Whenever there is a new portfolio manager, the branch manager appoints a coach and then invites the two to a meeting to make the introductions in person. Once the coach and the coachee agree on the needs, they select the topics they will work on from a checklist, which is stored online with the coachee guidebook for easy access.

A copy of the list is automatically sent to HR, the branch manager, and the coach and coachee. The duration of the coaching contract is normally three months, extendable for another month. Frequencies of the meetings range from once a week at the beginning to once every other week after the first month.

According to evaluation forms, 97 percent of the coachees say the coaching model helped them quickly learn about the products and services necessary to better serve customers. Ninety-two percent say it helped them adapt to their new roles more quickly.

Turkey at the Crossroads

Some people reading a book focused on global regions may ask why Turkey should merit its own chapter. The answer lies in the country's unique position as a crossroads—and perhaps a model for other countries in the future.

Many places regard themselves as crossroads of cultures and civilizations, but none has greater claim to that title than Turkey. A powerful regional presence in Eurasia, it has been open to strong cultural and economic influences from East and West for centuries. Istanbul, for example, is the only city that lies in two continents; its historical names—Byzantium, Nova Roma, and Constantinople—testify to the country's diverse cultural influences.

Turkey is eastern if you view it from the perspective of the West and western if you view it from the perspective of the East. Descending from the Ottoman Empire, Turkey has been a secular democratic republic since 1923. It is the only secular democracy in the world with a 99.8 percent Muslim population, the only predominantly Muslim member of NATO (since 1955), and the only predominantly Muslim country that is a candidate for EU membership. Its strength as a regional power does not come solely from its unique heritage and Islamic identity but rather from its strong ties to the West as well as its importance as a key hub for the transportation of goods—particularly oil and gas—between the East and the West.

Because of this unique heritage—and the difficulty of placing it squarely within any individual region—Turkey stands alone in this book rather than as a part of Europe, the Middle East, or Asia. In fact, Turkey is a little bit of each.

Business Context

Turkey is an upper-middle-income economy that has tripled its GDP since 2002, thus becoming the sixteenth largest economy in the world and the sixth largest in Europe in 2011. Aspiring to be one of the top 10 economies in the world by 2023, Turkey has recently been named at the top of the "next 11" growth markets after Brazil, Russia, India, and China.[1]

One of the biggest vulnerabilities of the Turkish economy is the account deficit: it currently stands at 10 percent of gross domestic product (GDP), making it one of the highest in the world. The foreign trade deficit is mainly due to Turkey's dependence on imported energy amid rising oil prices. While increasing domestic demand for energy is responsible for much of the deficit, it also serves as an engine for growth. Much of this demand is financed by short-term international capital flow, which is a problem. Another significant issue is the declining level of domestic savings, which at 12.7 percent of GDP lags far behind that of many other countries.

With a population of 75 million, Turkey is very young. Twenty-six percent of the inhabitants of the country are under age 14. Turkish households have a high dependency ratio, which leads to low savings rates. Also contributing to low savings is the low level of female labor force participation, currently 24 percent of the total female population above age fifteen.

Turkey was lucky to reform its financial sector during the 2001 economic crisis, which made it resilient to the global financial crisis that hit in 2008. Despite decreases in external demand and slowing international capital flows, Turkey has one of the fastest-recovering economies in the world. However, no matter how well the economy currently seems to be doing, with the European Union (EU) struggling to save its ailing members, Turkey still faces the risk of losing external demand for its products—the EU accounts for 50 percent of its exports.

Turkey lived through three coup d'états from 1960 to 1980 and had short-lived coalition governments from 1991 to 2002. Today's ruling party, the Adalet ve Kalkima (AKP), celebrates its tenth year in power with the support of 50 percent of the voters.[2] The AKP continues to enhance relations with the Gulf States, which has caused Turkey to enjoy an increasing popularity in the Arab world. The risk posed by a fragile EU may be partially offset by the Gulf funds pouring into the country for investment. It is also true that an increasing number of Turkish businesses are going to the Middle East for investment, especially in the construction sector. The recent Arab Spring has also been a factor in Turkey's popularity. Under an ambitious "zero problems with neighbors" policy, Turkey is trying to fill the role of mediator and peace broker, something greatly needed in the region. However, deteriorating relations with Syria and ongoing conflicts with Iran and long-time ally Israel are putting Turkey's mission at risk, undermining its regional leadership role.

Beginning in the 1980s, Turkey became much more focused on global relations and international markets, and as a result, the private sector started to grow. As international trade and foreign investment increased, so did interactions with mainly Western counterparts. The country began moving from an agriculture-based economy to a service-based economy. Today agriculture accounts for less than 10 percent of the GDP, even though 25 percent of the workforce is still employed in the sector.[3] Industry accounts for 27 percent and services for 64 percent of the GDP. The role of the state in the economy substantially decreased as privatization efforts increased, especially after 2000. A number of large enterprises have been privatized and US$48.2 billion has been raised in privatization revenues between 2003 and 2010.

The current business climate in Turkey is very encouraging for organizations looking for ways to grow domestically and internationally. Continued domestic growth looks positive based on the current stability in the Turkish economy and the growth of the middle-income population. Growth based on exports also looks promising based on Turkey's proximity to more than 50 countries: 1.5 billion people and a US$25 trillion market within a four-hour flight. Thus, it appears that current prospects far exceed the risks in Turkey, and the opportunities for growth are significant.

Organization Trends

Turkey's move to a service-based economy has shifted the focus from products to people as the key success factor for businesses. Organizations have begun to pay more attention to HR management as they have come to realize the importance of using labor and capital to offset the impact of rising costs undermining their competitiveness.

Businesses in Turkey had difficulty making long-term plans because of volatile political and economic conditions before 2002, especially while struggling with inflation rates as high as 100 percent.[4] In a stable political and economic environment, it is much easier to make long-term plans, which have positive effects on the HR profession. HR professionals are now able to align HR practices with the mid- and long-term strategies of their organizations. Before this period of stability, all they could really do was day-to-day operations and constant damage control.

Solid growth performance of the Turkish economy has led to increasing outbound M&A (merger and aquisition) activity in the past few years. Thanks to their flexibility and ability to adapt to new environments, Turkish companies have made 68 foreign acquisitions totaling US$7.5 billion in revenues in the past five years, according to a report released by Deloïtte Turkey in January 2012. In 2011 alone, Turkish companies made 26 overseas acquisitions worth US$2.9 billion.[5] Market and product diversification, brand acquisition, and raising competitive advantage through cost efficiencies have been the fueling factors for outbound M&A.

At the same time, the Turkish market stands as an attractive destination for investors. Total M&A deals in 2011 surpassed the record level of 2010 with 241 acquisitions. Middle-market transactions were dominant. In the absence of big-ticket privatizations, total volume was at a level of US$15 billion. Foreign investors have generated 74 percent of that volume through 138 deals.[6] As foreign investors' and private equity firms' interest in Turkey increases, issues such as good governance and investor relations become very important for organizations.

As more multinational companies come to manage their regional operations, including operations in Eastern Europe, the Middle East, and Africa, they tend to set up and update systems for more effective execution. Turkey has proven to be a location of choice for many of these companies. Coca-Cola, Pepsi, Microsoft, Unilever, Pfizer, Roche, GlaxoSmithKline, Novo Nordisk, Ericsson, and TeliaSonera Eurasia are some of the companies that have chosen Istanbul as their regional headquarters.

Aside from these multinationals, local companies in Turkey can be divided into two groups: institutionalized holding companies and family-owned, non-institutionalized companies. The institutionalized companies are trying to focus their diversified portfolios on a few core, highly profitable businesses. They tend to be regional or global players in their specific fields. For example, Koc Holding, one of the biggest conglomerates in Turkey, has chosen to focus on banking, energy, durables, and automotive, and has sold its insurance business to joint venture partner Allianz and its retail business to a global fund. Many family-owned companies attempt to institutionalize, but few of these attempts are successful as family conflicts block the transition.

Talent Trends

Significant growth means a big demand for talent in Turkey, and the war for talent is intense. Finding the right people with the right skills who also have fluency in English is difficult: Fluency in English is a particularly critical skill in the context of globalization.

With Turkey's youthful population (61 percent under age 34 and a median age of 29.7), high performers become leaders very young. The CEO of Vodafone Turkey, Serpil Timuray, who proved to be a very successful turnaround leader, was appointed as GM of Danone Turkey when she was 33, and she assumed her current role at Vodafone when she was only 40. Similarly, ING Turkey has made a very interesting transfer from McKinsey Turkey and appointed 34-year-old Pinar Abay to lead its 6,000 employees.

Though a coincidence, it's no surprise that both Timuray and Abay are women. A growing number of women are taking on leadership roles in Turkey. According to Grant Thornton's *International Business Report,* published in March 2012, women fill 31 percent of senior management roles in Turkey. This ratio is 10 points above the global average and represents a 6 percent increase from the preceding year, making Turkey the most improved on the list for the year. The numbers from Coca-Cola Marketing Turkey seem to back up the report findings: where 45 percent of employees at Coca-Cola Marketing Turkey are women, 73 percent of its managerial roles are filled by women—including that of the CEO. The report also shows that 34 percent of the leadership roles in finance are filled by women, followed by 21 percent in sales, 16 percent in HR, and 14 percent in marketing. The number of women in HR leadership roles seems to be quite low when compared with the number of women in the HR profession.

Implications for HR Practices in Turkey

In Turkey, company size is the main factor for both the presence and growth of HR departments. A study conducted in 2006 with the participation of companies in the Gebze Organized Industrial Zone (which accounts for 13 percent of total manufacturing capacity in Turkey) found that only 28.3 percent of companies that have up to 250 employees had an HR department; for companies with more than 250 employees, it's 71.7 percent.[7]

In addition to the size of the company, the globalization of the marketplace and increased inbound and outbound M&A activity is playing a significant role in the growth and maturation of the HR profession in Turkey. For those companies trying to attract international institutional investors, financial analyst reports on future performance are critical—and the growing importance analysts give to HR-related intangibles in predicting future success becomes even more important. Therefore, HR leaders of publicly traded companies seem to have found a new way to differentiate themselves: make sure you have the right HR metrics in place to collect data attractive to investors and communicate that data before it is demanded.

Currently, there appears to be a growing awareness of the need for these practices in Turkey, although actual execution greatly lags intent. As for M&A targets, corporate governance seems to be at the top of their HR agenda. On the other side, HR teams of companies ready to acquire new businesses try to strengthen their HR due diligence muscle.

To move up the value chain, an increasing number of companies in Turkey are trying to embrace innovation as an organization capability. Therefore, HR departments are looking for ways to make their organization cultures more innovative, investing in training and development activities that focus on innovation. Organizations are making structural changes to this end as well. "Head of Innovation" is an increasingly common title in Turkish companies. Eczacibaşi Holding and Yildiz Holding are two organizations that have created this position, and they have them report directly to the CEO.

Within the country, companies are very active in working to attract talent. They not only publicize their employee value proposition but also design innovative programs to attract young talent. Finans Up of Finansbank, Red Generation of AVEA, Talent Camp of Garanti Bank, Techno Idea of Turkcell, Thinking Club of Akbank, Business School of P&G, Career Test Drive of Eczacibaşi Holding, Discover FreeZone of Vodafone, the CAReer Talent of Mercedes-Benz, Idea Trophy of Unilever, and Imagine Cup of Microsoft are a few such programs designed to attract the best talent.

According to the results of the Most Admired Companies for University Students survey conducted in 2011 by *Bloomberg Businessweek* and Realta Consulting in Turkey, companies such as Turkcell, Mercedes Benz, Unilever, Coca-Cola, Microsoft, Turkish Airlines, Isbank, Garanti Bank, and Pfizer top the list. The results suggest that these companies are better at offering new talent what they are looking for in their prospective employers. According to the study, new talent is looking for good working conditions, development opportunities, support for entrepreneurship, utilization of their talent, advancement opportunities, finding meaning at work, work–life balance, and good pay. HR plays a key role in each of these areas. Many of the leaders who were interviewed for this book mentioned their desires to be listed among the top companies in this survey. Therefore, many companies are running programs especially designed to attract young talent and to stay ahead in the fierce competition for those people.

Awareness of the importance of HR is growing. Some companies do have world-class practices, but others lag behind, meaning significant variation from organization to organization. As one would expect, the multinational companies and institutionalized local companies tend to have more mature practices than the noninstitutionalized local ones.

The brief time since Turkey achieved a state of economic stability, along with recent significant growth, has also had a tremendous impact on the relatively immature state of HR practices in the country. The upside of this growth and the war for talent is that highly sought-after employees are demanding more of the HR function. That, combined with growing awareness of the need for HR to act as a business partner, bodes well for the profession, at least in most segments of the economy.

Review and Discussion of the 2012 HRCS Turkey Findings

The HRCS was conducted in Turkey for the first time in 2011. In the overall data, 3 percent of the study participants were from Turkey. In global terms, that is a significant sample size. However, variations among the participants make it less than entirely representative of the overall business situation in the country.

Fifty-five percent of the participants were female, which is in line with the overall total but quite high compared with the ratio of women in the Turkish labor force (24 percent overall, 18.5 percent in cities, and 47 percent in the services sector). As this is the first HRCS data for Turkey, it will be interesting to see if the country follows the global trend toward an increase of women in the HR profession.

Turkey stands out in the HRCS as almost half the participants (49 percent) came from companies with more than 10,000 employees. This is quite a high ratio when compared with the 25 percent overall total in that category. This also means that family-owned, noninstitutionalized companies are not well represented, and large local institutionalized companies and multinationals are overrepresented in the data.

Fifty-one percent of the participants have a graduate degree (almost the same as the overall number at 50 percent), and 46 percent have four-year degrees (8 percent above the overall total of 38 percent). These are very high ratios when compared with the overall education level in Turkey. According to OECD's 2011 Education at a Glance report, net graduation rates from high school, four-year college, and advanced programs are 44.8, 20.9, and 0.4 percent respectively. As compared with the overall populations, HR professionals in

Turkey are indeed highly educated, and the specific participants in the survey may have further skewed that percentage.

Only 9 percent of the participants have more than 15 years' seniority. This is quite a low number when compared with the 36 percent overall total. Forty percent of the participants have less than five years' experience, and this rate is quite high compared with the 24 percent overall total. This is a direct reflection of Turkey's population demographics. In addition, HR as a profession is a developing one with many openings for new graduates. People who accept these positions can move up the career ladder quite quickly. It is not unusual to see HR managers and directors in their late twenties and early thirties with no more than 10 years' total seniority.

As for the industries represented among the participants: 26 percent are from manufacturing, 25 percent from wholesale/retail, 24 percent from pharmaceuticals, and 11 percent from banking. The high ratio of participants coming from manufacturing and wholesale/retail might have some implications for the Turkey domain mean scores. The average ratios of employees to HR professionals in these two sectors are the highest after agriculture, which means the HR professionals working in these sectors might be involved in more operational, routine HR work, thereby decreasing their perceived effectiveness.

Effective HR Professionals in Turkey

Turkish domain mean scores that show the effectiveness of HR professionals in each competency follow exactly the same pattern as the overall total, with credible activist (4.04) scoring highest, followed by capability builder (3.82), change champion (3.76), HR innovator and integrator (3.76), strategic positioner (3.73), and technology proponent (3.64). The same pattern continues even when only associate ratings are taken into consideration, which means there is not much difference between the perceptions of participants and their associates. The associates' ratings are actually slightly higher than those of participants' across all domains.

Because credible activist has the greatest impact on perceived performance in Turkey (23 percent), HR professionals in Turkey should build relationships of trust and have both a strong business and HR points of view to be perceived as personally effective. Following credible activist is HR innovator and integrator (18 percent). HR professionals must know the latest insights on key HR practice areas related to human capital (talent sourcing and talent development), performance accountability (appraisal and rewards), organization design (teamwork and organization development), and communication. Knowing is not enough; they must be able to turn these unique HR practice areas into integrated solutions. Being a capability builder (17 percent) is also critical for HR professionals' effectiveness. HR professionals should be able to audit and invest in the creation of organization capabilities, which are actually a company's culture, process, or identity—such things as customer service, speed, efficiency, or innovation. Being a change champion (15 percent), to initiate and sustain change; and a strategic positioner (15 percent), to think and act from the outside in to translate external business trends into internal decisions and actions is also an important capability. Being a technology proponent (12 percent)—which means accessing, advocating, analyzing, and aligning technology for information, efficiency, and relationships—seems to have the least impact on the perceived effectiveness of HR individuals. These six domains of HR competency explain 42.5 percent of the effectiveness of an HR professional.

Being a strategic positioner appears to have less impact on an HR professional's perceived effectiveness in Turkey than in the field overall. Strategic positioner accounts for 15 percent of HR effectiveness (ranking it fourth among all competencies for Turkey) versus 17 percent of perceived HR effectiveness overall (ranking it second in the global norm).

In interviews with HR leaders, all of them stressed the importance of being a credible activist in the Turkish culture, where interpersonal relationships and networking are so important that good interpersonal relationships often matter more than performance. Being a credible activist is the most significant differentiator for HR professionals in Turkey.

Effective Business Performance

These six domains of HR competencies explain 8.4 percent of a business's success, but the impact of each individual competency on business success is different from its impact on individual effectiveness. Being an HR innovator and integrator seems to have the biggest impact on business success in Turkey (20 percent), followed by being a technology proponent (18 percent), change champion or credible activist (both 16 percent), strategic positioner (15 percent), and finally, capability builder (14 percent).

The HR professional mentioned at the start of the chapter who asked too many questions about the business is a good example of the credible activist. She is working for one of the fastest-growing local conglomerates in Turkey. The size and global reach of the organization have recently forced this conglomerate to change from an internally focused organization to an externally focused one. This switch includes transforming HR from operations center to trusted advisor and superb executor. Contrary to many of her peers, who have not yet adjusted to their new roles, this HR professional is making sure she attends all relevant meetings to better understand the business's needs. If she, as the business unit HR partner, is not invited to a meeting she thinks she needs to attend—and sometimes she is intentionally not invited by people who think the business is not hers—she immediately calls the head of the business unit, who makes sure she is asked to go. Once she understands the needs, she quickly mobilizes company HR people to address the issue. In short, even when she is not invited, she finds a way to make it onto the agenda and change it to create value for the business.

Improving HR operations, which falls under the technology proponent competency domain, seems to have a 5 percent higher effect on business performance than the overall average. This is one of the biggest deviations from the overall average among all factors. It thus may support the argument about HR being in transition from a focus on operations to a focus on practices.

Coca-Cola Bottlers, for example, is currently investing in a new HR IT platform that will ensure integration among all HR practices. Not only that, but as Alper Tokalp, the company's HR director, sees it, the new platform is a "talking HR" that enables HR to communicate effectively with employees and managers, allowing them to receive HR's know-how and guidance. Tokalp says, "Because this platform will improve our HR operations and connect people scattered in our region via technology, its configuration is of utmost importance to us. . . . We do not see this as an IT project—it is an HR project, so we needed a full-time person in HR who would deal with this project. We appointed a new HR technology manager." This is not a common title in Turkey; in fact, LinkedIn lists only one other person in the country who holds it. Tokalp says there is still a way to go as the company is not yet leveraging social media tools as much as it could to connect with its stakeholders.

There are, however, other Turkish companies that are doing good jobs with social media, especially to reach young talent. One of these is Yildiz Holding, a fast-moving consumer-goods giant. Its project Bizz@Kampus is sponsored by Biskrem, one of the company's baked-goods brands. Junior and senior undergraduate and graduate students can participate in the program in teams of three by registering through Facebook. They first read about Biskrem's target customers, marketing plan, product range, and market share. Then the teams are asked to create their own Biskrem product, which they have to describe in detail, including its sub-brand name, taste, shape, look, packaging, logo, and so on. The participants are asked to submit a presentation including sketches and images via Facebook. From the first round, 50 teams are selected to move on. In the second round, teams define their brand communication strategies and prepare a communication plan including events, social media initiatives, TV and radio commercials, outdoor activities, and promotions. After 10 teams selected in the second round submit their final presentations, they are invited to the holding headquarters to attend a one-day tour to better know the company and meet the leadership team. The winners among the more than 400 participating teams are given rewards and internship opportunities.

Building leadership brand, under the HR innovator and integrator competency domain, appears to have the highest impact on business results in Turkey, with a 6 percent deviation from the overall average. In paternalistic cultures like Turkey's, the subordinate-superior relationship resembles that between parent and child, and people respect authority rather than rules. A role-model leader is therefore critical in mobilizing people to get the results they need.

One large company in Turkey has taken an innovative approach in how to attract, retain, and engage high potentials through its new compensation system. Seeing that a traditional compensation system that takes into consideration only job size and performance is a problem in managing young high-potential employees, it introduced potential into the compensation equation via a nine-box performance-potential matrix. It identified the position in range (PIR) for each of the boxes with high, expected, and low performance on one side, and high, growth, and well-placed potential on the other. What this system enabled the company to do is give additional reward to high potentials. A person who used to be a high potential could have a possible PIR of 120 percent. But now high potentials' base salary can go as high as 130 percent. In contrast, a well-placed person with high performance will stay at 100 percent, receiving a bonus for high performance but not increasing the organization's fixed costs by acquiring a higher salary. Similarly, the company can now offer its high-potential new recruits (15 to 20 percent of all recruits in a given year) up to 120 percent of median base salary of their grade, replacing the former offering of approximately 80 percent for all new recruits regardless of their potential. The HR director said that this practice not only raises compensation-related engagement scores by 14 percent in the first year, it also increases people's awareness about the importance of measuring potential. Although the system is not linked to promotability, it is an effective vehicle for deciding which employees to invest in.

Stakeholder Focus and Business Performance

Approaching HR from the outside in will be a key practice for HR in the future. Having an outside-in approach to HR means totally understanding all the company's stakeholder needs and pursuing an HR agenda accordingly.

We have not yet met a single Turkish HR leader who claimed to be performing HR from the outside in. They all admitted that internal stakeholders—leaders and employees—were their main stakeholders. It was their satisfaction with the HR department's deliverables that came first. Some did put the needs of leaders ahead of employees, but many treated them as equally important. There is quite a balanced distribution overall with each stakeholder having a plus-or-minus 20 percent impact on business performance. However, the impact focusing on external customers has on business performance seems to be relatively higher in Turkey at 27 percent, and the impact of focusing on community seems to be much lower at a mere 10 percent.

HR leaders in Turkey believe that understanding the business and being able to turn the needs of the business into HR solutions is the most important demand business leaders have of HR professionals. Internal stakeholders have repeatedly told HR leaders that they do not want HR acting as policy police, rigid in approach and not really open-minded. Instead, they want HR to be creative and flexible to help the business get results. Rather than create obstacles via processes that only HR thinks are important, giving greater weight to external customers may be the solution to moving HR in a problem-solving direction to help the business succeed.

Because civil-society movements in Turkey are not as advanced as in the West, it is not surprising to see community emerge as a relatively unimportant stakeholder: Society doesn't have the enforcement it needs to be effective. However, the advance of technology is empowering community and giving groups and individuals a louder voice. Here are a few statistics for context: in 2011, there were approximately 32 million Internet users in Turkey; 2.5 million of those were over 45 years old, a 12 percent increase over the preceding year. Socialbaker, the company that monitors Facebook statistics, just announced that with its 31 million Facebook accounts, Turkey ranks sixth in all Facebook statistics by country and first in Europe.[8] With the increasing ease of access to information and social networking opportunities, community will take on a more important role for companies, employees, and HR professionals in Turkey.

The Impact of Focusing on Collective HR Performance

It is interesting to note that the focus of an HR department explains 26 percent of business performance, a significantly higher number than the 8.4 percent explained by the competencies of the individual HR professionals. Effective interaction with the board, effective management of external vendors of out-sourced HR activities, serving as a role model for the rest of the organization, and tracking and measuring HR's impact seem to have less effect on business performance in Turkey when compared to the overall total. On the other hand, investment in training and development of HR professionals, connecting HR activities to external stakeholder expectations, and developing an HR strategy that clearly links HR practices to business strategy seem to have more impact on business results.

Conclusion

As a true crossroads of East and West and with a stake in Europe, the Middle East, and Asia, Turkey offers a unique lens for looking at the future of global HR. In this round of the HRCS, it has established a baseline; subsequent studies will help to more clearly show the changes taking place in this dynamic country and its business and HR practices.

While the HR profession in Turkey cannot be lumped into one homogeneous practice, there does appear to be clear improvement and growth taking place, driven in no small part by the country's diverse, dynamic, and expanding business sector.

The HRCS data and interviews throughout the country show that HR professionals are meeting the challenges in their unique national context—and in many instances employing world-class, innovative solutions to improve the businesses that they support. It is an exciting time to be in the profession in Turkey, and the opportunities are great. The HRCS provides a road map for HR practice and HR practitioners in Turkey and focusing on the findings will help them to create greater value for their organizations as they focus their efforts and improve their competence.

PART THREE

SUMMARY AND INTEGRATION OF REGIONAL DIFFERENCES

COMMON AND CUSTOMIZED COMPETENCIES: SIMILARITIES AND DIFFERENCES AROUND THE WORLD

12

Brad Winn and Dale Lake

Any company is in essence a collective of the hearts, hands, and minds of its people; in the modern era, the company's financial, technological, or physical resources are secondary. So when we talk about HR competencies, we're really talking about the skills that great HR professionals use to build their firms. Leading, coordinating, motivating, aligning, training, developing, evaluating, and empowering the human dimension and culture of an organization is not rocket science—it is much more complex. It is even more complex for an organization set in an international context. Doing global HR competently is truly a magnificent challenge, especially considering how varied the human family is across the globe.

Consider the life experience of Mudada Mutizi in southern Africa. Mutizi was born in a grass hut in 1963, to a large family living below the world's standards of poverty. Yet he describes his upbringing as filled with joy and simplicity. As a young man he witnessed the political uprising of his race and the overthrow of the white minority rulers. He now has new freedoms, a family of his own, and a job that supports his family and his newfound identity.

Compare this with the life experience of Puneet Pandey in India. Pandey is director of global resourcing and training at HCL Technologies, a business-process outsourcing company based in New Delhi. He is literally one in a million in India, having earned an engineering undergraduate degree in the mid-1990s and completed his MBA after that. Pandey is naturally independent and driven to excel at work, putting his whole heart and almost every waking hour into pushing his company forward.

Compare this with the life experience of Miriam Essa Al-Ateek in the United Arab Emirates in the Middle East. Al-Ateek was raised in affluence and recently completed her MBA. Last year she gave birth to her third child and has now returned to the workforce, enjoying a professional career and the challenges of balancing work, motherhood, and community. She is constantly concerned about the welfare of her children, the quality of her work, and her ability to keep up with the demands of local community causes about which she cares deeply.

Given the vast differences in the nature and experiences of people and companies throughout the world, are there any principles that apply generally to the human and organizational dimensions of the firm? While important differences exist, we believe that the answer is clear: yes.

What does the HRCS research reveal about common HR competencies that may be important regardless of geography? With the almost unbelievable diversity among human beings on planet Earth, are there any basics that cross regions and cultures? And are there other competencies that are unique or have more impact in certain regions of the world?

This chapter explores these questions for HR professionals who are moving their careers and companies forward amid the vast complexities of the global context. While preceding chapters address the variety of HR practice through-out the world, this chapter focuses on questions of comparative practice—both similarities and differences.

The Case of Viterra Global

In the year 2000, a small agricultural co-op in Canada found itself with US$1.5 million of unsecured debt, insufficient senior-level HR experience, and the recognition that it needed a global presence to survive. Through a series of interventions, it transformed itself into the Viterra Company, the largest Canadian-owned grain handler, delivering to customers in more than 50 nations around the world.

Viterra is an example of a company that has successfully navigated the complexities of managing human talent and leading a global workforce focused on growing the business. It has learned how to integrate effectively across regions while accounting for regional differences.

In 2001, acting in full survival mode, CEO Mayo Schmidt set out to radically reduce the size of the company, sell off underperforming businesses, raise new capital, and convince the board to dissolve itself. Fortunately, however, Schmidt brought in human and organizational expertise in the form of a personal coach who pointed out that he was not going to "reduce the company to success." Schmidt agreed. With his personal HR coach, he entered into the following interventions:

- Schmidt prepared himself to be the leader of the whole organization by looking beyond the financial side of the firm, acknowledging the criticality of the human and organizational dimensions of the company.
- He acquired new personnel to complement his own skills.
- He transformed his office from a single CEO to the office of the CEO, which he shared with his top operations person and the head of HR.
- He developed a new vision and worked through the commitment process with all the top executives until there was buy-in throughout the firm.
- He developed a new performance-management system that held people accountable for objectives *and* values.
- He directly intervened with the culture, values, and guiding principles to help people separate from the old local co-op mentality to the new global reality.
- He oversaw the introduction of several new information technologies.
- He put in place systems responsible for maintaining continuous change.
- Finally, he repositioned the company for the international market.

The core competencies relied upon for Viterra's turnaround included change management, building international corporate capability, strategically positioning the firm to go global, integrating key personnel, supporting technology, and giving credibility to and elevating the role of HR.

The HR function grew beyond its primary focus on labor relations, becoming the third part of a three-person office of the CEO. It was charged with development (change champion), and interpreting global business context (strategic positioner). As stragtegic positioners, HR developed strategic acquisition playbooks, managed personnel in several different countries, and built company capability. It also ensured that its practices focused on the few but critical business issues (HR innovator and integrator).

So what were the results of additionally focusing on the human and organizational dimensions of the firm? Security analysts reported in 2009: "Viterra generated net income of $288.3 million for the year, up sharply from the $116.5 million earned during the same period in 2007."[1]

Today the company has the respect of the financial community, resulting from substantial cash inflows. Schmidt has been elected CEO of the year in Canada, and personnel turnover is very low in a highly competitive labor market. It has been six years since the transformation began, and profits have grown every year.

Two months into 2012, Viterra became the target of several global agricultural companies—maneuvering that culminated in its sale for US$8.9 billion, boosting its stock from $4 a share to over $15 a share.[2]

Global Trends

Viterra's transformation was successful in part because its CEO was able to detect high-level global trends, adapt quickly to changes in the global environment, build the requisite human and organization capabilities, and employ global talent and demographic trends to its strategic advantage.

Global Trends at 60,000 Feet

Nine of the chapters in this volume examine the current situations and trends within each region. One key conclusion emerges when the chapters are taken together: If there is one overarching trend, it is globalization!

Nonetheless, this is not a linear progression. Roughly, globalization follows the following path:

- Localities discover and exploit natural resources (minerals, oil, lumber, farmland, and so on), produce agricultural and other commodities, and begin developing a services sector.
- Markets for these natural resources, commodities, and services expand from local to national to international arenas.
- As these markets expand, local practices are pressed to become more homogeneous for ease of transfer (products, economies, systems, cultural practices, and the like).
- Markets that are most advanced in manufacturing, technology, services, electronic information, and so on exert backward pressure on resource providers, changing the providers' expectations toward products and services of convenience beyond mere survival.
- The needs of advanced regions often create chaotic changes in those regions where the primary resources originate. (For example, if Saudi Arabian oil was used only locally, it probably would be worth US$10 a barrel. And world demand for lithium affects the labor market in Peru, which has almost no local need for the element.)

Demographic Trends and Global Talent

Never before has the world been so flat and never before have organizations had such an exceptional opportunity to draw on a truly global workforce. Thomas Friedman notes that for the first time in history, talent has become more important than geography in determining a person's opportunity in life.[3] More than ever, companies are looking internationally for talent to outpace the competition. The worldwide talent market offers almost unlimited possibilities for finding the desired type of workers. The key for organizations and HR professionals is to understand who and where these workers are, and to competently fit and grow them within their companies.

According to Ernst & Young, despite overall population growth, the pool of working-age people is expected to decrease in many parts of the world.[4] Already, more Japanese workers are leaving the labor market than entering it. For the first time, the same phenomenon has arrived in Europe. It will soon hit Russia, Canada, South Korea, and China. Yet younger emerging regions are seeing the opposite effect. India has one of the youngest populations in the world: Nearly one-third of the population is under the age 15. Indonesia, Brazil, and Mexico are emerging markets that also have large, young workforces. These regions will have a competitive advantage if they manage to provide their youth with the skills and educations that the world needs. In particular, India is leading the trend of emerging markets with a young and skilled workforce.

In addition to trends regarding age and educational demographics, cultural attributes such as relationships, aggressiveness, orientation to authority, speed, and competitiveness are also important when considering global talent markets. Asian workers are often adept at teamwork, whereas Indian workers have a reputation for being more individually competitive.[5] These differences in cultural demographics can be an asset for multinational companies as they seek different kinds of talent and technical or leadership skills.

Different regions of the world are tapping into the potential of women in their workforces. Many emerging markets still face a lingering clash between historical gender role norms and the recognition of the values and contributions that female workers have on their economies and societies. The general trend is clear, however. Over time more and more women are entering the workforce, and many multinational companies are the beneficiaries.

Demographic trends are also active within the HR profession itself. Our data show dramatic change in the number of female HR professionals in the study over the past 25 years. This suggests that HR has changed from a male-majority profession to a female-majority profession. When we first began the HRCS in 1987, 23 percent of the participants were women. In 2012, that had risen to 62 percent, a dramatic increase. Regions of the world where female representation is even higher than the worldwide average include Australia and New Zealand (77 percent), Turkey (74 percent), China (71 percent), Asia

(70 percent), the United States and Canada (69 percent), and Europe (65 percent). Regions below the average include the Middle East (20 percent), India (35 percent), Latin America (54 percent), and Africa (61 percent).

As you might expect, education levels of HR respondents have increased over the past 25 years. For the first time, a majority of HR professionals in the study have graduate degrees (51 percent).

In the war for talent, organizations that understand worldwide demographic trends win. Global demographic and regional trends regarding gender, education, health, aging, technical capabilities, mortality rates, and cultural attributes and attitudes are critical factors as companies look to outpace the competition.

Given the diversity of peoples, cultures, and nationalities, and the sheer distances involved, it would seem unlikely that anything we could say about HR competencies could hold true around the world. This brings us back to the question posed earlier: Are there HR competencies that are common across regions and sectors? It also brings up the question: Are there HR competencies that are uniquely important in certain regions of the world?

Common Competencies versus Customized Competencies

Yes, providing great HR leadership in different geographical regions of the world is much more complex than rocket science. When we began to investigate HR competencies in 1987, we found that our results exceeded our expectations—and they have continued to do so through the years and the tens of thousands of professionals who have provided data. When we started we simply wanted to discover some basic clusters of skills that might form competencies to help all of us understand what the critical dimensions in the HR role are for individual effectiveness and for business performance.

This part looks at the generalizable nature of the data, or what we might call the "common global competencies"—those that translate around the world. It also looks at the nongeneralizable competencies, or places and situations where HR professionals may need "customized regional competencies."

Table 12.1   *Review of Competency Domain Scores*

	All Respondents	HR Participants	HR Associates	Non-HR Associates
Strategic Positioner	3.89	3.69	3.90	3.94
Credible Activist	4.24	4.14	4.21	4.30
Capability Builder	3.97	3.88	3.96	4.03
Change Champion	3.93	3.81	3.94	3.96
HR Innovator and Integrator	3.90	3.77	3.91	3.94
Technology Proponent	3.74	3.54	3.76	3.78

In addition, we now have data regarding how the effectiveness of the HR department as a whole affects business performance. In this section, the following questions are addressed: Are there differences by region regarding the department's effectiveness and business performance? What are the developmental implications of these findings for HR professionals and global companies?

The six competency domains—reviewed in Table 12.1—emerge from the data gathered in all regions, and thus they come closest to answering the question of what competencies are most important for excellence around the world. That is, "If I have an HR role—whether I live in India, France, Saudi Arabia, Brazil, or Canada—what key competencies should I build upon?" In the table, the scores reflect averages for all items within a given domain on a scale from 1 to 5, with 1 being "to a very little extent" and 5 being "to a very large extent."

Meeting the Mark: Global and Regional Impact on Individual Performance

The first clear pattern is that, generally speaking, being a credible activist has the greatest impact on perceptions of individual performance and technology proponent has relatively the least impact. The pattern is generally from

Figure 12.1   *General Pattern of Impact on Individual Performance*

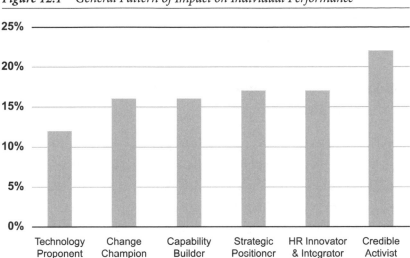

low to high as follows: technology proponent, change champion and capability builder, strategic positioner and innovative integrator, and credible activist. (See Figure 12.1.)

So if you want to increase your impact as an individual performer, you should make sure you have developed high-level competency as a credible activist, innovative integrator, and strategic positioner.

This pattern of relative impact holds true on average across the globe. But what if we break down the data by global regions? This pattern turns out to be generally consistent for most of the world. But interestingly, when we look at the relative strength of the impact of competencies on individual performances by region, we find some noticeable differences in certain areas.

For example, one intriguing difference is important for those HR professionals who live in or are assigned to China. Being a strong technology proponent in China is one of the more important competencies for individual effectiveness. This is quite a contrast compared with data for most of the rest of the world. With the exception of China, every other global region rates the technology proponent competency as least important to individual performance.

Further, being a credible activist does not have the highest impact competency for HR professionals' individual performances in the Middle East and China, nor is it as high as we would expect in Africa.

Delivering Results: Global and Regional Impact on Business Performance

In addition to identifying effects on individual performance, the data also reveal which competencies have a relatively stronger impact on business performance. This is important because being a great individual performer on a sinking ship will be completely unsatisfying if the applause drowns out as the ship goes down. Having identified the six competencies, the study asks: Which of these skill clusters have the most impact on business performance? The first pattern we notice is that, generally speaking, being an HR innovator and integrator has the greatest impact on business performance and credible activist has relatively the least impact. The pattern is generally from low to high as follows: credible activist, strategic positioner, change champion, capability builder and technology proponent, and HR innovator and integrator (see Figure 12.2).

Figure 12.2   General Impact on Business Performance

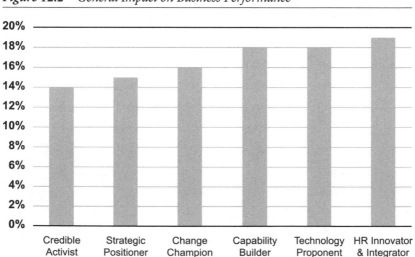

Thus, if you want to increase your impact on business performance, you should make sure you have developed a high level of competency as an HR innovator and integrator, technology proponent, and capability builder. This pattern of relative impact on business results is an average of what we see across the globe. The Americas (the United States, Canada, and Latin America) and China generally follow the global pattern.

But when we break down the data for other regions, we notice some interesting differences. For example, Europe differs from the rest of the world with regard to how the competencies affect business performance. The competencies of technology proponent and capability builder have a relatively stronger impact, whereas the critical activist and strategic positioner competencies have a relatively weaker effect on business results.

In Africa, the competency of change champion is a singular standout, the highest impact of any competency in any region in the world. And in Africa, having the competency of capability builder has a significantly lower impact than in any other global region.

Asia prioritizes the credible activist competency more highly than any other region when rating impact on business results. On the other hand, Asia discounts the impact of the HR innovator and integrator, which has on average the most effect on business performance throughout the world.

Other regions that differ from the norm relative to impact on the business performance include Australia, the Middle East, and Turkey. Australian companies are unusually high on change champion and unusually low on HR innovator and integrator. Businesses in the Middle East prioritize HR innovator and integrator more highly than we would expect and discount capability builder, as do those in Turkey.

In the United States, Canada, the Middle East, China, and Turkey, it is most effective to focus on the HR innovator and integrator competency. In Europe, Asia, and Latin America focus is on the capability builder competency. In Australia, New Zealand, and Africa focus is on the change champion competency. In India and China, focus is on the technology proponent competency.

Summary

The HR competencies and practices that are relatively common in affecting individual performances and careers are generally consistent for most of the world. That is, the pattern of relative impact generally holds for individual HR careers globally. To promote your individual career and be noted as a high performer in HR, you will want to have all the competencies in your quiver, but for real recognition you will want to ensure your place as a credible activist. Secondarily, you will want to focus on the competencies of innovative integrator and strategic positioner. What is interesting is that these priorities will generally work worldwide.

Affecting business performance is not so straightforward. The domains' relative impact on business performance depends on where you are in the world. To improve your impact on business results, you may need to customize your approach for different global regions. In this realm, as Table 12.2 illustrates, one size does not necessarily fit all.

In sum, which HR practices and competencies are relatively more important in different geographical regions? What are the unique regional aspects of HR? To build the business, HR professionals need to recognize regional differences and be adept enough to change focus depending on where they are working.

The HR Department: Working as a Team

Are the best individual players usually on the winning teams? The answer is a resounding no. In fact, when you look at international football (soccer), American football, or any other sport, the best individual athletes are often not on the winning team. The explanation is quite simple and well-known: In winning, great teamwork is more critical than individual superstar performance. It is not the best individual players who end up winning but rather the best teams.

Global HR Department Practices That Deliver Results

Our data confirm the value of teamwork in the world of HR. An effective HR department has four times as much impact on business performance

Table 12.2 *Highest-Impact Competencies for Business Performance by Region*

HR Competency	Africa	Asia	Australia and New Zealand	China	Europe	India	Latin America	Middle East	United States and Canada	Turkey
Credible Activist		High								
Strategic Positioner										
Change Champion	Highest		Highest							
Capability Builder		Highest	High		Highest		Highest		High	
Tech Proponent				Highest	High	Highest		High		High
Innovator/Integrator	High			High	High	High	High	Highest	Highest	Highest

(31.7 percent) as the skills or competencies of individual HR professionals (8.4 percent). Of course as HR professionals we want to hone our personal competencies, but we can't stop there. To maximize our impact, we
must be part of a unified, competent team. This is how HR truly creates
business value.

So what are the attributes of the effective HR department and its impact
on business results? Table 12.3 shows the impact of the dynamic dozen—the
12 key attributes of great HR departments.

These key attributes are essential for the HR team that wants to make
a difference in the business. HR leaders should ask the hard questions of

Table 12.3   *12 Key Attributes of Effective HR Departments*

Attribute	Mean (1–5)	Relative Weighting on Business Success (100 points)
Robust training	3.46	7.30%
Clear roles	3.65	7.60%
Credible board interaction	3.67	7.70%
Aligned structure	3.64	7.80%
Integrated HR solutions	3.50	8.20%
Accountable line managers	3.38	8.20%
Managed outsource vendors	3.49	8.30%
Cultural role models	3.42	8.40%
Measured impact	3.22	8.80%
External stakeholder focus	3.25	8.90%
Aligned HR strategy	3.61	9.20%
Aligned HR initiatives	3.62	9.70%
Multiple regression (R^2)		0.317

themselves and their teams with regard to the extent to which these attri-butes are embedded in their HR departments. These attributes—along with the relative impact they have on business success—are some of the key find-ings of our study:

- *Robust training* (7.3 percent). Training and development are not just for those outside HR; they make a huge difference for those within. We usu-ally think of HR as the department that conducts training for others, but it needs to take some of its own medicine regularly.
- *Clear roles* (7.6 percent). Clear roles and responsibilities are important for different groups within HR such as service centers, centers of expertise, and embedded HR. With clear expectations on how HR work is delineated and coordinated, departments can expect to significantly improve their impact on business success.
- *Credible board interaction* (7.7 percent). Interacting effectively with the board of directors is another measure of good HR teams. Building credibility in this relationship is perhaps one of the most delicate yet critical jobs of HR.
- *Aligned structure* (7.8 percent). Matching the structure of the HR depart-ment with the way the business is organized is another hallmark of excel-lence. Too often HR departments are structured around internal issues and not aligned with the structure of the company. At its best, HR should con-tinuously align itself with the way its business is configured.
- *Integrated HR solutions* (8.2 percent). Effective HR departments ensure that the different functions groups within HR work well together to provide integrated HR solutions. Initiatives, programs, and activities need to mutu-ally reinforce one another and be coordinated toward strategic business ends, rather than springing up as a series of new HR ideas-of-the-month.
- *Accountability of line managers* (8.2 percent). The key to multiplying your impact lies in holding line managers accountable for HR. As the classic Chinese proverb says, "Give a man a fish and he will eat for a day. Teach a man to fish and he will eat for the rest of his life." Successful HR depart-ments know that over time, teaching line managers and holding them accountable will yield the strongest results—and the only sustainable ones.

- *Managed outsource vendors* (8.3 percent). Effective HR departments do not walk away from outsourced HR activities; they manage their products and processes carefully. External vendors need to be continuously appraised and held accountable for how HR activities are supporting business goals.
- *Cultural role models* (8.4 percent). The HR departments with the most impact have taken the unique opportunities and responsibilities to become architects of the organizations' cultures. These departments ensure that they can serve as cultural role models for the rest of the organizations.
- *Measured impact* (8.8 percent). Highly effective HR departments track and measure the impact of HR. They take the time to develop balanced indices and then diligently track and publicize how and where they are making a difference.
- *External stakeholder focus* (8.9 percent). Connecting HR activities to external stakeholder expectations creates real business impact. All divisions of an organization, including and especially HR, need to keep their eyes on the prize: the good opinion of the customers and other important external stakeholders.
- *Aligned HR strategy* (9.2 percent). Great HR departments develop HR strategies that clearly link HR practices to business strategies. Start with the business strategy; next develop your HR strategy. If an HR practice is not contributing to the business strategy, just stop it. Remember: In a world of change, static policies tend to outlive their usefulness!
- *Aligned HR initiatives* (9.7 percent). Ensure that your HR initiatives enable the business to achieve its strategic priorities. An effective HR department works as a unified, competent team to drive home strategic priorities and business results.

The impact of these 12 HR department attributes is significant. In general 31 percent of the impact on business performance can be attributed to the variance in these factors, with the most important being strategic alignment, external stakeholder focus, and measuring HR impact. Do these well as a team and the organization wins.

Regional HR Department Practices That Affect Business Performance

Every region of the world shows a strikingly strong correlation between the 12 attributes of effective HR teams or departments, with especially strong impacts on business performance in Asia, India, Latin America, China, and the Middle East.

With regard to specific HR department attributes for Europe, the United States, Canada, and Africa, aligning HR initiatives has the most impact. For China and Asia, aligning HR strategies come first. For the Middle East, it is external stakeholder focus, while for India, measured impact is highest. For Latin America, the attribute of cultural role models has the greatest impact, and for Australia, clear roles is highest. Finally, for Turkey, robust training has most impact. These differences reflect the cultures and focus of HR in each of these localities.

Comparing the regions with one another, Australia shows a relatively strong impact on business success when emphasizing the attributes of clear roles and aligned structure. The United States and Canada show relatively strong business impact when HR departments get credible board interaction right. Africa shows the strongest impact on business performance when aligned structure and aligned HR initiatives are well done. Turkey shows the greatest impact when HR departments focus on robust training and external stakeholders. In China, the greatest impact comes from managing outsourced vendors well, and in Latin America from working well as an HR team to hold line managers accountable and be cultural role models. Asia is highest on aligned HR strategy, and India sees the highest impact on business success as HR teams focus on tracking and measuring impact.

While there are differences in the relative importance of each attribute by region, in no case are any of the attributes insignificant. In fact in every region of the world, working well as an HR team employing these 12 attributes can make a huge difference on the business performance of any company. You might ask, "To what extent does my HR department exemplify these attributes?" Gaining competence as an individual HR performer is necessary but not sufficient.

Being individually competent and being a part of a highly effective HR department, taken together, will create the winning team for both HR and the global business.

Conclusion

During the past two decades all of us have endured the phases that leadership as a concept went through, as book after book highlighted some aspect of leadership as though it were the whole: *visionary leadership, fast-track leadership, winning leadership, primal leadership, change leadership,* and so on ad nauseam. Finally, a few scholars developed research-based leadership as a concept. For the first time, this study defines HR as a total concept, sparing all of us from the faddism that can characterize leadership work.

This study shows that the fully competent HR professional anywhere in the world should demonstrate powerful skills in each of the six domains. The central question for the senior executive in HR becomes, "How do I design and implement a developmental program for the HR professionals in my organization in each of the regions for which I have responsibility?" Obviously, we conclude that the place to begin is with the six domains: strategic positioner, credible activist, capability builder, change champion, HR innovator and integrator, and technology proponent. Since these domains answer the question of *what* is to be developed, the remaining development paradigms become clear:

- "Where do my people and my department stand vis-à-vis others in my region and in the world?" Obviously this requires assessment using the measures developed in this book. Further, the opportunity now exists to include such measurement as a regular part of performance management.
- "What is the best way to turn such assessments into individual development plans?"
- "How do I develop continuous training, work experiences, task-force assignments, and other opportunities for individuals to expedite their learning in each of the domains according to the needs identified in their individual development plans?"

In addition to individual development, the HR context or culture can also be managed to support the six domains:

- Create in-house newsletters, seminars, training events, and special celebrations that focus on the six domains by highlighting outstanding examples.
- Develop values that support the six domains and make them explicit in performance reviews.
- Connect HR domains to external stakeholder expectations by including them in partnering arrangements.
- Track and measure the impact of HR.

Based on these findings and implications, HR professionals throughout the world should be challenged to learn to do HR from the outside in, which means understanding the social, technological, economic, political, environmental, and demographic trends facing their industries, as well as knowing the specific expectations of their customers, investors, regulators, and communities, and then building internal HR responses that align with these external requirements. Build a relationship of trust with your business leaders by knowing enough about business contexts and key stakeholders to fully engage in business discussions, by offering innovative and integrated HR solutions to business problems, and by being able to audit and improve talent, culture, and leadership. Earn trust by delivering what you promise.

In addition, make sure you understand the key organization capabilities required for your organization to achieve its strategic goals and meet the expectations of customers, investors, and communities. Learn to do an organization audit that focuses on defining and assessing the key capabilities your company requires for success and their implications for staffing, training, compensation, communication, and other HR practices.

Make change happen at individual, initiative, and institutional levels. Help individuals learn and sustain new behaviors. Enable organization change by applying a disciplined process to each organizational initiative. Encourage institutional change by monitoring and adapting the culture to fit external conditions. Be able to make isolated events into integrated and sustainable solutions.

At the same time, innovate and integrate your HR practices. That is, look forward into the future with new and creative ways to design and deliver HR practices. Integrate these practices around talent, leadership, and culture within your organization so as to offer sustainable solutions to business problems. Evolve your organization's HR investments to solve future problems. Master technology to both deliver the administrative work of HR and to connect people inside and outside to one another. Make social media a reality by using technology to share information and connect people both inside and outside your organization.

Finally, we would recommend that for both fully globalized and regional companies, heads of HR work with other companies to create regional consortia that could be mutually funded for the purpose of providing learning in the six domains. The board of directors of such training consortia should come from the participating companies. Such consortia could also develop other specialized HR courses for advanced professionals. A consortium reduces the overall cost of continuous development for individuals while providing a training center that can maintain its competitive edge globally. The consortium can also be located in an existing university but operate with its own funding through the consortium. Many prototypes of this idea already exist: for beverages, electronics, and various designs, for example. The HR executive programs at the Ross School of Business at the University of Michigan can serve as a prototype of the approach.

CHAPTER 13

FUTURE OF GLOBAL HR: WHAT'S NEXT?

13

Dave Ulrich

One of the first times one of the authors presented this competencies research, a participant in the workshop asked, "So what's next?" We were a bit aghast at having just spent a year defining questions, forming partnerships, collecting data, doing statistics, and creating an HR narrative from the research to be asked, "What's next?" We felt that we had just defined the competencies required for HR professionals to be personally effective and have business impact.

But we realize that neither the business world nor the required response is static. Change happens, and that is bound to require new competencies for HR professionals.

Looking back over the two and a half decades of this research, we can see a host of social, technological, economic, political, environmental, and demographic changes in an increasingly global context. When HR loses track of these trends and their organizational implications, its value diminishes—and this happens distressingly often. Ed Lawler and his team have found that HR departments are not changing as fast as the context in which they work.[1] Arthur Yeung and Alejandro Sioli both found in separate studies that HR issues matter more when the pace of change is high.[2] In the 2012 HRCS data, we found that HR matters not because of the pace of change in the industry but because of the organization's ability to adapt to change and to meet specific customer requirements. Organizations that are adaptable and competitive have HR professionals who demonstrate the HR competencies we have identified.

This chapter peeks into the unknown future of HR, following the logic we suggest for HR professionals who want to deliver value:[3]

- What are the contextual and stakeholder changes HR will need to understand and anticipate?
- What are the future requirements for HR in the areas of talent, organization, and leadership?
- What are the implications of business context and requirements on HR for future HR competencies?

Contextual and Stakeholder Changes

The chapters in this book model the context of the future, which will be globally driven, demographically diverse, technologically connected, and economically adaptable.

Globally Driven

Truly global firms have gone through a four-step process: national to international to multinational to global. National firms create products and services exclusively for in-country markets. When firms become international, they export their goods to other countries by developing a global supply chain, manufacturing globally, and opening sales offices or distributorships in other countries. International firms seek efficiency as they drive costs down through standardization so they can compete globally on the basis of price. Firms become multinational when they tailor their goods for different markets and build a presence in each local market. Multinational firms seek effectiveness as they customize services to local conditions. Truly global firms share knowledge, talent, capital, customers, and practices around the world. Global firms seek collaborations with networks that take advantage of synergies across borders.

In the future, companies will probably continue to move along this continuum. Small- and medium-size enterprises, often in Africa and Latin America, will evolve from national to international markets as family businesses grow.

In particular, many local markets in the Middle East, Latin America, Africa, and Asia are being grouped into regional entities. Multinational organizations will shift to becoming global networks. Even state-owned enterprises like those in China and India are likely to attend more to global practices as they learn from others in similar economic conditions.

The future global orientation has a number of implications. First, a global mindset involves more than any specific management or HR practice. Global thinking obviously occurs when someone moves to another country. But it also becomes mandatory for anyone in a local market who has global customers, who relies on a global supply chain, or who faces nondomestic competition. Second, global innovation occurs anywhere. We frequently hear people in traditionally global companies say that their most innovative work is being done in emerging markets that allow more flexibility and face greater demand for change. Their challenge is to use emerging-market innovation to enlighten mature markets. Third, in a flatter, more global world, work can be done anywhere with relatively similar quality but at much lower costs. Labor markets will be increasingly global since hiring for key positions can be done anywhere—and in many cases the work can be transferred anywhere.

The globalization of labor markets makes it difficult to justify hiring and locating work on the basis of mature market compensation. As work becomes more global in nature, so will pay rates. Since work can be done anywhere, a new global compensation equilibrium will raise the standard of living in emerging markets and may potentially lower the standard of living in developed economies. It will cause labor strife in mature markets when pay is reduced because it is impossible to justify being paid much more for essentially the same work. Finally, globalization will require more complex models of cause and effect. Political change in Europe, social reforms in the Middle East, education investments in Australia, and consumer demand in China all affect markets and organizations around the world.

To respond to these global realities, HR professionals need to become global thinkers. They need to make their organizations more global in mindset, processes, and standards. At the same time, they need to help their people and organizations recognize and adapt to local conditions. They should help develop the responsiveness of their companies to global happenings.

Demographically Diverse

Employee demographics have traditionally focused on race, gender, and lifestyle. With the globalization trends, the makeup of the workforce will shift dramatically. We often use some simple exercises in workshops to demonstrate some of these emerging demographic changes:

- How many of your fathers or mothers worked for one company? Generally a majority.
- How many of you will work for only one company? Generally 20 to 40 percent. How many of your children will work for only one company? None. (In three years, with tens of thousands of seminar participants, we have never had anyone say yes, anywhere in the world.) Next generation employees will inevitably have mobile careers.
- How many of your closest friends were born outside your home country? How many of your children's closest friends were born outside your home country? We live in a globally diverse world.
- How many of you have e-mailed or tweeted someone from another country in the past 24 hours? Work is global.
- Who were your company's three largest competitors 10 years ago? Who are the big three today? Who will they be in 10 years? Industries now compete across boundaries.
- How many of you know when Christmas is this year? Most people in Western countries will know; fewer in Eastern countries. How many know when Hanukkah is? Fewer. How many know when Ramadan is? Almost none outside Islamic countries. We live in an increasingly complex world of ethnic backgrounds and interests.
- At what age did your father or mother retire? At what age do you plan to retire? It is almost always older. What about your children? Older still.

While workforce demographic issues vary by region (for example, some parts of the world will soon face gender equity issues and some will not), the faces of the workforce will clearly change as the world becomes more of a global village. HR professionals need to be more sensitive to global demographics. They need to respect people with difference experiences, but they also need to unite those differences into shared organization agendas.

Technologically Connected

Information that creates knowledge that leads to decision making is the new hidden wealth of nations and the competitive advantage of organizations. Technology is what enables globalization and shifts the way people think and act. In China, the knowledge worker has begun to replace the manufacturing worker. As natural resources recede in importance, knowledge resources rise in the Middle East, Africa, and India. After centuries of fighting wars over land and the resources on and in the land, economic and social wars are fought through corralling and amassing information. Ironically, information itself is becoming commoditized; the ability to locate information is ubiquitous. Everyone has access too much of the same information. In today's global environment, some competitive advantage will adhere to companies that identify, import, bundle, share, and apply important information to make insightful decisions. The knowledge stakes have been raised as companies begin to use information as a key differentiator.

Cloud computing and social networking have made information, products, services, and relationships readily accessible. Looking forward, a challenge will be to filter and bundle overwhelming amounts of information into consumable chunks that lead to informed decision making. The analytics of Google, Amazon, and Facebook will need to turn data warehouses into useful insights. It is already possible to envision information and relationship access anywhere, anytime, to anyone. Work that has been defined by physically going to or from an office will change, with subsequent challenges for governance, performance, and relationships. We see this dramatically happening, for example, at Innocentive.com, a website that accesses knowledge on a global scale to solve challenging business problems.[4]

HR professionals need to use technology not only for more efficient delivery of HR transaction work but for better access to information about relationships and networks. In the future, the important field of HR analytics should start by specifying the competitive decisions that need to be made, then finding information to improve them.

Economically Adaptable

Rates of change differ in different parts of the world. Europe, Australia, North America, and other more mature markets anticipate slower economic growth, which requires large organizations to focus on driving down costs and streamlining operations. Africa, China, India, the Middle East, and Asia are growing rapidly and must focus on amassing financial and human capital to keep up with the growth. The role played by government also differs. In some regions, governments are taking a more proactive role in regulation and stimulation of targeted industries; in others, the role of government is reduced enabling private sector growth; and in still others, government is gridlocked and unable to set clear direction. Political stability and cooperation between government and industry will become increasingly necessary for investment.

With globalization, informed citizens, and ubiquitous technology, the cycles of change have shortened. Some regions still encourage leaders to have long-term visions and aspirations decades out, but most organization planning occurs in years or months. When it is nearly impossible to predict an ever-changing future, the so-called long term is increasingly shorter. Less attention is paid to long-term planning and more to short-term, opportunistic responsiveness.

HR professionals who anticipate economic and regulatory conditions will help their organizations build a capacity for change that outpaces competitors. Changeable organizations will be more likely to succeed over time and HR should lead and model those changes.

Future Requirements for HR

Given the prospects for external change, we anticipate a future where human ingenuity and organization capability, as guided by insightful line and HR leaders, will emerge as the new frontier of competitive advantage. Different global regions may take different paths to achieve competitive advantage, but the agendas around talent, organization, and leadership are similar.

In this changing competitive landscape, HR will probably become more granular, that is, increasingly broken down into more definitive, customized forms. Rather than one type of organization, we will probably see many types. In Africa, the Middle East, India, and China, for example, we envision three: privately owned organizations controlled by families and other relational networks; SMEs that are rapidly growing (and sometimes failing); and large state-owned enterprises and multinational corporations. Tailoring HR practices to each of these organization types will be important.

Granularity will also apply to employees. Along with mass customization, as products are tailored for specific markets and even individuals, we envision mass personalization of the employee value proposition. Employees, particularly high-performance knowledge workers, will create a tailored work environment that personalizes where they work, what they work on, and what they get from doing their work.

Yet even with emerging business conditions and HR granularity, we envision HR continuing to focus on three demands: talent, organization, and leadership. We continue to be struck by how much the HR profession has fallen prey to the talent trap, defining effective HR almost exclusively through improvements in talent. We strongly believe (and the research behind this volume shows) that without the right organization culture, capability, or processes, talent success is not sustainable. Great organizations outperform great individual people who are coping with ineffective organizations. The competitive challenge is to make the organizational whole more productive than the sum of talented individuals. Leaders have the charge of bringing talent and organization together.

Talent

By whatever name it goes, talent (workforce, people, human capital, competence) will be critical for the future. Talent ultimately results in productivity, which shows up in financial and customer results. Several trends seem likely to affect efforts to boost productivity through talent:

- *From sporadic investment in talent to disciplined and consistent investment.* Many regions of the world realize that more talented employees will be a key to their economic sustainability. This implies lifetime education, not merely a degree or certificate. Career-long investments in learning through training and development both on the job and through life experiences are likely to increase. The aging of the global workforce and the mandate for fast cycle-time in employee skill upgrading will both drive this trend.

- *From war for talent to Marshal Plan for talent.* The war for talent metaphor has dominated HR thought for more than a decade.[5] A war implies winners and losers. We like the metaphor of a Marshal Plan for talent, where investments are made so that everyone succeeds. This will focus talent not just on individual success but also on collective success, both within companies and across industries.

- *From competence to commitment to contribution.* Competence clearly matters; brighter people with greater skills generally can do more. Commitment also matters because those who work harder get more done. But we envision a shift toward contribution and meaning. When people find meaning and purpose in their work, they are more committed and demonstrate more competence— and they are more likely to stay with the company that offers this sense of purpose.

- *From work–life balance to life–work integration.* Today, as with our parents and theirs, work is often a place to go and to return from. With technology woven into our lives, however, work is becoming something that can occur almost anywhere, and this change will continue. When people go to work, they will be going to meet with others to solve problems together, but when they need to accomplish something by themselves, they will probably do so away from the traditional office setting—at home, in work clubs, in hotels, in customer offices, and so on. This increased life–work integration is likely to appeal to the next generation of employees, who seek more control over and flexibility in their work.

- *From domestic to global.* No one can escape global talent requirements. As knowledge work replaces physical work, the work itself becomes transportable. Since knowledge has no borders, employees may be sourced from any country in the world to solve knowledge problems. People also have to learn to work with others with very different backgrounds and cultures. Some regions, countries, and organizations may experience brain drain if they cannot find ways to attract and retain the brightest and most mobile talent.

- *From stable to flexible careers.* As noted earlier, few people entering the workforce will intend to stay a lifetime in a single company. Instead, they will expect to work on projects and tasks in different companies. Career mobility has implications for working in teams, for portable healthcare and retirement benefits, and for redefining loyalty.

These six talent trends do not capture the entire global granularity of talent, but they indicate some talent challenges ahead for HR professionals seeking to drive productivity.

Organization Capabilities

Organization capabilities represent what the organization is known for, what it is good at doing, and how it patterns activities to deliver value. The capability approach to organizations builds on other approaches. For the systems movement, capabilities represent the unifying maypole around which separate systems revolve. For the morphology or bureaucracy movement, capabilities represent the outcomes of the organization design. For the efficiency movement, capability logic broadens the outcomes of organizations beyond efficiency.

Shaping the right organization through a capability lens synthesizes four current approaches to organization assessment. Applying the *culture perspective* means finding the right organization values, norms, or patterns.[6] Applying a *process lens* means identifying and improving key processes such as new product development, continuous improvement, product diversification, order-to-remittance cycles, innovation, and so forth. These processes often stand out through balanced scorecard assessments of organization alignment.[7] Applying the *core competencies* logic focuses on upgrading functional activities like R&D, manufacturing, quality, marketing, supply chain, HR, and information technology.[8] And taking a *resource view* means identifying key resources that an organization possesses to create value.[9] The capability logic synthesizes and advances these approaches to enable HR to create the right organization.[10]

In recent years, assorted lists of generic and possible capabilities have been proposed. George Stalk suggests that organizations might have capabilities of speed, consistency, acuity (ability to see a competitive landscape), agility, and innovativeness.[11] Korn Ferry, the consulting firm, lists capabilities that build strategic effectiveness, identifying 20 of them in eight categories.[12] Ulrich and Smallwood began by identifying 10 core capabilities that organizations might possess and subsequently have added to this list.[13]

In the future, we expect to see organizations pursuing a number of critical capabilities:

- *Flexibility.* With changing technologies, demographics, political systems, and economic conditions, organizations will have to become more flexible. This flexibility may apply to speed of change in products or services, to work conditions or settings, to career paths, to planning cycles, or to other business processes. Organizations that have the ability to adapt quickly and continually will be likely to succeed.
- *Collaboration.* Work increasingly becomes a team sport; no single individual has the capacity to handle the complex global requirements of tomorrow's markets. Collaboration may occur across levels within an organization, within teams, across business units within an organization, with alliance partners around the world, and with online social networks. These multiple types of collaboration will change the way problems are identified and solved.
- *Social responsibility.* As Millennials move up the ladder, they will carry their values with them. These values will probably include an increased sensitivity to issues around the environment (matters such as carbon footprint or alternative energy), philanthropy and commitment to give back to the community, and flexible work–life policies, all which amount to a new employee contract. Organizations out to do good for their employees will need to do good to the world in which employees live.
- *Complexity.* Increased information, globalization, granularity, and other changes make the world more complex. Organizations that can find simplicity in complexity will be most likely to succeed. In today's world, this is the elegance of Apple's interface on the iPad and iPod, the simple design which has enabled millions to access the power of information. This trend is likely to continue not only in products and services but also in how organizations operate.

- *Integrity.* Corruption continues to be an issue in many parts of the world. In emerging markets it manifests as pressure to buy your way into the marketplace, and even in mature markets some leaders abuse their power and authority. Labor in many global markets is one of the most critical factors, so corruption in the hiring process may need to be addressed and overcome. In developed economies, integrity means complying with the letter and the spirit of law for the best interest of many and not just pursuing the best interest of the few, as leaders did at Enron and Lehman Brothers. Becoming transparent and accountable for HR practices can help build integrity as an organization capability.
- *Risk management.* In some organizations today, strategy discussions increasingly revolve around risk. The risks include environment, regulation, operations, economic, and culture. Organizations that can assess and manage risk as they move into new markets will be more likely to succeed.

We are sure we have not identified all the organization capabilities required for the future. Nonetheless, this list covers organization outcomes HR professionals should be attending to.

Leadership

Leaders have the dual responsibility of sourcing talent and creating organization capabilities. In this round of the study, we found that the ability to create leaders (individuals who get the right things done) and establish leadership throughout the organization is a critical competence and role for HR professionals. As we contemplate leadership for the business context we described, we see three trends:

- *From command and control to coach, collaborate, and communicate.* Leaders get things done through others. In complex, changing global organizations, leaders cannot govern by observing or telling others what to do. They have to get things done through a shared commitment to common goals. Management by mindset needs to replace management by objectives. When leaders can create a shared mindset, or commitment to a common goal and process to reach the goal, they get others to do the right things for the right reasons. Managing by mindset comes through coaching and communicating more than commanding and controlling. In particular, with the high expectations and flexibility held by the next generation, leaders who impose will lose talent; those who engage will gain it.

- *From why and what to how.* In our leadership work, we find that many leaders know why they should improve—they understand that better leadership boosts productivity, customer share, and financial performance. These leaders are often able to tell us what they should do to improve because their 360-degree feedback results, performance reviews, or personal insights have made the need clear. But they still don't do it. We think leadership in the future will increasingly attend to how leaders do what they know they should do. We call this *leadership sustainability* and believe that HR professionals should help leaders not only figure out why and what they should do but also how to do it.
- *From leader to leadership.* Leaders are the specific individuals who direct work, often at the top of a company. Leadership exists all the way through the organization, in both domestic and global markets. Effective leaders work to optimize their teams and individuals within their teams; leadership seeks to integrate the entire hierarchy of leaders to optimize organization-wide performance. Leadership becomes particularly important in emerging markets where local leaders need to replace expatriates.

When HR professionals grasp the importance of leadership throughout an organization, they ensure sustainability over time.

Future HR Competencies

If these projections are accurate, the competencies for HR professionals are relatively easy to identify. The world will change and so will many of the competencies of HR professionals. Based on our experiences in the past, we anticipate that by 2017 (when we will do the next round of the HRCS), probably 20 to 30 percent of the 140 behavioral questions will be different.

The HR professionals of a half decade from now are apt to need specific competencies in the categories of future change. Some possibilities:

- Context and stakeholder changes
  - Do you build the capabilities of a global organization?
  - Do you develop global thinking throughout your organization?
  - Do you transfer innovative ideas or practices from one part of the world to another?
  - Do you recognize the implications of external changes and translate them into HR practices and other business processes?
  - Do you create a truly global workforce based on where the work can be done at the highest quality, in the fastest manner, and at the lowest cost?
  - Do you use technology to collect, share, and use information that gives your organization a competitive advantage?
  - Do you help your organization anticipate important but frequently subtle external changes and ensure that such changes receive appropriate executive attention?
- HR granularity
  - Do you customize HR practices to specific employee needs?
  - Do you offer local solutions to global challenges?
  - Do you simplify corporate messages and processes in the face of an increasingly complex and globalized world?
- Talent
  - Do you invest in lifetime learning for key employees?
  - Do you focus on retaining top talent?
  - Do you focus on fully applying the collective skills, knowledge, and experience of your workforce?
  - Do you help employees find meaning and purpose in their work?
  - Do you offer employees flexibility about where and how they work?
- Organization capabilities
  - Do you create an organization that has each of the following capabilities:
    Flexibility?
    Collaboration?

Social responsibility?

Turning complexity into simplicity?

Integrity?

Risk management?

- Leadership
  - Do you encourage leadership sustainability?
  - Do you build integrated leadership capability throughout the entire organization hierarchy?

We know that these are not all the requirements for HR in the future. Others will undoubtedly emerge. Over the next five years, along with our global partners, we will listen carefully to the whispers of business and try to hear future challenges where HR professionals can make a difference.

Looking Ahead

This book has focused on HR professionals and leaders on every continent and across the world. We appeal to those who are interested in knowing how to add value through HR within their respective geographical regions as they understand and apply HR best practices from around the world. We also appeal to those who are interested in forging high-performing organizations on a global scale.

We are optimistic that the future of HR offers incredible challenges and opportunities. For HR professionals who intend to add substantive value in their appropriate places at the strategy table, we hope we have identified what needs to happen in each region and worldwide.

ENDNOTES

Chapter 1

1. Tata Group Financials. http://www.tata.com/htm/Group_Investor_Group Financials.htm. Accessed on April 6, 2012.

2. Kneale, K. 2009. "World's Most Reputable Companies: The Rankings." *Forbes*. May 6.

3. Tata Companies. http://www.tata.com/businesses/sectors/index.aspx?sectid =aZ72PXPwpaI=. Accessed on April 3, 2012.

4. Tata Group Mergers and Acquisitions. http://www.tata.com/htm/Group_ MnA_YearWise.htm. Accessed on April 3, 2012.

5. Fan, J. P. H., Wei, K. C. J, and Hu, H. 2010. "Corporate finance and governance in emerging markets; a selective review and an agenda for future research." *Journal of Corporate Finance*. 17:2: 207–214.

6. Prahalad, C. K. 2005. *The Fortune at the Bottom of the Pyramid*. Upper Saddle River, NJ: Wharton School Publishing.

7. Bowonder, B., Kumar, S. Kumar, R., and Sridharan, A. 2009. *Innovation and Innovativeness: The Tata Experience*. Mumbai: Group Publications.

8. "The World's Most Innovative Companies." *BusinessWeek,* April 28, 2008.

9. "India's Tata Group." In Global Giving Matters. http://www.synergos.org/ globalgivingmatters/features/0503tatagroup.htm. Accessed on April 9, 2012.

10. Interview with Satish Pradhan on April 12, 2012.

11. Brockbank, W. and Ulrich, D. 2006. "Higher Knowledge for Higher Aspirations." *Human Resource Management Journal*. 44: 4: 489–504.

12. Ulrich, D., Brockbank, W., Johnson, D., Sandholtz, K, and Younger, J. 2008. *HR Competencies: Mastery at the Intersection of People and Business*. Published by the Society of Human Resource Management and the RBL Group.

13. This summary is provided from a working paper from Merouane Merzoug, "The Environment for Global Business."

14. Kerr, S. 1995. "On the folly of rewarding A, while hoping for B." *Academy of Management Executive*. 9:1:7–14.

15. Ulrich, D. and Smallwood, N. 2007. *Leadership Brand*. Boston, MA: Harvard Business School Press.

16. *Ibid.*

17. For a detailed description of our analytical procedures, see Ulrich, D. Brockbank, W. Johnson, D., Sandholtz, K., and Younger, J. 2008. *HR Competencies: Mastery at the Intersection of People and Business.* The RBL Institute and The Society for Human Resource Management.

Chapter 2

1. "Stunning Cocoa Grab Could Hike Prices, Lower Quality." AolNews, July 19, 2010. Available online: www.aolnews.com/2010/07/19/stunning-cocoa-grab-could-hike-prices-lower-quality/. Accessed on April 22, 2012.

2. Pew forum, http://features.pewforum.org/muslim-population/.

3. Younger, Jon, Smallwood N., and Ulrich, D. "Developing as a Talent Developer." *HR Planning Journal.* On press.

4. Ulrich, D. and Smallwood, N. 2006. *Leadership Brand*. Boston: Harvard Business Press.

5. Ulrich, Dave, Smallwood, N., and Sweetman, K. 2007. *The Leadership Code*. Boston: Harvard Business Press.

6. Grochowski, J. and Lawrence, K. 2012. "Social Media and HR Implications." RBL Mini-forum White Paper. Available at RBL.net.

7. Plummer, D. C. and Middleton, P. 2012. "Predicts 2012: Four Forces Combine to Transform the IT Landscape." In Gartner Research: http://www.gartner.com/technology/research/predicts.

Chapter 3

1. Mathabane, M. 1998. *Kaffir Boy: An Autobiography*. New York: Touchstone.

2. Krause, K. 2010. *True Size of Africa.* FlowingData.com

3. World Bank. 2000. *Can Africa Claim the 21st Century?* Washington, D.C.

4. Schwab, K. 2011. *The Global Competitiveness Report 2011–2012*. Geneva: World Economic Forum.

5. Pennington, S. 2011. *University Rankings*. Johannesburg: SAGoodNews .co.za.

6. International Fund for Agricultural Development (IFAD). 2011. *New challenges, new opportunities: African agriculture in the 21st century*. Cape Town: ifad.org.

7. Waki, N. 2012. *Investors see Africa as most attractive destination–EIU poll.* London: Reuters.

Chapter 4

1. Warner, M. 2002. "Globalisation, labour markets and human resources in Asia-Pacific economies: An overview." *International Journal of Human Resources Management,* 13(3): 384–398; Rowley, C., Benson, J. 2002. "Convergence and divergence in Asian HRM." *California Management Review,* Winter, 44(2): 90–109; Harzing, A., Pinnington, A. (eds.) 2010. *International Human Resource Management,* 3d ed., London: Sage; Nankervis, A. R., Cooke, F. L., Chatterjee S. R., Warner M. 2012. *New models of HRM in China and India.* London: Routledge.
2. Wilson, P. 2010. "The future of work and the changing workplace: Challenges and issues for Australian HR practitioners." Melbourne: AHRI; OECD. 2012. *Global Statistics,* Geneva: OECD.
3. OECD 2012, *op. cit.*
4. OECD 2012, *op. cit.*
5. Wilson, P. 2010, *op. cit.,* p. 7.
6. ECD 2012, *op. cit*
7. OECD 2012, *op. cit*
8. Boxall, P. 2003. "HR strategy and competitive advantage in the service sector." *Human Resource Management Journal,* 13: 3: 5–20.
9. Blondell, J. 2009. "People driving business." *hrmonthly,* December.
10. Blondell, J. 2009, "People and business both come first." *hrmonthly,* December.
11. Ibid.
12. AHRI 2012. *HR Practitioner and the HR Profession,* Melbourne: AHRI.
13. Boxall, P., *op. cit*
14. Goodyear, L. 2012. "Turning the Tide: Australia's Best in HR & Business Leadership 2011." *hrmonthly,* February.
15. *Ibid.*
16. Mackey, K. and Boxall, P. 2007. "The relationship between high performance work practices and employee attitudes: an investigation of additive and interaction[0]effects." *International Journal of Human Resource Management,* 18: 4: 537–567.

17. AHRI/CEDA. 2003. "HR: Creating business solutions—A positioning paper." Melbourne: AHRI.

18. *Ibid.*, pp. 5–6.

19. Wilson, P. 2010. *op. cit.*, p. 3.

20. *Ibid.*, p. 12.

21. *Ibid.*, p. 3

22. Fisher, C., Dowling, P. 1999, "Support for an HR approach: The perspective of senior HR managers." *Asia Pacific Journal of Human Resources,* 37(1): 1–19.

23. AHRI. 2012. *HR Practitioner and the HR Profession.* Melbourne: AHRI.

24. *Ibid.*

25. *Ibid.*

26. *Ibid.*

27. Blondell, J. 2010. "HR on the bottom line." *hrmonthly,* December.

28. Nankervis, A., Compton, R., Baird, M., and Coffey, J. 2011. *Human Resource Management: Strategies & Practices.* Melbourne: Cengage Learning.

29. Howarth, B., 201, [0] "On the move." *hrmonthly,* September.

30. *Ibid.*

31. *Ibid.*

32. Blondell, J. 2010. "Transforming culture." *hrmonthly,* December.

33. Boyd, C. 2010. "Leading the way." *hrmonthly,* December.

Chapter 5

1. Yeung, Arthur and Shen, L. 2011. *Haidilao: Winning by Service Differentiation.* CEIBS case.

2. *Ibid.*

3. Wong, Richard. 2012. "Another Look at China's 12th 5-Year Plan." Presentation at ICEDR Workshop, Hong Kong.

4. Yeung, Arthur. 2012. "Going global as third round of strategic thrust: Dialogue with Xiang Wenbo." *CEIBS Business Review.* February, pp.101–102.

5. Yeung, Arthur and Dai, N. 2010. *Mindray: Chinese Talent, World Class Products.* CEIBS Case.

6. 2009. Huawei Social Responsibility Report.

7. Yeung, Arthur, 2010. *Organizational Capability: Secrets of Sustainable Business Success.* China Machine Press.

8. Yeung, Arthur & Brockbank, Wayne. 1995. "Reengineering HR through information technology." *Human Resource Planning Journal*, 18:2 pp.24–37.

Chapter 6

1. European Union Official Website. "Basic Information on the European Union." http://europa.eu/about-eu/basic-information/index_en.htm. Accessed on May 3, 2012.
2. The World Bank. "GDP per person employed statistics." http://data.worldbank.org/indicator/SL.GDP.PCAP.EM.KD. Accessed on May 4, 2012.
3. European Union Official Website. "Real GDP Growth Rate Volume." http://epp.eurostat.ec.europa.eu/tgm/table.do;jsessionid=9ea7974b30dd 8549af6fd90a4215b5a4bd09638f55ac.e34SbxiPb3uSb40Lb34LaxqRb30N e0?tab=table&plugin=1&language=en&pcode=tsieb020. Accessed on April 30, 2012.
4. Karsten Breum, Vice-President of Human Resources. A.P. Møller-Mærsk A/S. From an interview given on May 18, 2012.
5. Eurostat Press Office. "Euro Area Unemployment Rate at 10.9%." http://epp.eurostat.ec.europa.eu/portal/page/portal/publications/collections/news_releases. Accessed on May 2, 2012.
6. The RBL Group. "Top Companies for Leaders 2011." http://rbl.net/index.php/research/detail/top-companies-for-leaders–2011. Accessed on May 6, 2012.
7. Eurostat Press Office. "Hourly Labour Costs Ranged Between €3.5 and €39.3 in the EU 27 Member States." http://epp.eurostat.ec.europa.eu/portal/page/portal/publications/collections/news_releases. Accessed on May 5, 2012.
8. "Sarkozy, Hollande. "Advance in French Vote; Far Rights Le Pen Gets 20%." *World News on MSNBC,* http://worldnews.msnbc.msn.com/_news/2012/04/22/11331803-sarkozy-hollande-advance-in-french-vote-far-rights-le-pen-gets–20-percent?lite. Accessed on April 22, 2012.
9. Walker, Peter and Taylor, Matthew. "Far Right on Rise in Europe." *The Guardian* (UK), http://www.guardian.co.uk/world/2011/nov/06/far-right-rise-europe-report. Accessed on November 6, 2011.
10. Mayrhofer, W., Sparrow P., and Brewster C. 2012. *European Human Resource Management: A Contextualised Stakeholder Perspective.*

11. Westervelt, Eric. "In Norway, Law Promotes Women in Boardroom." *NPR* (Norway), http://www.npr.org/templates/story/story.php?storyId= 111673448. Accessed on August 10, 2009.

12. Maria Maria, senior director, Group Human Resources. A.P. Møller-Mærsk A/S. From an interview given on May 30, 2012.

13. OECD Official Website. "Work-Life Balance." http://bli.oecdcode.org/ topics/work-life-balance/. Accessed on May 4, 2012.

14. Oudhuis, M. and Tenglad, S. 2012. "Standardization and self-management a solvable dilemma?" Paper presented at the 6th Nordic Working Life Conference, Helsingør, Denmark, April 25–27, 2012. http://www.sfi. dk/Files/Filer/Nordic%20working%20life%20conference% 202012/General%20stream/SELF-MANAGEMENT_OCH_ STANDARDIZATION16april2012.pdf. Accessed on May 19, 2012.

15. European Union Official Website, *Fertility Statistics,* http://epp.eurostat .ec.europa.eu/statistics_explained/index.php/Fertility_statistics. Accessed on May 6, 2012.

Chapter 7

1. http://web.worldbank.org/external/default/main?theSitePK=659149 &pagePK=2470434&contentMDK=20370107&menuPK=659160&p iPK=2470429. Accessed April 17, 2012.

2. http://indiatoday.intoday.in/story/ICICI+ranked+45th+among+100+ most+valuable+global+brands/1/95113.html. Accessed April 21, 2012.

3. Interview with K. Ramkumar on April 16, 2012. Mr. Ramkumar is an executive director and member of the board of directors of ICICI Bank Limited.

4. Ibid.

5. http://zeenews.india.com/business/news/economy/professional-forecasters-lower-fy13-gdp-growth-to-6-5-rbi_56969.html

6. Chakrabarty, K. C. 2009. India's economic transformation. Inaugural address to the Antique India Markets Conference in Mumbai.

7. http://www.dbresearch.de/PROD/DBR_INTERNET_DE-PROD /PROD0000000000253735.pdf. Accessed on April 21, 2012.

8. "A special report on India." *The Economist.* November 11, 2008.

9. Bloom, D. E. 2011. "Population dynamics in India and implications for economic growth." Work Paper No. 65. Harvard Initiative for Global Health.

10. http://www.transparency.org/policy_research/surveys_indices/cpi/2009/cpi_2009_table. Accessed April 21, 2012.

11. Hewlett, S.A. and Rashid, R. 2011. *Winning the War for Talent in Emerging Markets*. Boston, MA: Harvard Business Review Press.

12. Kumar, N. 2009. *India's Global Powerhouses*. Boston, MA: Harvard Business Press.

13. Prahalad, C. K. 2005. *The Fortune at the Bottom of the Pyramid*. Upper Saddle River, NJ: Wharton School Publishing.

14. Kumar, *ibid.*

15. http://www.manpowerindia.net/hr-jobs.html. Accessed April 20, 2012.

16. Mr. L. Prabhakar played an invaluable role in orchestrating the availability of the specific cases throughout the remainder of this chapter. Mr. Prabhakar is the vice president of HR of the Agri Business Division of ITC Limited and is on the board of the National HRD Network.

17. Information for this case was contributed by Mr. Arun Leslie George, senior vice president and head of HR at Coromandel International, on April 22, 2012.

18. Information for this case was contributed by Mr. Ashutosh Telang, executive vice president and head human resources at Marico Limited, on April 22, 2012

19. Information for this case was contributed by Mr. Yogi Sriram, senior vice president—Leadership Planning & Talent Acquisition, Larsen & Toubro Limited, on April 22, 2012.

20. Information for this case was contributed by Mr. D. K. Srivasatava, corporate vice president and global HR head of HCL Technologies, on April 26, 2012.

21. Information for this case was contributed by Mr. S. Y. Siddiqui, managing executive officer administration, on April 22. 2012.

22. Information for this case was contributed by Mr. Krish Shankar, executive director—HR and member of the Airtel Management Board, on April 23, 2012.

23. Information for this case was contributed by Mr. Soumen Chakraborty, president—corporate of Dr. Reddy's Laboratories, on April 21, 2012.

24. Information for this case was contributed by Mr. Prince Augustin, EVP for Group Human Capital and Leadership Development, on April 22, 2012.

25. Information for this case was contributed by Mr. Pratik Kumar, executive vice president, human resources at Wipro and president at Wipro Infrastructure Engineering, on April 22, 2012

Chapter 8
1. Full list at: cpi.transparency.org/cpi2011/results/.
2. http://www.americamovil.com/amx/en/cm/about/intro.html?p=28.
3. PISA. 2009. Executive Summary, http://www.oecd.org/dataoecd/34/60/46619703.pdf.
4. http://www.latinbusinesschronicle.com/app/article.aspx?id=5601.
5. http://www.repsol.com/es_es/corporacion/prensa/notas-de-prensa/ultimas-notas/12052010-carabobo.aspx.

Chapter 9
1. *CEO Quarterly.* Q1, 2011
2. Med Jones, president, International Institute of Management. Interview Part 4 "GCC Economic Outlook." *CEO Quarterly,* January 3, 2011.
3. The CEO Magazine. Q1, 2011. GCC Economic Outlook 2011: GCC Opportunities and Risks. *CEO Quarterly*, pp. 28–30.
4. Forstenlechner, I. 2010. "Workforce localization in emerging Gulf economies: the need to fine-tune HRM." Personnel Review, 39(1), 135–152.
5. See, for example, Emirates Centre for Strategic Studies and Research. January 23, 2012, GCC Budgets and Economic Outlook for 2012.
6. Office of the Chief Economist. December 2011. The GCC: Economic Outlook 2012. Riyadh: Samba Financial Group.
7. World Economic and Financial Surveys. October 2011. Regional Economic Outlook: Middle East and Central Asia. Washington, USA: International Monetary Fund.
8. The CEO Magazine. Q1 2011 "GCC Economic Outlook 2011: GCC Opportunities and Risks." *CEO Quarterly*, pp. 28–30.
9. *Ibid.*
10. Al-Jazzaf, D. M., & Al-Mutairi, E. May 17–21, 2009. Kuwait Team's Report on Kuwait Vision 2035. Knowledge Economy Workshop. Alexandria, Egypt.
11. Economic Research Department, National Bank of Kuwait. August 19, 2010. Kuwait's new development plan. Kuwait City, Kuwait.

12. Key forecast for individual GCC countries. Samba Report, December 2011, page 7.

13. Saudi Arabia announced that it will phase out domestic wheat production by 2016 in order to save water. "The GCC in 2020: Outlook for the Gulf and the Global Economy." The Economist Intelligence Unit Limited. 2009. London.

14. Saudi to increase desalinated water production. *Technical Review Middle East*, 27: 3, 2011.

15. Nasser, A. 2012. "Human Capital Investment: Strategies for the Arabian Gulf." Keynote address at the 11th ASHRM International Conference & Exhibition. Abu Dhabi. March 26, 2012.

16. According to the report, Qatar National Bank SAQ : GCC population growth forecast to reach 50 million in 2013.

17. During the Day 2 (March 27, 2012) of the panel discussion at ASHRM2012 (the 11th ASHRM International Conference and Exhibition, Abu Dhabi, March 25–28, 2012), when asked, "Do academic institutions, professional services companies and consultants, possess the appropriate skills, methods and tools to adequately train and develop the workforce of the future?"—whether universities in the region do a good job at producing high-quality graduates—less than 1 percent of the audience agreed.

18. ASHRM2012 papers presented by Dr. David Hathorn, "Professional standards and their relevance to the Middle East," and Dr. John Maxwell, "HR Certification & Standards: The facts as they are!"

19. Katou, A. A., Budhwar, P. S., Woldu, H., & Al-Hamadi, A. B. 2010. Influence of ethical beliefs, national culture and institutions on preferences for HRM in Oman. *Personnel Review*, 39(6), 728–745.

20. Professor Philippe Fargues. Director, Migration Policy Centre, European University Institute (EUI) and Professor Nasra M. Shah, Kuwait University.

21. 2011. National Offices of Statistics. Fargues.

22. 2011. Socio-economic impacts of GCC migration—Professor Philippe Fargues and Professor Nasra M. Shah.

23. Hausmann, R., Tyson, L. D., and Zahidi, S. 2011. The Global Gender Gap Report. World Economic Forum Insight Report.

24. Women face a particularly difficult labor market situation. The ratio of female-to-male unemployment rates in most regions exceeds 1.0, but in the Middle East the regional ratio was as high as 2.3 in 2011. International

Labor Office. 2012. "Global Employment Trends 2012: Preventing a deeper jobs crisis." Geneva: International Labour Organization.

25. Elamin, A. M. and Omair, K. (2010). "Males' attitudes toward working females in Saudi Arabia [Electronic Version]." *Personnel Review*, 39(6), 746–766.

26. Hammouya, M. 1999. Statistics on Public Sector Employment; Methods, Structures and Trends. International Labor Organization, Geneva.

27. 2012. "Mobily Interacts with Twitter." January 22, *Arab News*.

Chapter 10

1. Browning, E. S. 2011. "Retiring Boomers Find 401 (k) Plans Fall Short." *The Wall Street Journal*. February 19. http://online.wsj.com/article/SB10 001424052748703959604576152792748707356.html Accessed from on June 3, 2012.

2. Cited from Progressive Debt Relief.http://www.progressiverelief.com /consumer-debt-statistics.html. Accessed at on June 3, 2012.

3. Anderson, S., Collins, C., Klinger, S., and Pizzigati, S. 2011. "Executive Excess 2011: The Massive CEO Rewards for Tax Dodging." http://www. ips-dc.org/reports/executive_excess_2011_the_massive_ceo_rewards_ for_tax_dodging. Accessed on June 3, 2012.

4. Donlon, J. P. 2008 "Lafley's Law: If You Want to Win Become a Game Changer." Chief Executive.net. http://chiefexecutive.net/author/j_p_ donlon/page/9. Accessed on June 3, 2012.

5. Hsieh, T. 2010. *Delivering Happiness: A Path to Profits, Passion and Purpose*. Hachette Book Group, Inc.

6. Lafley, A. G. and Charan, R. 2008. *Game Changer: How You Can Drive Revenue and Profit Growth with Innovation*. New York: Random House.

7. Lafley, A. G. and Charan, R. 2008. "The Consumer Is Boss." *Fortune*, March 10, pp. 121–126.

Chapter 11

1. 2007. Global Economic Paper No. 153. Goldman Sachs.

2. Turkey Supreme Election Board website, results of 2011 general elections, The exact number is 49.83 percent. www.ysk.gov.tr.

3. Annual Economic Report 2011, p. 31, 49. Turkish Ministry of Finance.

4. "Turkish Economy—Inflation, Association of Treasury Controllers." www.hazine.org.tr.

5. Turkey Outbound M&A Report. 2012. January, p. 3. Deloitte Turkey.

ABOUT THE AUTHORS

Dave Ulrich

Dave Ulrich is a professor at the Ross School of Business, University of Michigan and a partner at The RBL Group, a consulting firm focused on helping organizations and leaders deliver value. He studies how organizations build capabilities of leadership, speed, learning, accountability, and talent through leveraging Human Resources. He has published over 200 articles and book chapters and over 25 books. He edited *Human Resource Management* 1990–1999; served on the editorial boards of four journals, the Board of Directors for Herman Miller, and the Board of Trustees at Southern Virginia University; and is a Fellow at the National Academy of Human Resources. He has received numerous honors and wide recognition for his work. He has consulted and done research with over half of the Fortune 200 and speaks frequently in national conferences and company events. His e-mail is dou@umich.edu and The RBL Group can be found at http://www.rbl.net.

Wayne Brockbank

Wayne Brockbank is a clinical professor of business at the University of Michigan's Ross School of Business. At the Ross School of Business, Dr. Brockbank is a cofaculty director and core instructor of the Advanced Human Resource Executive Program, the world's number one rated HR executive program. He serves on the core faculty of Michigan's senior management executive programs in India. He has been on the visiting faculty at universities in other countries, including Argentina, Saudi Arabia, Kuwait, Australia, China, Indonesia, Great Britain, the Netherlands, India, Korea, and the Czech Republic. His research focuses on linkages between business strategy and human resource practices, creating high performance corporate cultures, and organization levers that drive business performance. He has consulted on these topics with leading companies on every continent. Professor Brockbank completed his PhD at UCLA where he specialized in organization theory, business strategy, and international business. wbrock@umich.edu.

Jon Younger

Jon Younger is a partner in The RBL Group and leads the firm's strategic HR practice. He has coauthored four books, many articles, and book chapters and consults widely in the Americas, Europe, and Asia. He has taught at the

University of Toronto, where he received his Ph.D., and has been a member of the executive education faculties of the Indian School of Business and the University of Michigan. He and his wife, Carolyn, divide their time between New York City and bucolic New Jersey.

Mike Ulrich

Mike's background is focused on research methods and statistical analysis. He holds both BS and MS degrees in statistics with emphasis on business analysis. Mike has experience in a wide variety of statistical methods, including ANOVA, sample and survey design, structural equation modeling, Bayesian hierarchical models, stochastic processes, and nonparametrics. He has worked on a variety of statistical projects from exit polling to the relationship between job performance and satisfaction.

6. Annual Tirkiss M&A Review 2011. January 2012. Deloitte Turkey.
7. Demirkaya, Harun. 2006. *The Organization of HRM*. p.18. Kocaeli University.
8. Facebook Statistics by Country. www.socialbakers.com.

Chapter 12

1. 2008. *The NBF Daily Bulletin*. September 11. Bloomberg/Reuters: Canada.
2. Bloomberg.com/news/2012–03–13/Viterra/s-soaring-on-takeover-talk-still -bargaining.
3. Friedman, Thomas L. 2005. *The World is Flat: A Brief History of the Twenty-First Century*. New York: Farrar, Straus and Giroux.
4. 2011. "Tracking global trends: how six key developments are shaping the business world." Ernst and Young Documents. EYG No. DK0061.
5. Das, Gurcharan. 2002. *India Unbound: The Social and Economic Revolution from Independence to the Global Information Age*. Sydney: Anchor.

Chapter 13

1. Boudreau, John and Lawler, Edward E III. 2012. "How HR Spends Its Time: It Is Time for a Change." Working paper, Center for Effective Organizations. http://ceo.usc.edu/bookstore/.

   Boudreau, John and Lawler, Edward E III. 2009. Achieving Excellence in Human Resources Management: An Assessment of Human Resource Functions. Palo Alto: Stanford University Press.
2. Yeung, Kwok On. 1990. *Cognitive Consensuality and Organizational Performance: A Systematic Assessment*. Ph.D. Dissertation, University of Michigan, Ann Arbor.

   Yeung, Arthur, Brockbank, Wayne and Ulrich, Dave. 1994. "Lower cost, higher value: Human resources function in transition." *Human Resource Planning Journal* 17(3): 1–16.

   Yeung, Arthur and Ulrich, Dave. 1990. "Effective human resource practices for competitive advantages: An empirical assessment of organizations in transition." Richard J. Niehaus and Karl F. Price (eds.). *Human Resource Strategies for Organizations in Transition*. New York: Plenum Publishing Company, 311–326.

   Hermans, M., Wright, P., Ulrich, D., and Sioli, A. 2009. "Enhancing HRM practices: A stakeholder approach." Best Paper Proceedings of the 2009 Academy of Management Meeting. Sioli, A. 2007. Human Resources Competency Study-Latin America. HR Summit, Bs.As.

Ulrich, D., Brockbank, W., and Sioli, A. 2005. "So! We are at the table. Now what?" *The Human Factor.* 2:1:46–55.

3. Many of our ideas on the future of HR come from others who have recently dealt with the topic: http://www.hrmreport.com/article/The-Future-of-HRóHow-to-Achieve-the–2020-Workplace-Today/

   http://www.hrpa.ca/Documents/HRPA_KB_CEO_Perspective_Research_Highlight.pdf

   http://hrpeople.monster.com/benefits/articles/1907-what-is-the-future-of-hr?

   http://www.deloitte.com/view/en_US/us/Services/consulting/human-capital/hr-transformation/hrtimes/17be064f2044b210VgnVCM2000001b56f00aRCRD.htm

4. https://www.innocentive.com/. Accessed May 12, 2012.

5. Michels, Ed, Handfield-Jones, Helen, and Axelrod, Beth. 2001. *The War for Talent.* Boston, MA: Harvard Business Press.

6. Schein, Edgar. 1992. "The study of organization culture has been synthesized in. . . ." *Organizational Culture and Leadership: A Dynamic View.* San Francisco, CA: Jossey-Bass..Deal, T. E. and Kennedy, A. A. 1982. *Corporate Cultures: The Rites and Rituals of Corporate Life.* Harmondsworth: Penguin Books.

   Kotter, J. P. 1992. *Corporate Culture and Performance.* New York: The Free Press.

   Cameron, Kim S. and Quinn, Robert E. 2005. "Diagnosing and Changing Organizational Culture: Based on the Competing Values Framework." The Jossey-Bass Business & Management Series, ISBN 13 978–0–7879–8283–6.

   Corporate Leadership Council. June 2003. Defining Corporate Culture. Corporate Executive Board. Retrieved from www.corporateleadershipcouncil.com.

7. The process approach to organization may be seen in the work "The Balanced Scorecard: Measures That Drive Performance," with David P. Norton. *Harvard Business Review,* January–February 1992. *The Strategy-Focused Organization: How Balanced Scorecard Companies Thrive in the New Business Environment,* with David P. Norton. Harvard Business School Press, 2000. *Strategy Maps: Converting Intangible Assets into Tangible Outcomes,* with David P. Norton. Harvard Business School Press, 2004. It is also found in process management work:

Smith, Howard and Fingar, Peter. *Business Process Management: The Third Wave*. Tampa, FL: Meghan-Kiffe Press.

Kohlbacher, Markus. 2010. "The effects of process orientation: A literature review." *Business Process Management Journal*; 16(1):135–152.

8. Approaching organizations as core competencies has been captured in work by C. K. Prahalad and Gary Hamel. 1996. *Competing for the Future*. Boston, MA; Harvard Business Press. Hamel, Gary. 2012. *What Matters Now: How to Win in a World of Relentless Change, Ferocious Competition, and Unstoppable Innovation*. San Francisco, Jossey Bass. Prahalad, C. K. and Hamel, Gary. 1990. "The core competence of the corporation." *Harvard Business Review*; May–June: pp. 79–91.

9. The resource-based view of organizations has a more academic tradition in work by J. B. Barney. 1991, "Firm Resources and Sustained Competitive Advantage." *Journal of Management*; 17(1) 99–120.

   Makadok, R. 2001. "Toward a Synthesis of the Resource-Based View and Dynamic-Capability Views of Rent Creation." *Strategic Management Journal.* 22(5) 387–401.

   Sirmon, D. G., M. A. Hitt, and Ireland, R. D. 2007. "Managing Firm Resources in Dynamic Environments to Create Value: Looking Inside the Black Box." *The Academy of Management Review*; 32(1) 273–292.

   Barney, J. B. 2001. "Is the Resource-Based Theory a Useful Perspective for Strategic Management Research? Yes." *Academy of Management Review*; 26.(1) 41–56.

   Wernerfelt, B. 1984, "The Resource-Based View of the Firm." *Strategic Management Journal.* 5(2) 171–180.

10. The concept of organization as capabilities was briefly introduced by Igor Ansoff and then advanced in 1990 in work by Dave Ulrich and Dale Lake, followed by many who worked to identify the key capabilities of an organization.

    Ulrich, Dave and Lake, Dale. 1990. *Organizational Capability: Competing from the Inside/Out*. New York: Wiley.

    Stalk, George, Jr. 1988. "Time—the next source of competitive advantage." *Harvard Business Review*, July–August, pp. 41–53.

    Stalk, G., Evans, P. and Shulman, L. E. 1992. "Competing on capabilities: The new rules of corporate strategy." *Harvard Business Review.* 70(2):57–69.

Lombardo, Michael and Eichinger, Robert. 2002. *The Leadership Machine*. Minneapolis: Lominger.

Collins, David J. 1994. "Research note: How Valuable Are Organizational Capabilities?" *Strategic Management Journal.* Winter, pp. 143–152

11. Stalk, G., Evans, P. & Shulman, L. E. 1992. "Competing on capabilities: The new rules of corporate strategy." *Harvard Business Review*, 70(2): 57–69.

12. http://www.kornferry.com/pdf/LTC/StrategicEffectivenessArchitect.pdf

13. Ulrich, Dave. 1998. "Integrating practice and theory: Towards a more unified view of HR." In Patrick Wright, Lee Dyer, John Boudreau, and George Milkovich (Eds.), *Research in Personnel and Human Resources Management*, Greenwich, CT: JAI Press.

Ulrich, Dave and Smallwood, Norm. 2004. "Capitalizing on capabilities," *Harvard Business Review.* June.

INDEX

ABOUT THE CONTRIBUTORS

Jade White
Jade White is managing director for North America East with The RBL Group, where he focuses on helping organizations transform performance through people. He has nearly 20 years of global experience in the HR field and has held leadership roles at Mars, Allianz, Capital One and Cendant with a deep focus in learning and development, talent management, OD, strategic HR and business partnering. Jade is cocreator of IMPACT, The RBL Group's Business Partnering Skills workshop, focused on developing the strategic alignment and partnering skills of HR professionals. IMPACT is featured in RBL's newest program, the comprehensive HR Academy, which leverages practical tools to address top organizational challenges with particular emphasis on credible activist and change champion. Jade has a master's degree in education and human development from George Washington University and a bachelor's degree in HR Management from the University of Richmond. He and his family reside in New Jersey. His e-mail is: jwhite@rbl.net.

Justin Allen—Africa
Justin Allen is a principal with The RBL Group and oversees RBL's work in Africa. He is dedicated to advancing the fields of leadership and strategic HR in emerging economies and has collaborated with leaders from the top companies in the world. Prior to his current role, Justin was the managing director of the RBL Institute where he built a sustainable network of senior HR leaders, coauthored the highly praised book, *HR Transformation*, and oversaw significant growth that led to the RBL Institute being named "The #1 Global Think Tank for Strategic HR." Justin came to RBL from GE where he was an HR Leader and also worked at GE Crotonville. Justin began his career as an international researcher in labor statistics and holds a master's degree in business management and organizational behavior.

Elijah Litheko—Africa
Rre Elijah Litheko has held the position of CEO of the Institute of People Management (IPM), South Africa, since 1995. Before joining the executive team, he led and facilitated the highly successful Black Advancement Leadership Programme and played a key role in the restructuring and transformation of the South African Forestry Company Limited (SAFCOL). Mr. Litheko currently serves on the University of Johannesburg's HRD Advisory Council,

the University of KwaZulu Natal's HRD Advisory Council, and the Human Resource Development Council of South Africa (HRDCSA), chaired by the deputy president of the country. He is also a board member of the Southern African Society for Cooperative Education (SASCE) and has received numerous awards for his contribution to the advancement of HR in the African continent. Mr. Litheko holds an MBA from the Demontfort University (UK), a BTech HRM from UNISA, and a Postgraduate Diploma in Labour Law, GIMT.

Anne-Marie Dolan—Australia

Anne-Marie is the manager of Research & Development at the Australian Human Resources Institute. Anne-Marie joined the Australian Human Resources Institute in 2000 and currently heads up the team managing AHRI's research, award and mentoring programs, and program development. She also consults a number of clients on capability and skill development projects. Anne-Marie has completed undergraduate and postgraduate studies in HR. Prior to joining AHRI, she held a number of HR positions in New Zealand in the education and government sectors. Anne-Marie also holds the position of HR Manager at AHRI and oversees the strategic and practical HR requirements for the organization, including recruitment, performance management, and professional development.

Alan Nankervis—Australia

Dr. Alan Nankervis is a professor of HRM at Curtin University. He has held senior academic positions at RMIT University (Melbourne), Curtin University (Perth), and the University of Western Sydney, and been a visiting scholar at universities in Canada, Thailand, and the United Kingdom. His research interests include strategic human assets management, the links between performance management and firm effectiveness, comparative HRM in Asia, and service industry management. He is currently the chair of the Australian HR Institute's (AHRI) national course accreditation committee.

Arthur Yeung—China

Arthur Yeung is the Philips chair professor of HRM at China Europe International Business School, the leading business school in China. His research interests focus on building organization capability for strategic implementation, globalization of Chinese firms, and leading large-scale organizational transformation. Before his return to academia, he served as chief HR officer of Acer Group and worked closely with the chairman to transform Acer for global competitiveness. As an author of several award-winning articles and 10 books, Dr. Yeung has been featured as one of the "Executive Development Gurus" by *Business Horizon* in the United States. In addition to serving as editorial board member of five international academic journals, he sits on the boards of several publicly listed companies in NYSE and HKSE. In China, he also leads a learning consortium with more than 70 CEOs to address issues related to the enhancement of organization capabilities. Dr. Yeung teaches regularly in executive education programs in association with Harvard, INSEAD, and Michigan.

Tao Wang—China

Tao Wang is vice president of 51job (NASDAQ:JOBS, www.51job.com), a leading human resource solutions provider in China. He leads a prominent training and assessment business team in China. He is also an experienced facilitator in the field of leadership and management training. Prior to joining 51job, Mr. Wang served as a senior consultant at Bain & Company and gained rich experience in strategic and marketing strategies development. He also served as a representative and the general manager of a joint venture company in Wuhan for TI Group Asia Pacific. Earlier in his career, Mr. Wang held various engineering and project management positions at the Ministry of Aerospace Industry in China. Mr. Wang received a bachelor in math degree from Shandong University and a master's degree in engineering from the Second Academy under the PRC Ministry of Aerospace Industry. He also holds a MBA from the Business School at University of Warwick in the United Kingdom.

Allan Freed—Europe

Allan Freed is a principal consultant with The RBL Group, a consulting firm focused on helping leaders and organizations deliver results and increase value. Allan's current work helps organizations identify and build capabilities required for the execution of strategy through leveraging human resources and improving leadership performance. Allan has worked with HR executive teams in a large number of Europe's top companies to apply RBL's award-winning databases and research to assess alignment between business strategies, HR practices, and HR competencies. His e-mail is afreed@rbl.net.

Christine Cleemann—Europe

Dr. Christine Cleemann is assistant professor of Strategic HR at the Copenhagen Business School and consulting partner of The RBL Group since 2009. She is well respected for her teaching and consulting work in HR strategy, talent, and people innovation and HR professional development. Prior to joining the RBL Group, she played a key HR role in a corporate turnaround, building and executing a new strategic HR organization at the global forwarder, Damco. Dr. Cleemann successfully managed a corporate HR development redesign involving 300+ internal HR professionals at Denmark's leading provider of tele-communication solutions, TDC. She then served as general manager of Global HR Capabilities in the multinational energy and transportation corporation, A.P. Møller-Mærsk.

Even Bolstad—Europe
Even Bolstad is managing director at HR Norge, the Norwegian member organization for human resources. For the last several years, he has led the transformation of HR Norge toward becoming a leading source of knowledge in the Norwegian HR community and a successful European HR association. He is a Naval Academy graduate with an MBA and is also educated within labour law and leadership development. In addition to HR, Bolstad had his working experience within finance, strategy, communications, logistics, and negotiations before turning to general management and HR Norge. He has served as president of IIRA/ILERA Norway and has been a board member at the Norwegian Directorate of Labour and the European Association of People Management. Mr. Bolstad is a frequent speaker at Norwegian and European HR summits, and he is a much-used commentator and columnist in Norwegian media.

Håvard Berntzen—Europe
Håvard Berntzen is senior advisor HR at HR Norge, the Norwegian member organization for human resources. He is an eager trendspotter and researcher in the HR field and is head of conference development for HR Norge. As the main contact person of the European sample at the HRCS 2012, he aimed to increase the European participation in the study compared to previous years. He has a BA in Communication from the University of North Dakota and an MSc in Leadership and Organisational Psychology at the Norwegian School of Business, in addition to many courses in Psychology from the University of Oslo. He is a relations builder and is known for high quality and high commit-ment in his work. In addition to HR, Håvard has previous work experience in the field of journalism, social work among juveniles, and in the music busi-ness. He resides and works in Oslo, Norway.

L. Prabhakar—India
L. Prabhakar is the vice president of human resources at the agribusiness division of ITC Limited, a leading Indian conglomerate, and is a member of the Management Committee of that business. He has been associated with ITC for 17 years in different capacities across businesses and in their corporate offices. He has also worked with TVS Motors for four years and Murugappa Group for three years. He has a master's degree in personnel

management and industrial relations from XLRI, one of India's premier management schools. Keen on strengthening the HR profession, he actively engages in sharing his experiences through articles, presentations and networking, and by mentoring young HR professionals and students. He has been actively associated with National HRD Network, India's leading body for HR professionals, and is currently the national treasurer. His other interests are in the area of social responsibility with focus on livelihoods and employability.

Michel Hermans—Latin America

Michel Hermans is a professor of Human Resources Management at IAE Business School in Argentina. He obtained his BSc and MSc degrees in Business Administration from the Rotterdam School of Management in the Netherlands, and is currently working toward completion of his PhD in industrial and labor relations at Cornell University in the United States. Michel's research interests are strategic and international human resources management, in particular HRM in Latin America and HRM in interorganizational work arrangements. His work has been published in Research in Personnel and Human Resources Management, Academy of Management Best Paper Proceedings, and Harvard Business Review Latin America. Additionally, he has contributed several chapters to books on HRM. Michel has taught in programs at Fundaçao Getulio Vargas (Brazil) and IPADE Business School (Mexico) and consulted with numerous companies throughout Latin America.

Alejandro Sioli—Latin America

Alejandro Sioli is a professor of Human Resource Management and Organizational Behavior at IAE Business School in Argentina. He has a degree in industrial engineering from the Universidad de Buenos Aires, an MBA from IAE Business School, and a PhD from IESE—Universidad de Navarra in Spain. Alejandro has been the HRCS academic partner for Latin America since 1997. He served as the academic codirector of LAHRP (Latin American HR Partnership), a joint initiative of IAE, and the Ross School of Business at the University of Michigan. His research and teaching focus on HRM and organizational transformation processes. Alejandro has been a visiting professor at the University of Michigan and has taught in all programs offered at IAE. Additionally, he has taught at schools throughout Latin America including IPADE (Mexico), Inalde (Colombia), IDE (Ecuador), ISE (Brazil), ESE (Chile), IEEM (Uruguay), and IESE Business School (Spain). He has done extensive consulting work with multinational and local companies in Latin America, the United States, and Spain.

Adam Rampton—Middle East

Adam Rampton is a principal consultant and managing director for The RBL Group—Middle East. In these roles, Adam regularly partners with clients throughout the region to advance business objectives through leadership development and strategic alignment of human resources. He is able to draw on his professional experience, including both business and HR leadership roles, to bring practical solutions to his clients. Prior to joining The RBL Group, Adam also worked for General Electric (GE) where he graduated from GE's HR Leadership Program and held roles of increasing responsibility in a variety of industries including financial services, healthcare, and oil and gas. Adam earned an MBA from the University of Notre Dame and has over 13 years of results-focused experience partnering with global business leaders. He is fluent in Romanian and is currently based in Dubai, UAE.

Fouzi Abdulrahaman Bubshait—Middle East

Fouzi Abdulrahaman Bubshait is currently the senior HR director with the leading mining company in Saudi Arabia. His career spans three decades and includes various HR managerial positions in the oil and gas industries. His interest in the development journey of young people is reflected in his role as chairman of the Quality of Academic Programs Subcommittee of the Industry—King Fahad University of Petroleum and Minerals(KFUPM) Partnership. Fouzi is the immediate past president of the Arabian Society for Human Resource Management (ASHRM). During his presidency, the membership of ASHRM increased from 400 to 4,000 and chapters were established throughout the GCC. Fouzi's academic qualifications include: an MSc in HRM from Texas A&M University, an MSc in HRD from the University of Minnesota, and a MSc. in Computer Science from KFUPM.

Andrew Lindsay Cox—Middle East

Andrew Lindsay Cox is currently a senior strategic consultant with a major oil and gas company in the Middle East. His 40-year career includes a multitude of project management and consulting roles in a variety of industries in several different countries. He has a special interest in strategic management, organizational performance, and effective HR. Andrew was the principal contact and "driver" for the HRCS in the Gulf Region. His efforts contributed greatly to putting the region "on-the-map" in this regard. Andrew is the immediate past director-at-large of the Arabian Society for Human Resource Management (ASHRM). During his tenure, he was vice-chair and developed the programs for two successful regional conferences. Andrew has an MSc in Strategic Quality Management from the University of Portsmouth. He is a member of the

Australian Institute of Project Management, a Certified Quality Practitioner—Chartered Quality Institute (UK), and a senior member of the Australian Computer Society.

Keith E. Lawrence—North America
Keith recently completed a career of 32 years at Procter & Gamble, the world's largest consumer products company. He worked across a number of billion dollar brands-including Pampers, Olay, Crest, Charmin, and Pantene. His assignments encompassed both line leadership as well as all aspects of human resources across multiple functions. He led global efforts to define leadership at P&G, integrated employees joining from multiple acquisitions and numerous organization redesigns and start-ups. He pioneered such breakthrough concepts as "Winning at the Employee Moments of Truth" and the creation of Best in Class Organization Transformation approaches. During this work Keith partnered with several other companies, including Toyota, General Mills, McKinsey, GE, and Right Management. His current practice is focused on enabling organizations to deliver and sustain extraordinary performance while enabling the dreams and aspirations of their members.

Pelin Urgancilar—Turkey
Pelin Urgancilar is a consulting partner with The RBL Group based in Istanbul. An expert in organizational diagnosis and enhancing employee engagement in organizations through integrated HR services aligned with strategy, Pelin helps leaders build intangible value in their organizations by helping them clarify strategies, build a talent base, and create a high performance and innovation culture. Before working with The RBL Group, Pelin worked for Hay Group as a business development manager for five years and held managerial roles in sales and marketing with service companies in Turkey and the Middle East for six years. She has been working with leading pharmaceuticals, FMCG, and telecom companies in Turkey, Eastern Europe, and CIS. A graduate of Uskudar American Academy, Pelin holds a BA in international relations from Marmara University in Turkey.

Michael D. Phillips—Turkey
Michael D. Phillips is a principal consultant with The RBL group. He has worked with clients throughout the world with a focus on creating high-performing individuals and organizations. He is a much sought-after consultant, lecturer, facilitator, and trainer. He has designed and implemented talent and performance management systems for companies in many countries and in numerous languages. A former university professor, Mr. Phillips is an educator at heart and in his career he has worked with every level of learner from grade school

students to corporate CEOs. An expert in change management, he is the author or editor of numerous articles, books, and journals. He holds a PhD from the University of Chicago and is the former managing director of the Center for Leadership Solutions. Michael lives in the Wasatch Mountains of Utah with his wife and three children.

Bradley A. Winn

Bradley A. Winn is a consultant, scholar, and director of the graduate HR Executive Program at the Jon M. Huntsman School of Business, Utah State University. As a recognized organizational and public policy leader, Dr. Winn has served as assistant commissioner for academic affairs, vice president for institutional planning, and provost & academic vice president for the Utah State Board of Regents, Utah Valley University, and Snow College, respectively. He also served as an elected legislator in the Utah House of Representatives and policy and budget analyst for former Utah governor Michael Leavitt. Brad began his career in business and industry as an engineer for ATK Thiokol's space shuttle booster program and as a manager at Novations business consulting firm. Joining with scholars from around the world, he focuses his research on positive organizational leadership, strategic change, global workforce leadership, and entrepreneurial sustainability. Brad Winn is a popular, award-winning professor who presents regularly at national conferences and events. His e-mail is: brad.winn@usu.edu.

Dale Lake

Dr. Dale Lake received his doctorate in social psychology from Columbia University where his dissertation won an outstanding research award from the American Institutes for Research. Dr. Lake's books include: *Organization Capability, Managing a State's Education, Perceiving and Behaving, Measuring Human Behavior* and *Organization Change: A Comprehensive Reader.* He has extensive consulting experience in such areas as strategic implementation, sourcing, team building, global team development, organization design and human resource management. Between 2000 and 2012, Dr. Lake has served as a consultant to Viterra, where he has helped to redesign the company and guided the organization to new vision, mission, and values orientation. This led to a merger that doubled its size and accelerated its growth. In 2012 Viterra was purchased for over $12 billion more than it was worth in 2000. He has served on the faculties of New York University, Boston University, The State University of New York at Albany, and the University of Michigan Institutes for Social Research.